WINDOW GARDENING
THE OLD-FASHIONED WAY

Tried and True Methods for Turning Any Window, Porch, or Balcony into a Beautiful Garden

EDITED BY HENRY T. WILLIAMS

Skyhorse Publishing

Skyhorse Publishing books may be purchased in bulk at special discounts for sales promotion, corporate gifts, fund-raising, or educational purposes. Special editions can also be created to specifications. For details, contact the Special Sales Department, Skyhorse Publishing, 307 West 36th Street, 11th Floor, New York, NY 10018 or info@skyhorsepublishing.com.

Skyhorse® and Skyhorse Publishing® are registered trademarks of Skyhorse Publishing, Inc.®, a Delaware corporation.

Visit our website at www.skyhorsepublishing.com.

10 9 8 7 6 5 4 3 2 1

Library of Congress Cataloging-in-Publication Data is available on file.

ISBN: 978-1-61608-704-3

Printed in the United States of America

Fig. 1.—Decorative Bird Cage and Flower Stand.

INDEX.

PART I.

PART II.

PLANTS FOR WINDOW GARDENS.

PART III.

PARLOR DECORATIONS.

PREFACE.

It is a great pleasure to write to an audience of flower-lovers—they are so eager, so enthusiastic and so delighted with any hints or suggestions which will help them in their efforts to make home more beautiful.

The taste for Window Gardening, and the plant decoration of apartments, is becoming almost universal; scarcely a cottage or villa but has its attempts, whether simple or elaborate, to decorate the windows, the porch, or the balcony with some few flower pots or climbing vines; it is a sign of healthy sentiment, for the presence of flowers always aids in the development of refinement and an elevated taste.

Desiring to foster this fancy for window ornament, a number of flower-lovers have united with me in the effort to produce a book specially devoted to this subject, aiming to make it simple, practical, and adapted to the use of amateurs and beginners in the cultivation of indoor plants.

Several gardeners and professional writers have contributed articles on special subjects, and we have combined our experience and information in a careful manner, endeavoring to produce a volume as accurate and complete as time and space would permit.

The result is now before the public in this richly illustrated, tasteful volume; and it is hoped that among this goodly number of pages and engravings, every one will feel that their time is well spent by gaining some hints of use and good service.

Acknowledgments of kindly assistance are due to C. L. Allen, "Daisy Eyebright," Thomas Meehan, Robert Demcker, J. L. Little, Jr.; also to the publishers of some foreign Illustrated Horticultural works, inaccessible to the general reader, whose names are mentioned in the Index.

Should the reader feel pleased with this little testimonial to one of the most beautiful of all departments of flower culture, the author will not regret his effort to add some definite encouragement to the more extensive development of Rural Taste.

THE EDITOR.

CHAPTER I.

ITS PLEASURES — INCREASE IN POPULAR TASTE — REFINING INFLUENCES.

No home of taste is now considered complete without its Window Garden. Indeed it may be said that Window Gardening is one of the most elegant, satisfactory, yet least expensive of all departments of Rural Taste. As a useful means for developing a taste for plant-life and a love for flowers, I count nothing so effective as this simple style of gardening; for who has not noticed that where flowers reign, grace of mind and manner soon follow. One of the advantages of Window Gardening is its *simplicity,* open to every one and impossible to none. Thousands of persons confined to their homes for the greater part of their life have no greater rural estate than that which the Window Garden affords. To watch the unfolding leaves and budding flowers, the development of branch after branch, is a study of the reality of plant-life, exquisitely interesting to the soul who finds in it its only world of pleasure and sentiment.

It is a form of gardening too, of *permanent use and value.* The Window Garden is independent to a large degree of the varying seasons, for it can be made attractive every month in the year. The advent of Spring, Summer and Autumn, only render the plants of the Window Garden more luxuriant and make the flowers more brilliant, but they do not die with the first frost or cold wind in winter. When the prospect without is dreary, we can still look to our fern-cases or window-boxes or hanging-baskets and behold in them objects of increased admiration, because they are so charming in their contrast with the desolateness without, and are genial remembrances of greener days gone by.

The universal popularity of Window Gardens, whether large or small, simple or elaborate, is the evidence of a growing taste for flowers and ornamental plants in all circles of society. We have only to notice in all our large cities, towns and villages, how frequent window decorations have become, sometimes seeming as if not a single house was without them in many of our most fashionable avenues. In European cities the citizens indulge even more extensively and passionately in their plant pleasures than we do ; every home is decorated from the workingman's window, and its few flower-pots of balsams, to the fernery and tile jardinieres of the aristocratic mansion.

In Brussels, says M. Victor Paquet, " the balconies are turned into greenhouses and miniature stoves, gay with the brightest and greenest foliage. And in Paris there are many contrivances in use by means of which the rarest and most beautiful plants are produced. Passifloras cling to columns in the upper floors; water plants start into blossom in tiny basins curiously contrived in solid brick-work, and limpid water flows down a miniature rockery from whose crevices start up ferns and lycopodiums."

The rooms of the Parisian are gay with flowers replaced freshly every day, and in the denser parts of London, black with its smoky atmosphere, may be found some of the choicest of plant-cases. An English writer visiting such a locality once was ushered into a room where the darkness was almost felt, but every window was occupied with a plant-case in which plants were growing in an astonishing manner. Ferns of the greenest and freshest hue, orchids never surpassed, were there in redolent health and vigor. He was told to his great surprise that the cases were hermetically sealed, and that no water had been ad-ministered for months.

There is a never-failing charm, too, in the outside decorations of the house or Window Garden. The trellis-work of the balcony may be made ornamental with green foliage and its homeliness tastefully hidden. The ivy will cover the un-painted wall and make it still more artistic. The verandah can be soon covered with the most luxuriant of profuse blooming creepers. Unsightly objects, bare gardens, and plain fences can all be relieved. In fact no home is devoid of the means of tasteful decoration. And so many and easy are the forms of window embellishments at the present day, that we know of no better device for increas-ing the elegancies and attractions of indoor life.

Window Gardens, too, are *educators of taste.* In our large cities it is noticeable that the fair occupants of the wealthier homes are themselves practically inter-ested in window ornament. It is quite the fashion for their own hands to fill with pretty plants, of their own arrangement, jardinieres of costly tile, or else place them in baskets of rustic yet most artistic make. After a little time when they have grown to appropriate height, or the drooping plants have attained suffi-cient length, the full beauty of the Window Garden is apparent. Visitors are entranced with their wondrous beauty and are free with their exclamations of delight. The passer-by on the sidewalk stops for a moment to look lovingly upon the cozy bower of bloom just inside the glazed window pane. When pass-ing away, he still keeps it in mind, and long afterwards cherishes the memory of this artistic beauty spot. Flowers and plants, by their beauty and fragrance, are always in harmony with rich and costly furniture, pictures or statuary.

A simple flower stand near the window, a hanging basket over head, all shedding their perfume, add day by day brightness to the other genialities of the home; and all through the wintry months, furnish food for pleasant thoughts ; a single plant of the Ivy trained on the wall, or festooned over the window, is a joy to all beholders.

Flowers, plants too, often supply the place of children in bereaved homes; for their soul-refreshing, heart-inspiring, and eye-brightening influences, are joys to wean the thoughts from pain or sorrow.

Some mother perhaps cherishes fondly in her home, a few beautiful Fuchsias placed on a stand upon the window sill. She never tires of looking upon their graceful shapes, or the brightly colored jewel blossoms drooping downwards, for they remind her of the delight they once gave her little child before it went to its angel home. The value to her of these treasures, with their brilliant colors and snowy waxen petals, rose-colored or purple corollas, cannot be measured with the ordinary expression of language.

Among the most gratifying signs of floral taste, is the evidence of their introduction into *school rooms*. The teacher is perhaps fond of them and knows their influence. Their very delicacy, forbidding rough handling, serves to impose a wholesome restraint upon the children; if ever they are tired with their study, a few glances at the windowsill, and its pots of bloom, wreathes their faces with genial smiles, and they go to work again with willing hearts and refreshed thoughts. The curiosity of children, too, is proverbial, and many a girl learns more of nature from the living specimens before her, than from the dry details of her book of botany.

Not less important can we consider flowers and plants, as the best and most practical educators of *healthy sentiment*. They are always suggestive of purity and refinement. Nothing is so conducive to cheerfulness, or creates efforts to make home attractive, like their presence in the household. Constant associations with such objects of floral beauty, fits people to rank high as useful members of society. A floral writer has already expressed these sentiments in a most charming manner :

"They are a spring of sunshine, a constant pleasure. We would have flowers in every home, for their sunny light, for their cheerful teachings, for their insensibly ennobling influence."

As an *amusement* for the *invalid*, Window Gardening through the form of plant cases, is very appropriate. We call to mind an instance of one compelled in consequence of a bodily infirmity, to take up a residence in the city.

He had enjoyed for a long time in the country the pleasures of the green-house, and endeavored whilst in the city to replace it once more. A small but inexpensive three light green-house was erected in the back yard, open, airy. There he gratified his taste for floricultural subjects by gathering together an interesting collection of valuable ferns and orchids. In an upper room was arranged a capacious fern case, and there the invalid would spend many days during the winter recumbent upon the sofa dilating upon the pleasures of being able to watch the growth of a vigorous intertwining mass of curious forms of foreign ferns, many of them productions from distant portions of the globe, New Zealand, India, Mexico, Japan.

In our country homes, how common to see the plant stand before the window with its dozen or so pots of Geraniums, Primroses, Azaleas, &c., while an invalid sister or mother reclines in the easy chair, watching it for hours with delight, unmindful of the snow driving past the window pane.

The refining influence of the flowers is no where more apparent than in our *humble cottage homes ;* for there it is the young maiden cherishes her few pet flowers, with a deeper affection and truer love than even the skilled gardener. There is something so attractive in their very looks that none can resist their sweet and winning influence. Perhaps it may be because so few are disappointed in them, or expect them to yield a measured commercial profit. So no one's enthusiasm is gauged by dollars and cents.

In some of the strangest of conditions, there is often the most delightful dis play of floral bloom ; the prairie log cabin may often contain a flourishing win dow garden, with as choice specimens as that of the rich amateur.

Few are so poor but they can find room for a few boxes and pots to grow plants and beguile the long winter hours. They should be in the window of every sit ting room, in every school-house, that children, as well as parents, may be educa ted to the appreciation of their beauties, and their taste more readily cultivated and encouraged.

The *effects of window gardening* become more clearly seen each succeeding year. Many who have not the slightest idea of how a plant grows will obtain from the florist a simple basket of Ivy. Once living, it needs little further atten tion ; yet the eye of the proprietor often wanders upward to it, and as the tendrils reach out, twining around the basket, upward or downward, his senses are gradually interested, and in time other plants follow, who in turn are studied. These tempt others, mere visitors, to try the same experiment, and so the con tagious enthusiasm for flowers steadily spreads. In every state the love for flowers and plants is on the increase. The business of our florists is three times larger than five years ago. Our cottagers are devoting more time to the ornamen tation of door yards with these floral gems, and the window sill of many a cot has its sugar bowl or cracked tea pot, doing duty for a flower pot, while we have often seen the discarded fruit can, in some wayside ranchman's cabin in the inte rior of the Rocky Mountains, blooming with balsams or portulacca. All classes respond to but one sentiment, "FLOWERS, GIVE US FLOWERS."

Beside the delights of window gardening in opening new resources of amuse ment, recreation and instruction, which nothing else can give to the home circle, is the added advantage that it is *easy; but very little time is required for their culture.* Some window gardens are elaborate, expensive, and are suited only for those of scientific taste, but by far the most successful are those in our every day homes, with the simplest of flowering plants. There are many more easy plans for house gardening than difficult ones. The little physical exercise needed, is a relief to mental pursuits, and a variety to domestic duties, while the daily growth of each plant and flower, which constitutes the chief delight of the young flo rist, and the beauty and elegance of his little garden, form a crowning gratifica tion for his well spent hours, and stimulate an honest and desirable pride.

In some of the poorest quarters of London there may be found at any time handsomer Balsams than any professional ever raised, while some of the finest new Chrysanthemums ever produced it is said have originated in the window garden of some of these humble citizens.

A quaint old English writer calls this form of home pleasure, " *Fenestral Gar- dening,*" (*Hortus Fenestralis*) expressive of the decoration of rooms with green drapery from the garden. Many are deterred from the commencement of a window garden, or the care for cases of plants, on account of the supposed *trouble*.

There are really but few requisites to success. If any are ignorant of the plants or their proper arrangement, read these pages and learn how many simple forms may be adopted to make every house garden alive with plant beauty, and yet require only a half hour per day. A hanging basket or two, a window box or row of bulb glasses, a wardian case or fernery, all are easy. Once set, they need little care. In the other departments of propagation and culture, a little time, patience, and, best of all, trials of experience, will soon render the knowledge easily acquired.

To have some few choice, fragrant, beautiful flowers in mid winter when there is no green thing in sight, save the dense evergreen of the forest, or the garden hedge of spruce, prompts many to an assiduous care, and a hearty devotion to such plant treasures. Yet the recompense is worth the labor.

The matchless beauty which nature once bestowed on the gardens without, is now restored and perpetuated within ; and to many a fair finger deftly handling the tender plant, the exquisite embroidery of the leaf, or coloring of the flower, will form objects for the eye to rest upon with unwearied delight.

Fig. 2.—Design for Window Garden.

CHAPTER II.

CONSTRUCTION, LOCATION AND DESIGNS FOR WINDOW GARDENS.

The Window Gardener has choice of a great number of designs for the gratification of his taste. The Window Box of Evergreens, Ferns, or Ornamental Plants; the Jardiniere, the Hanging Basket, the row of Bulbglasses, the Plant Cabinet, the Fernery, Wardian Case or Conservatory, may all be his: while Flower Stands, Etagere and Mantel Piece Gardens, and other floral elegancies, are of great variety and tasteful construction. Nothing, however, has so decided an effect as broad leaved plants in the window sill.

Our engraving opposite (Fig. 2) is a sketch of a library window, about 3 feet wide, and 6 high, with book shelves on either side, and a closet below for pamphlets. The window sill is made of extra width, say 14 inches. Here is placed a simple tray of about 3 inches in depth, made to fit the sill exactly: the interior is coated entirely with tin and rendered proof against leakage. The tray is filled with fresh mould from the woods, and then the plants are put in. At each end is an English Ivy, and the spaces between are filled with native hardy ferns, which usually are found out doors near our woods, remaining green down to the coldest winds and frosts of Autumn.

If the front of the box is too plain it may be decorated with a few acorns, and strips of chestnut.

About midway up the window is thrown across a miniature rustic bridge, upon which is still another but narrower tray, with lighter and more delicate ferns, such as the maiden's hair. This rustic bridge may be decorated with a lattice of the bright red dogwood, mingled with the white shoots of the linden. On the top of the window, as a cornice, some rustic branch from one of our wild forest trees, may be selected, twisted and crooked; yet affording numerous brackets for climbing plants to rest upon. Upon this moss-covered bark the Ivy of the lower box is expected soon to grow up to and crawl over, throwing its tendrils right and left, and filling it full with green foliage. A little hanging basket from the rustic archway, fills out the uniqueness of the picture, and the landscape view beyond is in a measure enhanced by the agreeableness of the standpoint from which we view it.

In some of the finer parts of London, where Window Gardens are dressed in highest elegance, there is a very popular form of Window Garden, consisting of a glass case, projecting beyond the window sashes, somewhat like a little glass bow-window. (Fig 3, 4.) These are made in every style, with rustic work in front, or of an architectural character to harmonize with the style of the building.

The sills, too, are made broad, and thus afford peculiar conveniences for their safe position. Wealthy citizens who return from the country at close of the summer find these glass gardens ready filled, and charmingly arrayed with ferns, evergreens and flowering plants, which will last throughout the entire winter. In the spring time these give place to Roses, Fuchsias, Pelargoniums, and a variety of other plants suitable for each season. They are exceedingly simple, and besides affording a world of gratification to the inmates of the house they are a great addition to the exterior ornaments of the building. They are not common in this

Fig. 3.

country, and it would be quite an object for some dealer in horticultural elegancies here to make a specialty of them, for as soon as known they will be greatly in demand. The construction is as follows : The lower window sash, if omitted entirely, and the glass case inserted in its place, is of sufficient height to reach to the upper sash. The base should be of one stout slab of slate, resting upon the lower window sill, and extending outward from 1 foot to 2 feet, and the same distance inward. If the window is large, 2 feet each side of the sash will not be too large. An iron frame is then cast of just sufficient length and width to set upon the slab, which may be fastened firmly to it. The glass sides are fitted into the frame be-forehand, which is curved at the top, and a tray inside filled with soil holds the plants. In many cases the plant case is double, (*i. e.,*) the lower window sash is not removed at all, but shuts down upon the slab of slate, and the plant case is divided into two parts, each rising and curving upward to the window. Such cases can be made by any manufacturer of glassware and metal casting, but should be well and tightly fitted; as, also, very thick glass should be used as a protection against the weather. For the purposes of examination and cleaning or handling

Fig. 4.

the plants, a glass slide or door can be provided in the side within the room. These designs will be found most suitable in our changeable climate for mild weather only, as we fear they would not afford sufficient protection against cold. To some the objection might occur that they hide the view of the street from the interior, but this, with others, might be just the desideratum wished for; yet it will be found in time that it excludes light and air to a considerable degree. Another item must be provided for. Water must necessarily be used for the plants, and there should be a place of escape. The box for holding the soil should be from 4 to 6 inches deep, and the bottom must be covered with broken pieces of charcoal or bricks about the size of walnuts, then a sprinkling of sand and other pieces of brick broken still smaller to about the size of a pea should be mixed with peat, and with this compost the box may be filled up. Cases of this kind are usually found in London, already prepared with plants, only needing the proper dimensions to be soon fitted to any window.

The best plants for these cases are ferns, which require but ordinary attention, and the cultivator will also observe not to place them in a southern window; a

Fig. 5.

northern or western one will be much better for they need little or no heat. As these cases cannot be heated, so no plants should be placed in there which require artificial warmth.

A very pretty design has been originated by a German gardener of a combined window case aquarium and fernery. (Fig. 5.) This occupies the window from the sill to top of the upper sash. The tank within contains slate slabs of considerable height, say one-third of the whole window on the outside of the case, the inner side nearest the room being of glass to afford a view of the interior. This slab is necessary to avoid the effect of the sun's rays which, when passing through a globe or aquarium of water, concentrate upon the floor and burn the carpet. Specimens of rock work are introduced at the sides or in the rear of the case; on their top are placed some pots containing ferns drooping over and covering the vacancies all up. If conveniences are at hand a little fountain may be introduced, and be constantly throwing up its tiny streams of water. All this requires great pains of preparation. The window completely shuts out the street view and is lighted only from the top, yet is a great curiosity and with some will be worth the trouble.

For planting in such cases as the two just described, the best plants will be the common English Ivy, (*Hedera helix,*) which thrives in confined places of this description and rapidly throws up its green foliage. The *Lygodium scandens* and *Lygodium Japonica* are lovely climbing ferns and need copper wires to be trained

Fig. 6.

to. *Trichomanes radicans, Hymenophyllum Tunbridgense Asplenium Fontanum* are moisture lovers and generally used in furnishing tanks for the aquarium. A suggestion worth heeding is to be remembered: do not commit the error of procuring too large fish for the aquarium; small varieties such as the gold carp are most suitable, and for every two gallon capacity of the water tank, put in one carp. Of water plants the best is *Vallisneria spiralis*, which will grow among pebbles if left undisturbed. *Confervæ* may be introduced and allowed to run over the rock or sides of the aquarium.

A very pretty home design, hardly called a Window Garden, yet affording room for some decoration, is that of a bee hive in the window. Such a hive was actually placed in front of one of the library windows of the late J. C. Loudon, the famous landscape gardener. This window was protected by a verandah, and the front of the hive was placed on a line with its pillars, and was consequently protected from perpendicular rain, but as the excessive heat of summer is equally injurious as rain, he had the hive protected from that and from the sudden influence of either heat or cold, by a casing of broom and heather intertwined. For examining the bees at work, the back of the hive next the window had a sliding door of wood covering a square of plate glass, so that when the door was lifted the bees could be seen at work. The engraving (Fig. 6) also affords to any one an idea of decorating the outside of the window with climbing vines; the *Wistaria* being much the most permanent and rapid growing. This will be found a most inter-

Fig. 7.

esting feature to children and visitors, and it will add much to the convenience of position if the window is low and near the ground.

One of the problems every window gardener has to solve is, to allow his plants all needful light, air and warmth, and yet protect them on the one hand from either the dry heat of the living room warmed by a furnace or stove, and on the other side from penetrating draughts of cold air.

This has been solved in many cases already, by the building of plant cabinets, which occupy not only the whole recess of the window, but are built out somewhat into the room, and the entire interior inclosed with glass sides or doors as a partition from the room. In every case that has come to our notice, where plants have been separated alike from the dry injurious air of the living room and the outside atmosphere, there has been the highest success. It is easy to attain a good uniform temperature, and the noxious fumes of the gas from stove, grate or gas burners, are fully protected against. The design introduced here, (Fig. 7,) is a glass case constructed in front of a window and projecting into the room with a door opening into it so that it can be easily entered. It would be well to build the floor of this house of wood, and a little higher than that of the room so that if necessary it can be removed without injury to the house. The lower portions of the case to the height of about two feet should be of wainscot. Inside the

Fig. 8   Fig. 9.

cabinet this paneling is lined with leaden troughs communicating with each other, and having a slight slope towards another trough lower than all the rest; it should be so contrived, that any water drainingfrom the pots or boxes containing the plants, may run off into the lower trough which should have no flower pots in it.

In these troughs should be placed wooden or slate boxes filled with earth in which climbing plants are placed alternately with Orange Trees, Camellias or flowering shrubs, so that they can be seen from the room. It is supposed, also, that the outside window is a bow-window or at any rate projects beyond the sides of the house. It should also have a sliding window at the top or bottom in case ventilation is desired, but cold air must not be admitted without imperative necessity. This design may be on too large a scale for ordinary purposes, but it serves to illustrate the idea that plants always thrive best when placed in rooms entirely by themselves. In such a cabinet a most glorious opportunity is afforded for decorating the sides of the interior with climbing vines, the ivy, convolvulus, or any other with showy colored flowers.

Ffg. 10.

Fig. 1].

Fig. 14 is still another design actually in use in one of our central New York homes. Here is a bow window filled with two boxes supported by legs, each box ten inches deep and filled inside either with earth or separate pots, the interspaces being filled in with moss or earth. The aim is to give a chance to plants with fine contrasts of foliage; Pelargoniums, Petunias, Heliotropes, Fuchsias, Amaranth, Coleus, Begonia, Geraniums, &c. In one end is a Maurandia climbing vine; in the other is a Mexican Cobœa, both twining and drooping over the wires which rise from the centre of the box, and curve towards the sides affording a delicate drapery of green. A hanging basket of moss hangs over each box, the one filled with Oxalis and Tradescantia, the other with Ice Plant. In the vase hanging just over the middle is placed a Kenilworth or Coliseum Ivy. On various brackets below are placed dishes of Ivy, Ferns and Moneywort. A few tall plants may be introduced to advantage, say one large pot full in the centre of each box. In one pot Caladiums, in the other Calla Lilies.

Belgian Window Gardens.

These are built outside the window altogether. A slab runs out directly from the window sill supported by brackets, and upon this is put a miniature green-house, constructed of glass roof and wooden sides like designs Nos. 8 & 9. These brackets below are generally very ornamental. Two or three shelves are placed inside on a row next to the window well supported and covered with pots. Care is taken not to let the case go too high to obstruct the light from entering the room, and ventilation is secured in Fig. 8, by lifting up slightly the lower portion of the glass roof. The plants are watered and arranged from the rooms within, as the windows do not slide up and down, but open inwardly on hinges.

Fig. 9 is ventilated by a door at the side or in front. An awning may be provided in case of unusual

Fig. 12.

heat from the sun, which will aid in keeping the atmosphere cool, and prolong the flowering considerably during the winter time. A thick covering is needed in cool days, or a vessel of hot water may be placed inside, where vapor will warm the little room greatly.

Figs. 10 & 11 represent a good continental style of a bow-window, where plants are out of the way of ordinary passing about in the room. Shelves are arranged around the entire window, and upon them are placed the pots of plants. In this case they should be of highly ornamental foliage, and free growth. A curved settee is placed just inside the row, and in front, just at the entrance of the recess, is a table for books.

Fig. 12 is a design for a rustic window box, permanently fastened to the outer side of the window case, decorated with Fuchsias, Ivy, Achyranthus, and drooping vines. An awning with brightly colored stripes adds greatly to the beauty.

Among the more wealthy residents of German cities, a plant cabinet is often found like Fig. 13. This is so made that its back is entirely open, and it can be pushed up close to the window, fitting it snugly. It is elaborately decorated, and quite costly. The door opens into the room, and the tops are ornamented with pots of Cacti and Agaves. This is much the handsomest design for a plant cabi-

Fig. 13.

net ever illustrated. The interior is filled principally with plants of stately growth, Coleus, Calla Lily, Canna, Maranta, Dracæna, Dieffenbachia, &c.

There are other designs of still more simple nature, which may be found in succeeding pages of this book. Window boxes are by far the simplest and most popular, but are adapted mostly to the indoor culture of bulbs. We have noticed frequently the late introduction of tile boxes, filling the entire width of the window, and placed just inside the panes of glass, filled with nothing but young plants of the Arbor Vitae. Their delicate, feathery green foliage contrasts well with the white curtains just behind, and the whole form one of the easiest, yet most unique styles of window gardening.

The Location of the Window Garden.

A good location or exposure is desirable. There are plants which love the shade. Pansies, Sweet Violets, and some of the variegated plants, will grow and bloom if not placed directly in the sun's ray ; but Roses, Geraniums, Heliotropes, Verbenas, Daphnes, Azaleas, &c., must be near the glass, and under the direct influence of the light, if we would have them flourish. An exposure where the sun can strike unobstructed from its first appearance above the horizon in the morning, until one or two o'clock, P. M., is much the most desirable. A southern or southeastern window is the best, next is an eastern exposure, then a western one, and the north worst of all. At a northern one, little but Pansies and Sweet Violets will grow, though Camellias delight in a cool, moist atmosphere, and will often flourish at such a window with but little sunshine. The plants must have all the sunshine you can bestow upon them, but at night they should be kept in the dark ; and as all plants in summer are cooler at night than in the day time, those that are grown in windows should also be cooler. This point is perhaps not as well understood as it should be, for there are persons so fearful

Fig. 14.—A Sitting Room Window.

that their plants will become chilled, that they turn all the heat of their furnaces upon them at night, and the gas-light joined with it, increases the irritation ; so that the plants are kept in an unnatural state when they ought to be at rest, for plants need sleep and do sleep ; so the effect of unreasonable light and heat is very exhausting. Drop the curtains over the plants to exclude them from the light of the room, or pin newspapers around them during the evening. Nothing is so handy and useful in protecting them from frost as newspapers. They will frequently preserve a plant when the mercury falls nearly to freezing point. Neither should plants be chilled. Avoid the extreme of rendering them too cool, but maintain a good medium temperature. Rooms whose thermometer reaches 80 to 85° during the day, and then falls to 30 to 35° at night, will never keep plants in good health.

Size of Windows.

The larger the better if you want to grow many plants. Bow windows are always liked, and generally considered the best, as they afford exposure to the sun at all hours of the day, if they face the south. The larger the panes, also the better. The best style of window, not bow, is to have a good sill, say not less than six inches wide on each side of the sash ; if eight or ten inches, so much the better ; this affords room for a fine sill or rustic window box, which may be changed at intervals from the inner sill to the outer one jutting beyond the edge of the sash. Boxes for this style of window should be six inches deep. Sometimes double boxes may be desired, one on each side of the window, in which case the outer box should contain low growing evergreens, and the interior one bulbs. It is usual, also, to cover the sills with paper before setting the boxes down. Still this is not necessary where there is no danger from leaking. If the window is low, and near the ground, climbing vines may be trained upward over the window ; this is more fully described under head of balcony gardening.

Our windows differ so much in size that every one must shape their preparations entirely according to their conveniences ; but if a sill, either permanent or temporary, can be constructed on the outside of the window, it will be found of convenient and constant use.

CHAPTER III.

General Management of Window Gardens.

In-door plants naturally require more care than those grown in the open air, for nature supplies all the needs of the latter; but the secrets of successful growth and profuse blooming in the house are enumerated in the following few essential rules of management:

1st. Give them plenty of light during the day, and darkness with a cooler temperature at night.

2d. A good supply of fresh air, when the sun shines brightest and warmest; in mild days the upper sashes may be lowered a little, and the cool air will blow over the plants instead of directly upon them.

3d. Perfect cleanliness, which is very important, for if the plants are covered with dust, they cannot grow, and will frequently die; their leaves are their lungs; frequent syringing will keep the leaves moist and clean.

4th. A proper amount of moisture; a dry atmosphere is fatal.

5th. A good compost or soil, in which their roots can luxuriate and send forth vigorous branches, leaves and flowers.

6th. Get good healthy plants to start out with; plants that have been blooming all through the summer, or for several months previous will not do well; new ones are best, or plants that were used the previous winter, and have rested during the summer, will also answer, but in general it is best to get new plants.

7th. Keep only a few plants; too many in the window will make close crowding; pots should never be set two or three deep on top of each other.

8th. A uniform temperature of 60° to 70° in the day time and 40° to 45° in the night, should be steadily maintained.

9th. Different places should be provided for different plants. A sunny window with a temperature of 45° to 50,° will suit roses, geraniums, &c., best; Begonias, Coleus, Cissus discolor, want a still warmer place of 60° to 70°, and yet but little or no sun light directly upon them. On the other hand, Heliotropes, and Bouvardias want all the sun possible, with a temperature in the daytime of 60° to 75°.

Sunlight.

Plenty of sunlight is the gardener's first requisite. If the location for this purpose is not right, the plants will not be healthy. If the plants are well placed in a good light, then the pots must be turned occasionally so that all sides may receive it equally. It will be well also to put flower stands or racks of pots on wheels, so that the whole may be changed at once, or wheeled away, if the room needs cleaning. Care must be taken to avoid rapid transition from darkness to the light, for sudden and violent changes are as trying to plant life as human life. Too much warmth will destroy tender leaves nearly as soon as too much cold. Then again, plants should be placed as near the light as possible; in rooms far away from the glass window, the plants will be weak, pale and of spindling growth. If they could receive light directly from overhead, they would be better than from the side. The ordinary variations of day and night have their corresponding effects on plants, since it is said that they inhale under the influences of light, and respire in the dark. The glass of the window should also be rubbed or washed clean. The most gaily colored flowers will be produced at a south window, but a north window has its advantage, in that it may be used for plants already in bloom, and will keep them much longer in perfection. For north windows, Camelias, Cytisuses, Primulas and Alpine Auriculas, will find the cool moisture they need, and will bloom in great beauty if properly attended to and kept from frost. Bulbs, if placed in the sunlight, will have their brilliancy of color greatly enhanced, yet if not changed occasionally in position, their flower stems will bend over and have an unsightly appearance.

Temperature.

The greatest success will be found to come from a uniform temperature of 45 or 50° at night, and 60 to 75° in the day time; 80° is too hot except for only some plants of semi-tropical character. Under no circumstances should the temperature go below 35°. If your living rooms, where your plants are placed must be considerably warmer than this in the former part of the night, then set the plants on the floor, shade from the light until the time of retiring, and then return them to the window sill or flower stand. Perhaps from no other cause than this, too great heat, during the day and long continued at night, our city grown plants grow so sickly and lanky in appearance. Once or twice a week will be sufficient for turning pots around. If this little item is not attended to, you cannot grow finely formed plants, and more than half their beauty depends upon their shape. If a closet or small room opening out of the sitting room can be devoted to plants and yet be well lighted, they will flourish far better than in the common room, for they can have a cooler atmosphere and less dust.

The same object could however be accomplished in a far more tasteful manner by enclosing the window recess with another glass window or partition. The outside glass protects the plants from the cold, the inside ones from undue heat and gas, while between the two there is a happy mean in which plant culture cannot fail to be successful. If however this is not done, and the window panes are made of double glass there will be little danger of their freezing on a cold night. It would be well to have one pane fitted with a hinge, which can be opened to air the plants. But to avoid this a heavy curtain can be placed at the window, and pulled down at night, to protect from cold air, while newspapers may be pinned around the plants to protect them from the bright light of the evening. The amateur must also study the characteristics of his plants, for one temperature will not answer for all. The Rose needs a cool atmosphere, yet moderately moist. The Fuschia is fond of both warmth and moisture, but needs occasional shading when the sun is too hot. The Coleus prefers plenty of heat and moisture, and would be satisfied never to have the thermometer go below 70° by night or day. The Geranium seems to accommodate itself to all circumstances, being the most easily grown of all window plants, and apparently needs only plenty of light and air, and average warmth.

Plants at night.

Plants need rest. Uniform darkness at night with lower temperature, is one of the conditions of treatment, but sometimes there may be a sudden change of temperature in the outer air, and in consequence thereof some one or more plants of the window garden may be frozen. Do not throw them away, but cut the branches back as far as frozen, or near to the soil, then water slightly and do not let the plant get quite as warm as before; if it has any life it will soon show buds and branches. Plants should be treated very much like human beings; a frosted finger should be warmed gradually, so should a frozen plant. Some plants if frosted, like Fuschias, will sprout from the roots and make a strong growth; others will send out strong, healthy flowering branches from the stem near the roots. A very simple plan to restore frosted plants is to transfer them at once to a dark cellar and shower them plentifully with water; keep them here two or three weeks and they will gradually recover their health again.

Another point is often discussed, whether *plants are injurious in rooms at night.* We think it unwise to have too many in a room; a few here and there are of little influence. Strong scented plants are injurious to have in the room at night. The Tuberose, Hyacinth and Jessamine, &c., are too sweet to be allowed to remain in a bedroom at night, and should not be patronized for this purpose by invalids. The sensations of the individual are often a good guide. After sleeping in a room with plants, the morning finds the sleeper inactive, feeling as if his night's rest had been heavy, the air of the room also does not seem pure, and the perfume peculiar. All the indications are sufficient to show the air is vitiated, and fresh air is needed as much by the individual as the plant.

Fresh Air.

Ventilation is absolutely necessary; therefore give it. Whenever the weather is mild open the window. *Too little fresh air* and too much warmth are formidable obstacles to success in house gardening. Plants that are kept shut up in warm rooms become very sensitive and are far more liable to suffer from a sudden fall in the temperature; but if they are frequently exposed to the fresh air they are better able to bear these changes of climate which often occur so unexpectedly. Those who live in close heated rooms can never make their flowers bloom in winter with any vigor. Some think that any atmosphere not inconvenient to men and women is good enough for the plant. It will live just as the human being lives, but it does so in sufferance rather, for it will not grow and bloom in perfect beauty. A very few handsome flowering vines are much to be preferred to spindling plants, pictures of misery, like their owners, overheated and crowded into close unhealthy unventilated quarters. In our fever to provide sufficient warmth in our rooms against the cold, we stop up every crack in our windows, every crevice of our doors; then with furnaces, grates or stoves at almost fever heat we get warmth enough to bid defiance to the chilling atmosphere. Rarely are we satisfied with a temperature in the room of less than 75°, and this must be constantly maintained from early morning till late at night. A draught of fresh air would quicken your blood and put a little more spirit into your countenances; still you aim to avoid it. Yet for the sake of your plants do it at least once a day. Throw open the doors and air the room thoroughly. This can be done at time for meals when it is usually vacant. The windows should not be opened directly upon the plants. Some other window or door away from the plants may be opened. It should be done also at the middle of the day when the outer air is mildest.

Cleanliness.

Here close attention is again required. Plants require regular care. They cannot be watered and cared for once a week and the rest of the time left to themselves, but they demand a daily amount of time to be spent upon them. Every morning when house cleaning is in order, the plants must be watered and cleaned. You will see how necessary this is, if you look at the nature of the plants, how they live. Like our skins, the leaves of plants are perforated with hundreds of minute pores through which they breathe, exhaling oxygen and inhaling carbon, and also giving out and inhaling moisture. If these pores are filled up with dust the plant cannot perform these functions and its life either ceases or stands still; it is not possible for it to grow or bloom. The dust of our living rooms is very injurious to the health of every plant. Unless it is removed, you may as well give up all hope of making your window favorites succeed. Frequent washing and watering are absolutely essential. For close handling of leaves, a soft sponge is of great service, for it can be used in the parlor without danger of dripping from the watering-pot. Wash each leaf separately and see that both sides of it are clean. To shower a plant turn it sideways over a tub of water or a sink; sprinkle it thoroughly with the watering-pot. If the plants are too large to handle in this manner set the pots or tubs into a larger one and either sprinkle or syringe every branch and leaf. You must improvise summer showers if you would induce summer growth. It is not enough to water the earth in the pot. The whole plant requires it. Frequent waterings are the most beneficial culture that you can bestow upon your plants. To be sure they are not easily given and will entail upon you some work.

When sweeping and dusting your rooms, throw newspapers or a light cloth over them; this will prevent the dust from settling upon the leaves, and help materially toward keeping them clean.

Whenever a warm rain falls, and the temperature stands at 50° or 55,° set all the plants out of doors, and they will be greatly refreshed and strengthened. It does not follow, however, that the whole plant is watered by being thus placed out doors; the leaves of the plant may be broad and shield the pot and roots; so do not forget to give these a chance also. If the leaves of plants are very dirty, warm water with a little soap and the use of the sponge or syringe, will remove all dirt. Exposure to the fresh air is not as dangerous as many would suppose, provided the temperature is mild. They are, in fact, benefited by such exposure and become far more hardy and able to resist sudden changes of temperature, much better than if kept constantly confined to the room.

Very few have any idea of how fast the dust accumulates in a room; it is in fact one of the greatest enemies the housewife has to contend with. A short time only, suffices to see the leaves of a plant covered with dust; if it is not removed, they soon get brown and wither; and it is really delightful, after giving them a good washing, to see how bright and shining are the leaves and how greatly they have been invigorated.

Watering Plants.

When shall I water my plants? is a vexed question, asked perhaps more frequently than any other by the beginner. This depends entirely upon the nature of the plant, for some need more water than others, and yet a soil thoroughly wet is totally unfit for plant-growing. The real idea each cultivator should aim for is to supply the plants with water, which may drain rapidly through the pots, yet sufficient be retained to give a good moist soil for the plant to live in. If the water passes away rapidly it will need replacing frequently. It is generally a sign of health when the soil is well drained and the plant uses up the supply of water quickly.

Watering should be supplied with a careful hand, for many parlor gardeners have an unrestrainable belief in the hydropathic process. To them there is only one orthodox rule: if the plants will wither up or are troubled with insects and do not grow as healthy and freely as they might, they drench it with a flood of cold water; so it is a fact, that more plants perish in the hands of the inexperienced, from having too copious a supply than too little. There are others again more cautious in their applications of water, who are, on the other hand, totally heedless of drainage, and let the water stand in the saucers under the pots, or in boxes without drainage, causing mould and sogginess of soil, rendering the roots weak and unhealthy.

The purposes of watering should be better understood. 1st. Water supplies to the roots fertilizing matter, contained in itself, and 2d. It converts the nourishment of the soil into a liquid form more readily fit for absorption by the roots. The roots can obtain it only when the soil is dampened.

Never give water when the soil is moist to the touch, but wait until it is dry.

Few plants thrive if water is around them constantly; yet Lobelias, Callas, Ivies, etc., are very thirsty and like to drink at their own will. Indeed they will not bloom or grow well unless you allow them so to do.

The healthiest plants require water the most frequently; and yet it may appear a contradiction to say that the plants which contain the most watery tissues, grow in the dryest places. The Cacti often supply moisture to the wild cattle of the plains of Mexico ; the animals break through their thorny exteriors with their hoofs, and then eat the moist morsels contained within, which quench their thirst.

Water, cold from the well or pump, is not suitable for plants, unless of a temperature of 60°. Rain water is best, for this is supposed to contain some little ammonia from the sky.

The best rule in all cases is to use water warm to the hands. Some florists advise water no colder than the atmosphere. We believe it generally best to use it *warmer*. In cool mornings it should be lukewarm, say not under 55°. Some cultivators say they have used hot water for sickly plants heated to a temperature from 110° to 170°, and have believed this to be the cause of their subsequent luxuriant growth and production of flowers of the greatest beauty ; but trials like this are not to be encouraged, and warm water of 75° to 90°, will do just as well and have far less danger from scalding. Over 90° is neither necessary nor safe. A lady is said to have once watered her plants with the tea that remained in her pot after the breakfast was finished. Her plants grew in wonderful beauty and luxuriance, and she attributes it to the magic effects of the tea ; yet she has forgotten it was better due to the warmth of the water than any fancied virtue. Some plants demand more water than others. Fuchsias, for instance, while in bloom often require water both morning and evening, and nearly all plants desire more when in flower than at any other time. The supply of water must be regulated according to the demand of the plants. Calla Lilies will absorb water two or three times as quickly as any other plant of the Window Garden. If rainwater cannot be easily obtained and hard water is the only source at hand, add a little soda to it and let it stand for a while ; use a small piece, say a small nugget of the size of a pea, to every gallon ; on that pour about a pint of boiling water and then fill it up with cold water. It will be quite warm, and a thorough drenching overhead and in the pots will vastly improve their color and health. A drop or two of hartshorn will also correct hard water somewhat. In watering, never wet merely the surface, but moisten the whole ball of earth in the pot. If the ball should yet be very dry set the whole pot in a pail of warm water till it is soaked through. The morning is the best time of the day for watering. A common hand-brush made of broomcorn dipped into warm water and shaken over the plants will imitate a summer shower, but its tiny drops may spatter against the window glass. A toy watering-pot, such as is used for children, is very useful for Window Gardening. If oil cloth is laid under the stand it can be used without much if any injury to the carpet or furniture. Care should be taken that the pots have good drainage, for then all surplus water will run into the

Fig. 15.

saucer, which may be emptied as fast as filled. In warm mild weather when plants absorb a great deal of moisture it will do no harm to leave a little in the saucer. Among other details to be observed in watering, the following items of caution are to be observed: Some plants should never be wetted on the leaves. Take the Begonia Rex, whose foliage, so large and grand, has an exquisite coloring; if its leaves were to be sponged with cold water, and the plant left out on the balcony or open air, it would probably die very soon; but a Camelia can be treated the same way and not be injured in the slightest. The reasons for it are good. The last plant has a hard shiny leaf, which can resist rough treatment; but the other has a succulent tender leaf easily affected. The novice then may generally find it true that plants with soft porous and hairy leaves should be very cautiously wetted overhead, but plants with hard varnished leaves may be watered frequently. Tepid water should be invariably used even down to the height of summer. If plants get infested with vermin, a sponging with soap and water made into a lather, will clear them. Then follow with clear water to remove the soap. It is also a good rule to observe that the colder the weather the less water must be given; and when plants are at rest, done growing, they need very little indeed.

Plants in cases may be watered once a week, for evaporation there is confined, but in open rooms once a day is sufficient. Some plants, who delight in very moist situations, need it twice a day. Never water when the sun is hot.

If the soil of the pot gets too hard, loosen it a little with a fork, or plunge it into a tub of water. Take pains to have good drainage, and beyond this little trouble will be experienced.

The Philosophy of Watering

is worth studying. Plants are constantly throwing off or evaporating moisture from their leaves, and at the same time the roots must be taking up an equal supply. If then on examining the soil in a flower-pot, you discover that it is moist for an unusually long time, you may be sure that something is wrong, either the roots do not take it up readily, or drainage is imperfect. Healthy plant action needs air as well as moisture. A soggy soil excludes air, and, as a result, our plants soon show drooping leaves and unhealthy branches. Drainage is to plants what digestion is to the human system, keeping everything in perfect action. Water and air enjoy a healthy circulation unimpeded, and plants which are growing freely and vigorously, with strong roots, will take up the moisture of the pots regularly. Mr. Meehan, who has studied plant physiology more thoroughly than any other American, sums up this subject in the following concise paragraph:

" A wet soil is totally unfit for plant growing. A plant standing 24 hours in water is irreparably injured. A Hyacinth, to be sure, will live one season in water; but all the matter of the flower which goes to water is prepared the year before, and after flowering, the bulb is exhausted and almost worthless.

" A good soil for plant growing, therefore, is not one which will hold water, but one in which water will pass away.

"The soil itself is composed of minute particles, through which air spaces abound. The water must be just enough to keep these particles moist, and the air in the spaces is thus kept in the condition of moist air. The roots traverse these air spaces, and it is, therefore, *moist air* which roots want, and not water.

"If it were water simply which plants wanted, we should cork up the bottom of the hole in the flower pot, and prevent the water getting away. Instead of this, we try to hasten the passing of the water through as much as possible, by not only keeping the hole clear, but often by putting broken pieces in the bottom to hasten the drainage. A plant will generally be the healthiest, therefore, which wants water the oftenest. If it does not want water, it is in a bad way. And more water will make the matter worse.

"How often to water them, will be according to how easy the water passes away. If, when you pour water on earth it disappears almost instantly, it would be safe to water such plants every day.

"The constant aim of the cultivator should be to keep the soil of such a consistence that a moist atmosphere shall always be present in the air spaces existing through it.

Moisture of the Atmosphere.

The atmosphere of our houses, as we have intimated before, is not only too dry for successful plant culture, but it breeds insects of various kinds which will injure their growth.

We have noticed that plants kept in kitchen windows where the air is charged with moist vapors from the boiling of water over the stove or range, and where the outside doors are frequently opened, and fresh air supplied, will often develop into surprising luxuriance and beauty. We can call to mind even now a farm kitchen in the coldest portion of our most northern states, where Roses, Carnations and Verbenas, grow finely, and are covered with a summery profusion of buds and flowers. These are usually the most difficult plants to bring into bloom in parlor windows, because they are apt to be so infested with minute red spiders, and the green aphis, scale or mealy bug.

It is the moisture in the air which tends to restrain and drive away such disagreeable intruders. The heated air of the house can be kept moist by placing an evaporating pan upon or in our furnaces, and over our stoves we can place a large fire-proof dish that must be daily filled with water.

If the surfaces of the soil in pots is covered with moss, it retards the evaporation of water; this practice is generally advisable only for those plants which require much water, such as Calla Lilies, Fuchsias, Camellias, &c. Pots that are imbedded in moss are always kept moist, and if a table is constructed just the height of the window, with a rim fastened around each side three inches in depth, and the whole lined with zinc, the pots can be set in it, and the moss stuffed in on all sides. When watering is needed, set it back from the window and sprinkle with a fine watering pot.

The Soil.

The most easily available material for a compost by the ordinary gardener, will be rich loam, sand, and thoroughly decayed cow manure. This should be mixed in the proportion of one half of the loam to one quarter each of the sand and manure. Leaf mould is also another grand material which every plant loves to grow in, and it will pay to secure a good quantity of it. The older and more decomposed the manure and leaf mould, the better they are, and every plant grower should keep a well prepared compost heap for his plants. A good compost, when all the material is handy, is composed of one fourth of the above elements of leaf mould, sand, loam and manure. To those who live in cities and can not get this conveniently, it is best either to buy your plants already potted, or go to a good florist and buy a good quantity of right compost; he can usually supply it at cheaper rate than it can be purchased anywhere else.

Keep this heap well filled, and no one must fail to bear in mind that the soil of every one of his pots needs changing and replenishing, or else it becomes exhausted, and the plants dwindle and languish for needed food.

Garden loam is often used by those in the country and found to answer, but if it should contain any clay, a little sand must be added. The sand itself is of no fertilizing effect, but is valuable in assisting the aeration of the soil and helping the drainage. Well rotten turf is another handy and valuable material, containing considerable quantity of vegetable mould. If used, put the coarser pieces at the bottom along with some pebbles or broken pieces of crockery, then fill in the finer mould to about half an inch from the surface. The soil must not be allowed to cake up, but be occasionally stirred up deep, so that air may have access to the roots.

Leaf mould is more highly prized by gardeners than anything else that can be procured. Every autumn the leaves are gathered in heaps, wheeled by the barrow load to a good location, and there left exposed to the rain and the action of the weather for sometimes two or three years. Here it decomposes and becomes rotten. Then it is mixed with good turf mould, also left to rot for a year or two, and finally chopped up; then add the sand, decomposed manure and some peat well minced to small pieces. This is considered the very best material for pots, or borders in green-houses or conservatories. A good pile of it is always maintained. It is rather an advantage than otherwise to have a few lumps in each pot ; they prevent the soil from becoming too solid.

A compost for *Camellias, Roses, Geraniums, &c.*, should be one part river sand, one part leaf mould, two parts turf or garden mould. For *Cacti,* use two parts coarse sand, three parts leaf and turf mould, one part peat, and a little broken plaster.

For *Azaleas, Ericas,* and most *New Holland plants*, take four parts peat, two parts sand, one part garden or turf mould, one part leaf mould.

Soil for bulbous roots should be light ; place them in the centre of the pots, about half imbedded in the light earth, then cover them with leaf or fine turf mould.

For drainage purposes, put in the bottom of each pot either a layer of powdered charcoal, or small broken pieces of brick or old mortar to the depth of at least an inch ; over this there may be a slight sprinkling of sand ; still it may be omitted if it has previously been well incorporated in the compost. In general it should never be less than one fifth the whole material of the compost, and one fourth will be best in most cases.

Forest mould scraped up under the branches of pine or other forest trees, or the soil taken from under the sods of droppings in cow pastures, will be found useful in imparting a vigorous growth to plants.

Amateurs sometimes choose earth from the back yards of their city residences ; this is rarely ever suitable, and often its effects can be seen in the half dead and weak look of the plants, who seem to be languishing for nourishment. This soil is rarely ever fertilized, and usually is either the filling in from the street or cellar. It may be fit to grow grass upon, but not to put in the pots of house plants.

There are some plants which require an imperative admixture of peat and loam, such as Ericas, Azaleas and Daphne. There is no substance which can be substituted for it, and produce success. Earth for pots should rarely ever be sifted, put it in just as it is ; lumpy and crude, so much the better.

In potting your plants and planting them out, be very careful to press the earth very tightly and closely around the roots and stalks of the plants ; half the secret of successful pot culture lies in *potting plants.*

Hard wooded plants should be potted rather firmly, and soft wooded ones should be left rather free and loose.

In repotting plants, take the plant that is to be repotted, turn it upside down, with your left hand across the mouth of the pot, and the stem of the plant between the fingers, give the pot a few raps on a pan on the table, lift up the pot and you have the plant and the ball of earth in your hand.

Examine it carefully, and if any worms appear, pick them out, or if the earth is full of healthy roots, and they are matted around the sides of it, the plant requires a pot one size larger than that in which it has grown.

Place the ball of earth and the plant directly in the centre of the new pot, and fill it up all around with fresh soil, pressing it firmly down either with the fingers or a flat stick ; cover the " ball " with fresh earth half an inch in depth ; strike the bottom of the pot several times against a flat substance, and again press the soil tightly around the roots. Loose planting is a fruitful source of the non-success attending the gardening of amateur florists. Place your plants in the shade for two or three days to allow their roots to become accustomed to the charge of quarters. A healthy, abundantly rooted plant, requires a pot one size larger, but, if the plant you turn out should not show its roots on the outside, it needs no change of quarters, still it may need fresh soil, and if the earth seems poor and gritty it is best to give it..

If in examination of your pots you should find some plant injured by injudicious waterings, its roots rotten, and soil soddened, then cut or tear away the decayed parts, turn out the wet soil, take a pot of the smaller size, and with a lighter soil give it another chance for life, watering it sparingly until the foliage shows its return to health and strength.

Never pot a plant that has its ball of earth quite dry, for you cannot give it water afterward. All the water you pour upon it will run down the fresh soil at the sides of the pot, leaving the plant to perish with drought. Sometimes in potting plants, you will find a large brown root coiled up in the pot like a snake. Cut it off close to the main root and put this plant in a pot of smaller size, and very soon fresh and more nourishing roots will take its place. Such roots are often found in pots of Geraniums. This piece of root can be made to grow by cutting it into 3 inch lengths, and planting them in pots of sandy loam, leaving a quarter of an inch of the root uncovered, and keeping them warm and moist.

In placing plants in pots in the open air, either sink them in the borders or on the grass. Be sure to scatter coal or wood ashes underneath them, to prevent worms from entering the pots and the soil from becoming clogged.

Fertilizers for Stimulating House Plants.

All plants will grow much finer if stimulants are given, say at least once a week.

A very fine liquid fertilizer can be made out of horse and cow manure. Take an old bucket for the purpose, put into it several shovels full of manure, to which add one pint of charcoal dust, this neutralizes its odor, add to it plenty of boiling water, let it cool, and apply to the plant. It should not be given too strong, but about the color of weak tea. The bucket can stay filled up with water for six weeks or two months as it is needed, then throw away its contents and begin again.

Guano water, a decoction of Peruvian guano, makes a good stimulant. It should be applied once a week to the roots, taking care not to touch the leaves with it. To one gallon of hot water, add one large tablespoonful of guano; stir until it is dissolved. Hen manure may be substituted and used in about the same quantity.

When used carefully, either are excellent, and give the plants a bright, vigorous green.

Ammonia water stimulates growth very satisfactorily. Dissolve ¼ ounce of pulverized ammonia in a gallon of water, and it will prove more grateful to the plants even than rain water which also contains ammonia. A teaspoonful of *aqua ammonia* added to a gallon of warm water will be of same efficacy. *Flour of bone,* when it can be obtained in the form of powder, easily soluble in water, is still more suitable, for it contains other elements of plant nutrition. Used in moderate quantities, not over a tablespoonful to a gallon of warm water, it will give the plants a healthy impetus; give a sufficient quantity to wet the whole ball of earth and pour off the surplus water that runs into the saucer. A special fertilizer used to advantage by some, is composed as follows : take of sulphate of ammonia four ounces, nitrate of potash two ounces, white sugar one ounce, add one pint of hot water; when dissolved cork tightly and add a teaspoonful to every gallon of water used for watering; six or eight drops of this liquid can be poured into the water of a hyacinth glass, and the flowers will be much finer.

All these special stimulants must be used with caution, be well diluted, applied not oftener than once a week, and once in three weeks will be sufficient for the hyacinth.

Pinching.

Plants should be kept in good shape by pinching off their shoots from time to time, so as to avoid an outward spindling appearance; straggling branches can never be handsome; but if their shoots are nipped or pinched in every month or so, they will grow bushy and have many more blossoms and leaves. Fig. 16

Fig. 16.

shows a good pruning scissors. Fuchsias and Pelargoniums are generally stopped once or twice before they flower. When the shoots have grown about three leaves their ends are pinched out; this gives three or four shoots instead of one, and increases the proportion of blossoms, but keeps the plant dwarf. The *training* of plants is also a matter of taste, usually the form of a half circle is most preferred. Fuchsias trained to single stakes and allowed to droop down are natural objects of beauty. Every gardener has his fancy. Nothing is so pleasing as to see a rose trained to stakes in pots bent completely back to the pot, in the shape of a semi-circle—every branch covered with buds just ready to bloom.

General Suggestions.

1. All plants have a season of rest ; therefore discover what season is peculiar to each, and transplant at that time. 2. The best time for taking cuttings is when the plants are in their most active state of growth, and this is before flowering. 3. Profuse bloomings exhaust the strength of plants, therefore cut off all flower buds as soon as their petals fall, and do not let the seed pods mature unless you desire to raise seeds. 4. All bulbs and tubers should be planted before they begin to shoot; if suffered to form leaves and roots in the air, they waste their strength. 5. Never remove the leaves from bulbs after flowering until they are quite dead. As long as the leaves retain life they are employed in preparing nourishment and transmitting it to the roots. 6. Window

plants are more liable to be injured by frost than plants in the ground, because the fibres of the roots cling to the sides of the pots and are more quickly affected by the chilling air. 7. The faster a plant grows, the farther apart are the leaves, the more distant the side branches, and the more bare appears the stem. Richness of foliage can never be attained when leaves become thus scattered. By keeping a lower temperature, especially at night, there will be a slower and more desirable growth, and conducive to compactness of habit to plants. 8. No plants can bear sudden contrasts of temperature without injury, therefore bring nothing directly from a heated room to the cool open air. 9. By checking the growth of leaves and branches you throw more strength into the flowers; this is why the terminal shoots of many plants should be pinched off to increase their vigor. 10. Avoid excessive heat. Plants often languish in a hot temperature while their owners cannot imagine why they do not grow, forgetting that the atmosphere is already too warm for even human beings. Suggestions like these will show that although Window Gardens require some skill and experience in good management, yet there is nothing abstruse or difficult to prevent any one from undertaking the care of one which needs only a reasonable degree of thought and attention to make it a constant delight.

CHAPTER IV.

SPECIAL CARE OF WINDOW GARDENS.

In Winter.

The beauties of the flower garden are gone, and we are now left to solace ourselves with any green thing we can coax by artificial help to grow and bloom during the long winter months, till spring returns again. Naturally enough we hate to lose the sight of the flowers, and graceful flutter of the green leaves, so we strive to prolong our joy, as far as possible, under many difficulties through unsuitable seasons.

During the winter seasons the chief requisites of success, are plenty of sunshine, an atmosphere not too dry or close, a mild uniform temperature, and especial attention to cleanliness, watering and daily care.

Plants which receive only a few moments of attention a day and then forgotten, soon become a disgrace, and the window garden becomes a nuisance.

In the open ground plants will flourish if left to themselves, but when grown in a pot, they are under artificial restraints and conditions, and must become an object of constant attention. This very necessity of the case renders window gardening of so much greater interest than out door gardening.

Plants at night should be in the dark, as that is their natural condition so that they may rest, and yet it is equally important that they should be freely exposed to the sun as long as light lasts.

So, especially in the winter months, when there is comparatively so little sunlight, place them as closely to the windows as they can be well managed, if not, they will become unsightly, drawn and weak. The more light that a plant receives the more freely can it absorb carbon and breathe out oxygen; so if you wish your plants to be purifiers of the air, be sure that they have plenty of light, and keep both blinds and curtains from obstructing it.

The necessity for air in *the winter* is no less imperative than the demand for light. In order to cultivate Geraniums successfully, a constant supply of fresh air is very needful. Roses, Verbenas, and indeed all plants demand it.

When plants are first brought into the house they should not be stimulated, but allowed a little time to become accustomed to their new quarters; and they will often wither a little from the want of fresh air, so let the windows be open all day, if it is sunny, and accustom them by degrees to the change of temperature.

It is not desirable to allow them to remain out too late in the season, but they should be housed before any danger of frost arises; a slight chill will frequently injure them greatly, especially the Coleus, and all sub tropical plants unused to our cold autumn winds.

They can be placed on a protected piazza, and covered at night with some mats or sheets, but the true lover of house plants does not feel at ease until all her pets are standing in their winter quarters ; then the cold chilly winds may blow, and Jack Frost's icy fingers pinch with blackening touches all that they can reach; the household flowers are safe beyond his dreaded touch.

Do not crowd your plant stands or windows, give to each plant room to stretch forth its branches and leaves, if you would have it bloom in vigor and beauty ; untidy straggling plants are always detestable.

Every dead leaf must be removed and every fading flower, and the leaf must not remain in the pots, but be taken away; cleanliness is so important that no damp leaves or decaying flowers should be left. Window plants suffer chiefly in the winter months from indiscriminate waterings, allowing them to go dry for two or three days and then soaking them for a week.

Many a lady cannot imagine why her plants do not grow and bloom as luxuriantly as at her opposite neighbor's. But it is the lack of daily atttention that makes the difference. One lady buys her plants because it is the fashion to have them in the windows; the other loves her plants as a part of herself, sees in them an individuality ; a glimpse perhaps of something beautiful beyond this world's plain realities, and it is not a care for her to attend to their necessities, but rather a privilege.

In the winter time the familiar question is asked over and over again: " How am I to know when my plants need watering?" Watch them carefully, and they will tell you; wilted leaves, drooping branches, and yellow shades show that they are water-clogged ; they must be allowed a respite.

Turn up the soil as heretofore directed, with a stout hair pin, and if it is dry give more water ; if not, abstain from it.

Success in window gardening depends greatly in never permitting the plants to suffer from any neglect.

When you water, give it copiously, and if the next day the plants have enough pass them by ; but there are always some in a window or a stand of plants that desire it, so carry round the watering pot every day, take the time either before or after breakfast, have a special hour, and never forget it. There is more danger of giving too much water during the winter, than in the spring and summer, because the evaporation is much less.

In winter there should be no water left in the saucers ; with the exception of aquatics they require it.

A small toy watering pot such as are sold for children's use, is of the greatest assistance; it will sprinkle the surface of tiny pots without wetting either stands or window glass.

A piece of oilcloth is an excellent protection to carpets, and should always be placed under every window and plant stand.

It is best to select a cloudy day for giving your plants a thorough cleaning, thereby imitating nature, as she seldom washes her vegetation with the sun shining upon it.

A pail of warm water can be brought into the parlor, and each plant thoroughly wetted in it, the surface of each leaf well moistened, without making any disturbance with the arrangement of the room.

Plants perspire like human beings, only the amount is seventeen times as great, according to Mr. Hale's computation.

In the Hydrangea, the minute orifices in the space of an inch, are found to be one hundred thousand.

Protection from Frost.

During the winter our tender plants are liable to become frost-bitten in spite of every precaution we may take in their behalf. When the mercury out of doors settles to 25° and 30°, some little branches and leaves will droop, and the soil in some pots may become solid in doors.

If this happens, all is not lost. Take the blighted plants tenderly, and dip them into cold water, not icy cold, but drawn from hydrant or cistern; then place them in complete darkness where not a ray of light can penetrate, and in three days at the utmost, you will find them fresh as ever, every leaf upright and green, while if they had been left in the light, every leaf would have fallen. Several times we have had this experience with our plants and have always revived them.

If the pots are set back at night from the windows on a piano or table, they will often escape freezing.

If a window opens on to a piazza, the plants can be protected by pinning a thick comforter outside of the window, or tucking it into the blinds.

Double windows are highly essential in a cold climate to keep off the intense cold, but they should always have an opening, a pane of glass with a hinge, or some means by which the room can be aired daily; the weekly cleaning is not often enough to open the windows.

Do not forget to shade them from too much light and heat in the early part of the evening.

The great secret of success in window gardening, consists in overcoming as much as possible the disadvantages under which the plants labor, and rendering their position and treatment as much as possible like those growing in the open air.

Spring Culture of Window Gardens.

March is the first month that treads upon the flowery border of spring; it is the beginning of the sunny season which shall awake the sleeping bulbs, plants, shrubs, and indeed all vegetation.

March, April, May and June, are very busy months, for in them we make large additions to our collections of plants by propagating new varieties, both by seeds and cuttings.

Of course with all your fancy for new things, you will not forget to secure some few pots of good old fashioned flowers. They may be dear to many from only childish associations, having proved their value by the many years in which they have been cherished. No true lover despises them.

The culture in the spring months differs but little from that of the winter; more air can be given, and often the windows can be let down from the top for the whole day. Remember that if the thermometer stands at 55° and 65° out of doors, and the sun shines brightly, too much fresh air is impossible; but have the windows closed by three o'clock, for by that time a chilly wind often springs up in April, which would prove injurious to many tender plants, in a rapidly growing condition. Later in the season there is no danger. Great attention must be paid to general cleanliness; now is the season to promote rapid growth, but if the plants cannot breathe freely, they are in a decidedly consumptive state, and must pine away. To prolong the blooming of plants, every fading flower, even if it is but one in a cluster, should be cut away.

To keep the flowers of Azaleas from falling, it is an excellent plan to drop a single drop of gum water underneath the flower, where it sinks into the calyx; now is the time for their most profuse bloom, and they can be made more ornamental by this process.

No flowers should be left with water standing in their saucers, but if the plants are sunk in boxes or moss, there is no need of using saucers, which are hard to keep clean.

Be sure and attend to the weekly washing; it is quite as essential to your plants as to your household cleanliness.

A small sized brush such as painters use, will be found of great service as it will wash off the tiniest leaf and stem.

Water must be given plentifully during the spring months, and it is well to supply it till a few drops ooze out from the bottom of the pot; but don't water while the sun shines full upon the plants.

Rain water is always the best for all vegetation. We especially recommend warm water in cold latitudes, as it cannot help but prove more invigorating to the roots. The sun does not shine every day; often it is withdrawn for a week, but if the soil is warmed with the water, it will not check the growth of the plants as much. This rule does not apply so closely to conservatories; there the plant can be sprinkled as though they were growing in the open ground, and warm water is not so much of a necessity in a greenhouse, where the whole temperature is adapted to the needs of plant-life. But this is not the case in window gardens, and we think its use the greatest benefit to them. Early in April, or in the later days of March, the plants that were stored in the cellar for safe keeping should be brought to the light; the decayed leaves and dust must be carefully brushed away and picked off, and the plant repotted, ready to start forth afresh.

The more hardy plants, like Roses, Geraniums, Pansies, etc., etc., can be put out of doors on warm days to enjoy an hour or so of fresh air and sunshine, at noontime; or if a warm rain falls, all the plants can go out and drink in fresh life with every drop. But don't let them remain out too long; a chill in April is often fatal to Heliotropes, variegated leaved plants, Fuchsias, etc. One must be governed by the climate.

In March or April, according to your latitude, it is well to look into the subject of repotting the plants that have stood in the window. If the plants have had the requisite care and attention during the winter, they have made many new roots and must now have larger pots if you would have them grow to the best advantage.

Water the pots freely so that the ball of earth will slip out easily, and have your fresh potting soil moist to the touch. Never pot a plant with its ball of earth quite dry, for you cannot give it a good watering in that state. All the water you may supply will run down the fresh soil at the sides, and the plant will experience the fate of Tantalus of old, and literally starve to death, although its nourishment is in sight. If you use new pots, let them be soaked in water over night if possible, and at least three or four hours before using them. If your pots are old, let them be thoroughly washed, and cleansed from all green mould and soil.

It is not needful to provide larger pots when the first roots show themselves; but when they have twined and interlaced their tiny fibres, then they require more room. Often a light rap upon the edge of the pot, will be sufficient to turn out the ball of earth; but if not, a thin bladed knife can be run around close to the pot for an inch or two from the top, and this will bring it out easily. Turn it out with your hand and examine the roots; if they are closely curled about it, the plant requires a pot one size larger. Fill the pot with rich compost and put in the ball and plant directly in the centre, for a plant growing sideways in a pot looks very badly; fill up all around the sides of the pot, packing the soil down firmly with the fingers, cover the ball to the depth of a quarter or half an inch, leaving a vacant space of half an inch more to the edge of the pot for the purpose of watering to advantage.

When you turn out the plant, the roots will sometimes appear decayed, and the soil poor, dried, and gritty; then wash it all away, removing the dried roots, and give fresh, rich soil, pressing it firmly about the roots, but keep the same sized pot.

Perhaps you will find your plants injured by injudicious watering, the roots rotted, and the soil sodden. Cut off the roots as much as possible without removing the whole of them, and plant them in much smaller pots with a sandy soil, and they will regain their health.

As the weather grows warmer in May, many plants can be placed in balconies or on piazzas, and shielded from chilly winds and cold nights by mats or blankets, or they may be removed to cooler rooms where the sunshine will be sufficiently warm to keep them healthy. This is far better than roasting them in the hot rooms that many will live in, spite of all remonstrances to the contrary.

Sweet Verbenas should be brought from their winter quarters early in March, and they will soon put forth their light green, deliciously perfumed leaves.

The plants that will flower most profusely in these months **are :**

Azaleas.	*Heliotropes.*
Abutilons.	*Lantanas*
Acacias.	*Libonia Floribunda.*
Anemones.	*Lobelias.*
Auriculas.	*Mahernia Odorata.*
Achimenes.	*Maurandias.*
Bouvardias.	*Myrtles.*
Begonias	*Oranges.*
Calla Aethiopica.	*Oleanders.*
Cinerarias.	*Pelargoniums.*
Cyclamens.	*Primroses.*
Daphnes.	*Petunias.*
Dielytra.	*Pansies.*
Epiphyllum Truncatum, etc.	*Roses.* *Tea.* *Hybrids.* **Bourbons.**
Fuchsias.	*Bengal Roses.*
Gardenias.	*Verbenas.*
Geraniums, in all varieties.	*Violets.*

The Mush plant (*Mimulus Moschatus*) is an universal favorite.

For culture in outside window boxes, the best are *Violets*, early flowering *Snow Drops*, early flowering *Anemones, Forget-me-Nots and Primroses.*

Summer Culture of Window Gardens.

June, July and August, do not require as much labor as the busy months of springtime. To be sure the cultivator needs to give daily attention lest the plants should become dried up from want of water; and must also tie, stake, prune, air, and weed with great care.

Water will now be required in greater quantities, and it need not be any warmer than standing in the sun will make it. The evening is the best time to apply it, because the plants will drink it up during the night to their great advantage, while if given in the morning, the sun's rays will claim their share, and by quick evaporation much will be lost in the atmosphere. There are some plants that will desire, and must have water twice in the twenty-four hours. Fuchsias, Callas, Lobelias, etc., should have water both night and morning.

After the first of June, the plants will enjoy all the fresh air that can be given both night and day, in nearly all latitudes. Calceolarias and Cinerarias will be benefited by being kept cool, which can be done by placing them on damp moss, or refuse tan bark, and covering the surface of the pot with it. By the middle of June they can be placed in a cool, shady window, and all the stems that have flowered should be cut off, or if planted in a cool border, they will furnish more roots which can be divided in September or October.

By the end of May, in many localities, many plants will flourish better outside the window than inside; Geraniums, Pelargoniums, Fuchsias, Roses, Heliotropes, etc., etc., can be placed in boxes and vases on piazzas or balconies, or a garden can be made on the roof.

Large strong boxes can be attached to the outside of the windows, and all the plants set into them. In this way much care is avoided, for the plants can be watered with a syringe or watering pot, and the *debris* of withered leaves and stems is more easily cleared away. The plants can also be kept much freer from insects, and will grow more luxuriantly. Manure waterings can be given weekly. A tablespoonful of guano in a gallon of water, which should stand in the sun two or three days before being applied, is the easiest to procure, but all or any of the manures alluded to before, can be employed. When the flower buds appear, stimulants are much needed ; and if no other can be procured, try this. Put a teaspoonful of *aqua ammonia* into a gallon of water, and sprinkle it all over the leaves and surface of the soil. Cut off all faded flowers ; this greatly helps to keep the plants free from mildew, and increases their healthy condition ; every yellow leaf should be taken off as soon as perceived.

If ever a plant becomes thoroughly dry from oversight or neglect, place it in a deep pan of rain water (if possible,) and let it remain for an hour or longer, until it is thoroughly soaked, but do not let the pot be entirely covered with the water. Hot water will frequently revive faded cut flowers ; cut off a small bit of the stem, and then immerse the end into very hot water ; you can see the petals smooth out from their crumpled folds, the leaves uncurl, and the whole branch and flower resume its beauty. Colored flowers revive the most completely. White flowers turn yellow, and the thickest textured petals come out the best from this hot foot bath.

For preserving flowers in water, there is nothing so good as finely powdered charcoal. It keeps the water from all obnoxious odors. As a general rule too much air and too much light can not be given ; yet when in full bloom the direct rays of the sun will cause delicate flowers to fade rapidly, while if they are shaded from the noon-tide heat, their beauty will be much prolonged ; but during the night the more fresh air they breathe is the better.

If house-plants are plunged in pots into the borders, care must be taken to either close up the outlet at the botom of the pot, or else to put bits of plank or shingles under them, or set them upon small stones. This is needful on account of the tendency of their tiny rootlets to force their way out of the pot, and when the plant is removed, they must necessarily be cut off, thereby causing it to droop *or wither*, and greatly injuring its growth.

It is not advisable to let your plants run to seed. You desire to secure flowers, and to do this you must not let the plant fulfil its mission of leaves, buds, flowers and seeds in natural order, but by cutting off all the faded blooms, stimulate it to shoot forth fresh branches and buds, and strive to do its duty.

In order to secure seeds that are worth planting, it is needful to pick off all the later buds, and throw the whole strength of the plant into forming seed that will prove worth the raising.

Do not omit the practice of washing your pot plants in the summer, thinking that the rain will do it for you. It will help you doubtless, but if the leaves are bushy, many of them will not have their full share, and should still be syringed and washed with all the help of thumb and finger, sponge, brush, or garden syringe.

. Keep the soil well stirred up in these months, for if you desire healthy plants the air must have access to the roots, and the surface of the pot must not be allowed to cake. There are many annuals that make fine pot plants both in summer and winter, but in June, July and August, they will give you most brilliant flowers at a very small cost. Boxes of Portulacca, Asters, Phlox, Stocks, Balsams, Pinks, Schizanthus, Zinnias, etc., are highly ornamental and within the reach of all flower lovers, while each of the above named flowers make handsome single plants in pots.

We can hardly give a list of flowers that bloom in these months, for their name is legion, and embraces many of those mentioned heretofore.

The Lilies are in their glory, and there can be no finer pot plants raised than the various varieties of Japan Lilies, Tigridias, Amaryllis and *Vallotta Purpurea Superba,* all of which are mentioned in the chapter upon bulbs.

Late in August, cuttings can be struck from all bedding-out plants that are desired to be kept during the winter. At this season they strike root very freely, and will frequently become fine plants by December.

Gloxinias and Achimenes are most desirable additions to summer blooming flowers. The Gloxinias are particularly beautiful and brilliant. Their exquisite coloring and freshness is unequaled.

Achimenes are, also, a genus of splendid plants, which will be described in Part II. They are unrivaled in beauty of coloring and form. They produce the most beautiful masses of blossoms in vases and baskets, over which they festoon their glorious flowers and trailing branches.

Autumn Culture of Window Gardens.

For this season there is little to be added to the directions already given for the culture of house plants in previous months. The plants that are intended for winter flowering should all be repotted and prepared for their permanent quarters early in September, so as to become fully established in the pots before the season is cold and gloomy. The roots must be attended to as heretofore directed, and if they cling to the surface of the pot, one of a larger size should be substituted, and fresh earth given. Be sure to procure good soil, and to press it tightly about the roots, and crown of the bulb, or stem of the plant.

Do not attempt to cultivate too many plants, remembering that one strong, handsome shaped healthy plant is worth more than ten or twelve sickly things, that are lanky, scraggy and never blossom.

Give your plants the morning sunshine. It is far better than the afternoon, and if the windows open, both to the east and southwest, so much the better for the plants at both windows; yet, if no other location can be procured, the afternoon sun is far better than none at all.

Never use glazed pots or crockery and painted ware, unless the common pots are set into them for ornamental purposes.

Stimulate once a week with some one of the various liquid manures alluded to.

Avoid extremes of cold and heat, and give all the air that is allowable, according to the temperature out of doors.

Of course, each gardener must regulate her plants, according to the latitude in which she lives. If, on the Pacific slope, the dust that is so tenacious during summer and autumn must be the greatest enemy to contend with, while on the Atlantic coast the chilly, bleak east winds are the greatest drawbacks to successful plant culture. In the west, the cold winds blow from the Rocky Mountains.

No set code of rules can be given, and common sense must govern window gardening, as well as in all the branches of domestic economy.

A large sponge will do duty for a watering pot, or a hand brush broom dipped into water and shaken over the plants; but sprinkling must be given in some shape, at least, once a day.

If the pots are thoroughly washed with hot soap suds, all tendency to green mould will be prevented.

Make the water that is given, warmer now than in the summer. Put your finger into the saucer, and see how cold it is, when it drains through the outlet. And if quite cold, give water of a greater warmth.

Plants that are in a state of rest, should have but very little water during the autumn.

Bulbs must be started for early flowering in September and for Easter, blooming late, in November.

Roses should all be repotted with rich soil: full two-thirds of entirely decomposed cow manure and leaf mould, so decayed as to crumble in the fingers, should be added, to one-third of good sandy loam.

As most of the desirable flowering plants will be treated of in their respective chapters, it will only be a repetition to notice them here, or to give a list of them.

CHAPTER V.

Insects, and How to Kill Them.

The previous anxieties of the gardener are but light compared to the deadly warfare he is now forced to wage against the tiny insects which not only infest his house-plants, but the soil in which they grow and bloom.

The red spider is the most minute, yet the most dangerous foe wherewith we have to deal. Hot and close parlors and sitting-rooms, are its delight, and it weaves its tiny webs about the casements waiting until the plants are ready to feed it.

He is a treacherous invidious enemy seeming to lie in the window frames quiet and warm, but ready to seize upon our rarest Roses, most valuable Fuchsias and Carnations, as soon as they are placed in their winter quarters.

It is the tiniest of red mites; the merest grain as it lies in repose under the leaves of the plant it has chosen for its dwelling, but when the leaf is closely examined, it rushes wildly about, apparently knowing that it is doomed, and its minutes are numbered.

Though these pests are so minute, one can easily discover their presence; for the upper sides of the leaves grow brown and sire, and the plant loses its healthy appearance.

A thorough sprinkling and washing may drive away the intruders, but if the heated and close atmosphere is still continued, plenty more will be generated.

Red pepper has been found decidedly obnoxious to it. It should be dusted upon with a pepper castor, holding the plant bottom side upwards, while another person dusts on the pepper. Of course you must take care not to let it fall in any quantity upon the soil of the pot, lest it should injure the roots.

A decoction of quassia will also act fatally upon insect life, if used in the following proportions:

Boil one ounce of quassia wood in three pints of water until but a quart remains; when luke warm, either dip in the infested plants, or sponge off each leaf with a sponge or brush. Let them stand fifteen minutes or so, then dip the plants or wash them off with clear water, as the decoction of quassia, if allowed to remain on the leaves, will injure them.

Tobacco smoke is also a good preventive to some insects, but this red spider does not seem to heed it.

The *aphis* or green fly, does not affect a liking for tobacco, for it intoxicates it, and causes it to fall from the leaves and branches of all plants. Hold a lighted cigar under the leaves of your Roses, etc., not so near as to curl them with the heat however, and see how they will fall down completely stupefied; but, if left to themselves, they will revive, and slowly return to their leafy homes. Place a paper under the leaves when you apply the smoke, and then you can easily destroy them.

If a plant is very much infested with these noxious pests, take the pot in your hand and spread a paper under it, then with a feather or small wing, brush off the insects and burn them all up. Then dip the plant into warm water, to kill the eggs, and with a weekly washing, smoking or sprinkling, not an insect will be seen.

A conservatory plant-stand, or window garden with plants covered with these insects, plainly announces the neglect they have received. The old maxim seems to come here again in play, *i. e.* "An ounce of prevention is worth a pound of cure."

If plants were as carefully washed and tended as many pet animals were, there would be no need of any remedies against insects.

Conservatories can be kept free of all insects by being smoked once a week with tobacco. Close all the windows carefully that lead into the house, take the largest size flower pot-saucer, put a shovel full of blazing coals into it, and pour over them an ounce of tobacco, letting it smoke well ; if it is slightly dampened the smoke will be more dense. Let it smoke for half an hour, then open the window out of doors, and let the smoke go out. Choose a bright fair day when half an hour's outside air will not injure the plants, and you will keep all of them fresh and vigorous.

The *mealy bug,* is a white mealy looking insect, but very destructive to plant life. It does not dislike tobacco, but has a hatred to whale oil soap. A quarter of a pound dissolved in five quarts of water, and syringed on to the plants, or sprinkled with a watering pot, will force it to disappear.

Like the aphis, it can be brushed off with a chicken's wing.

Brown scale will sometimes attack Roses, Daphnes, Oranges and Pittosporums, but it is not nearly as common as the above mentioned insect. Bad ventilation and dark places are its chief cause and *habitat ;* frequent washings and picking off with the hand, are its only means of destruction, as it thrives on tobacco smoke, and makes no objection to the disgusting odor of whale oil soap suds.

Thrips is a dark brown or whitish yellow fly, very active on the wing, and greatly injurious to many plants. It will not thrive where tobacco smoke is given to plants, and is most likely to be found where plants are placed thickly together, in a shaded window.

The *Verbena mite* is a most tiny insect, smaller than the red spider, and quite as disastrous in its ravages. It cannot be seen with the naked eye, but viewed through a microscope, it appears as large as a house fly.

If it attacks your plants, it appears like a black rust so thickly does it congregate together. It delights in Heliotropes, Petunias, Verbenas, etc., and is closely allied to the insect which infests the Plum, Peach and Cherry trees.

Neither sulphur, tobacco, or whale oil soap are obnoxious to it, but it will run away from the " Grafton Mineral Fertilizer," and a thorough sprinkling of the dry powder on the leaves or stems well moistened, will make the insects dislodge their hold, not to return.

There is another mite whose color varies from green to black, and is as particular in its attentions to Carnations and Pinks, and so rapid in its movements, that it has been named the " Carnation Twitter." It is very destructive to all the varieties of plants above mentioned, and it affects the leaves like the spider, making them very unhealthy in appearance, and as yet no means have been found to destroy it.

If plants grow vigorously, are healthy and well cared for, the ravages of insects are not to be much dreaded ; and if they do appear they can be quickly routed. Undoubtedly we must fight if we would become the owners of hand some, finely formed, profuse blossoming plants; and she who devotes the most time to them, will be the proudest of the flowers she rears.

Sulphur and tobacco are powerful remedies in the hands of an amateur, and will often not only kill all the insects, but destroy all the plants. As almost every amateur usually undertakes to try some experiment for himself, so we record the experience of a lady who writes us :

" Years ago, when we had the charge of a small conservatory, we tried the effect of sulphur thrown upon hot coals to kill infested plants. Every insect succumbed before its direful fumes ; so also did the plants; hardly a leaf remained on the stems the following day, and the poor leafless branches spake to me in terms of sad reproach through their mute lips. I was then a tyro in the business, and greatly desired to have every thing done *thoroughly*.

" Thus I learned, that there is no teacher like experience, his school is a hard one, he is a stern disciplinarian, but when his lessons are once learned they are not forgotten, but are indellibly printed upon the pages of memory.

" Luckily for my conservatory, it was denuded of its leaves in May, and soon the poor forlorn plants were set out into the borders where they could recuperate and regain the foliage denuded by so strong a sulphur bath.

" Again : I tried tobacco tea, and in it steeped each treasured Rose, each loved Fuchsia, and they looked so worn and weary after it that I was heart sick with my efforts in their behalf. Since then, I have been very shy of trying such experiments, and content myself with hand brushing and washing, but still more with the daily care, the constant loving attention which is much the surest and the safest for flowers."

White mites may frequently be seen infesting the soil in pots. They seem to be the larvæ of a small black or brown fly, and are very injurious to the well-being of the plants. Lime water, salt and water, and hot water, have all been tried. The first two were inefficient to injure them, and the last killed the plants. Now we turn in a goodly supply of warm water, and when we see wriggling specks of white, take up the pot and turn off the water. Give another supply, and turn that away, and continue to do so until not one remains. The third or fourth day the process is repeated, and by this means the troublesome mites are destroyed.

Wood ashes will sometimes drive them away. They appear to be on or near the surface of the pot. Red pepper carefully dusted over the outside of the earth will kill them, and then the earth containing it can be removed, lest the pepper might prove too heating to the roots. Salt is said to drive them away. We tried it as recommended, and killed half a dozen of our finest Carnations, so concluded not to try such rash experiments on choice plants. Again, in using the red pepper, of course you must not put on a full spoonful, but only a slight sprinkling over the surface, where the worms lie the thickest.

If angle worms are in the soil, they can be removed by turning out the ball of earth and picking them out, and if a fine hair pin or knitting needle is thrust into the soil, they will all come to the surface and can easily be dislodged.

Lime water will also drive them out and help the growth of the plant, keeping the foliage fresh and bright. It can be applied once a week without damage to the plant, and can be made by slacking a small piece of fresh lime in hot water, then adding cold, and stirring it well. The water will only dissolve just so much lime, and the residue will remain in the pail or firkin used to dissolve it. More water can be turned on to it, and so continue until it is all taken up. Then bottle the water and cork up for use. Keep the bottles where they will not freeze. A little of the undissolved lime can be put into every bottle, and when the water turns out discolored, more can be added to it.

A tablespoonful of spirits of camphor, added to a pint and a half of water, will make a good wash to keep off insects. But with proper care and good management these antidotes need not be employed.

Fresh water well applied, fresh air at proper times, and cleanliness at all times, are the best preventives one can employ against insects.

CHAPTER VI.

Propagation from Seeds, Cuttings, etc.

At present most of our Window Gardens in cities are filled with plants bought from the florist. Of course one half do not know how they are grown, and hence do not well know how to take care of them.

Every window gardener, it seems to us, should understand the first principles of plant life, and learn for himself how they are propagated.

Nearly all plants that are desirable for window gardening can be raised either from seeds, cuttings or by grafting. Bulbous roots are propagated chiefly from offsets, and the new varieties are produced from the seeds. Other plants are also increased by offsets or separating the roots, but their number is comparatively few.

Warmth, moisture, proper temperature and a soil suitable to promote the sprouting of the germ, and a shady situation until the seeds have swelled, are essential to the vegetation of seeds.

For window plants a greater degree of warmth is needful. Unless the air is from 66° to 70°, and some bottom heat is supplied, your success will not satisfy you. Seeds of tender plants require hot house treatment. Moisture must not be withheld at any time; yet, if it is in excess, the seeds are apt to decay before they sprout. A thick piece of flannel wet with hot water, and laid over the soil and pressed lightly down upon it, will ensure the needful moisture, warmth and darkness. Warm water should be given over it, letting it permeate slowly through it. It must be lifted daily to see if the tender seeds are starting; the flannel must be removed before the leaves appear, and a pane of glass which will exactly cover the seed box or pot placed closely over them.

Too deep planting is a fruitful cause of failure with amateur seed raisers. The depth of the soil must be proportioned to the size of the seed. Petunias, Primulas, etc., require the least sprinkling of sandy loam.

A good general rule is to cover the seed only to the thickness of their own diameter, yet this would not hold good with Sweet Peas, for they grow better when planted three inches in depth.

With very fine seeds it is best to press them lightly into the surface of the soil with the fingers, then shade from the sun three or four days either with cloth or newspapers, and sprinkle over the coverings, not letting them become dry at all, yet not killing the germ of the seeds by too much water.

Most tyros in plant culture fail by sowing their seeds in soil that is too wet or too dry. All seeds sown in pots are more difficult to manage than those raised in a hot bed or in the border on account of the danger of drying up. The ancient maxim again comes up, "that if a thing is worth doing at all, it is worth doing well." So in plant culture it is just as easy to do it right as wrong. The soil should be light and sandy; clear sand, such as the masons use for making plaster, is just the thing with which to cover the seeds, and to mix with the loam. The soil should not be all of sand, because it will dry too quickly. Nor must it be of clayey loam, because it will keep too wet, and will not let the air circulate freely enough to make the seeds vegetate. But a good loam mixed with sand will answer our purpose exactly.

Fill the pots with it and leave quarter of an inch of clear sand at the top, for the minute seeds, and half an inch for those of larger size. Abutilons, Pelargoniums, Coboea, etc. Set the pots in water up to the rims to let the soil become thoroughly wetted, then place them to drain for half an hour or more. Plant the seeds on the surface, sprinkling over them and pressing lightly upon them sand proportionate to their needs.

The sand must not be allowed to dry at all, and we find that nearly all kinds of seeds will germinate more quickly in it than in loam, though a mixture of both may be desirable in some cases when the care is not constant. Shallow cigar boxes are preferable to pots; they will hold much more, can be handled as easily, and make the best seed pans that we know of.

The soil for planting seeds should be as fine as possible. It is a good plan to bake it in an old pan in the oven, then sift it through a good sized sieve, which can be made out of an old milk pan, by boring holes through the bottom of it. Soil thus prepared is far better than if taken directly from the garden, yet in all cases it is better to buy it of the florists, then you know it is just right.

When the second tier of leaves show themselves, it is time to transplant the seedlings, into the pots or boxes in which you intend them to grow and bloom.

There is some art in watering seedlings as well as plants, as there is great danger of the tiny sprouts becoming water clogged or "damped off."

It is often better to water little pots by placing them in shallow pans of water, and letting them suck up moisture for a few minutes. Boxes can be moistened by pouring the water against the sides of them, holding the spout close to them, and letting only a small stream fall from the nozzle, thus gently wetting the whole surface.

The pane of glass that is to be kept over the young plants, can be edged upon one side to give more air, and prevent their growing spindling, and wire drawn.

Bell glasses are much better however, and are largely used in England and in France where they are called *cloches.* They are conical, rising to a sharp point in the middle, and are of cheap construction. Seedlings raised under them flourish finely, and there is little need for watering tiny plants; for when the edge of the glass is within the rim of the pot, the moisture becomes condensed upon the sides of the glass, and moistens the soil by trickling down upon it.

Another desirable way is to pack the pot in which the seeds are planted, into another pot of larger size, and fill up the space with moss, refuse hops or tan bark, which can be kept both warm and moist with hot water. A little of it can stand in the saucer which holds the largest pot, and thus an equitable state of moisture can be preserved.

Hard shelled seeds, like Canna, Acacias, Cypress Vines, etc., will germinate much quicker if they are soaked in boiling water for an hour or so. Turn it upon them boiling hot, and let it stand until cool, then plant the seeds. Some gardeners prefer to pour boiling water upon the surface of the soil prepared for them, rather than upon the seeds. Either way will succeed, but it is essential to soften the horny substance which envelops the seeds, if you desire them to grow.

Verbena seeds require soaking in warm water over night; turn the water upon them, and let the cup stand in a warm place.

Many beautiful plants can be raised from seeds as easily as from cuttings, and be more highly appreciated because they are all your own, developed by your patient care and attention.

Begonias, Callas, Oleanders, Cyclamens, Calceolarias, Gloxinias, Primulas, Carnations, Lantanas, Coleus, Heliotropes, Geraniums, Cinerarias, Pelargoniums, Camellias, Abutilons and Cacti, etc., can all be made to grow into fine plants, but it requires constant care and patience to cultivate them.

Some of them are very long in germinating, others in blooming, and they require much time, for the least neglect will often prove fatal to them.

Cuttings.

There is little trouble raising plants from cuttings; a few rules are essential, and a little care and time are requisite, but any one can make them strike root.

They can be struck either from woody pieces without leaves, but all ready to send them forth, or from young green shoots.

The first mentioned will rarely fail to grow, but they grow slowly, taking sometimes a long time to start the first leaf, while the nice green shoots will quickly become respectable plants. But it is well to know that if the branches of an old plant are broken down, the hard woody stems will produce in time, fine plants.

Take a hard old stem of Geranium, Fuchsias, Myrtle, Heliotrope, Sweet Verbena, or any desirable plant, and cut it so as to leave one or two joints or eyes on a piece, (a joint is the slight thickening of the branch whence the leaves and side branches will come out), set them into a damp sponge or moss, keeping it moistened, for four or five days, a week may not be too long, but keep them in a dark cool place. A slight callous will then be formed, and the cutting will be all ready to put forth fresh roots as soon as it is potted.

In carrying cuttings from place to place, it is best to wrap them in a damp sponge, leaving out the upper leaves, and covering the sponge with oil silk or enamel cloth. All cuttings strike root more quickly in sand than in loam, and if the bottom of the joint touches the side of the pot or box, it hastens its growth.

Bottom heat is quite as needful to propagate cuttings as seeds, and the heated cases referred to in another chapter would give every amateur a desirable hot bed at a slight outlay. To raise cuttings from a fresh or succulent branch, it is needful to take one in a proper condition to secure success.

Mr. Henderson says, that if a cutting bends, it will not grow easily, but if it snaps off it is ready to make root, and become a vigorous plant. This test does not always apply to woody stemmed plants like Myrtles, Sweet Verbenas, Daphnes, Roses and Azaleas, but their growth is usually finer if the wood is easily broken.

Whether the cuttings are of hard or succulent growth, they are similarly planted, and they can be inserted all around the edge of a pot not over an inch apart, and nearly as deep as the second eye.

CHAPTER VII.

PROPAGATING BOXES, HEATING CASES AND COLD FRAMES.

There are always some plants that are very difficult to start without some bottom heat, and all amateur gardeners cannot possess a hot bed. But the heated case affords to them the greatest facilities for striking cuttings, raising seeds, and bringing well established plants into rapid growth.

A home made case may be made in the form of a double cube, say twelve inches wide and high, and eighteen inches long. A concealed tank of zinc filled with hot water, will give out and retain the heat from twelve to twenty-four hours without changing the water. No lamp or extra heat need be used, and the cases are perfectly clean and unobjectionable, while they can be with a little mechanical skill, rendered very ornamental and agreeable objects for any parlor or sitting room.

It is best that the entire frame work be made of wood, and the sides and top consist each of a pane of glass fitted into the frame; or in other words, it is a small glass show case with open bottoms. One of the sides may be arranged so as to slide out to give greater ease in arranging the plant within and for cleaning the glass. The top may be movable, fastened by hinges, and lifted up one or two inches occasionally for ventilation. When the plants are in bloom, the entire side or top can be left open all day.

The wood work may be either painted or be constructed simply of black walnut, oak, and oiled; either will look well.

In some of our horticultural stores there are cases already constructed for propagating purposes which fill the exact need.

Figs. 17 and 18 are manufactured of galvanized iron, one being about three feet

Fig. 17.

long and two wide, the other one foot by eighteen inches. A shallow boiler about the size of the bottom is fitted in each case filled with water, and heated by the flame of either a lamp or gas jet beneath. The top is of glass and can be lifted at any time fresh air is needed. A thermometer completes the equipment. It is very simple and successful. The heat can be run up to any desired point and the lady who uses it can soon initiate herself into the mysteries and practice of rooting, cutting and propagating fine bedding plants.

Fig. 19 is a propagating box made of earthen ware, with grooves in the top for a pane of glass to slide up and down with a cover. The heat thus generated can be retained for a considerable length of time by closing the glass top. They are very suitable for starting soft wooded cuttings in sand.

Fig. 18.   Fig. 19.

A forcing stand may be erected like this in Fig. 20. It consists of a wrought iron frame of ornamental design with two stories. In each story there is a row of double pans, the bottom one containing water which is heated by a patent kerosene lamp, keeping the temperature of the inner pan about 100°. In this inner pan are placed mould, sand or loam, wherein the pots are plunged. The heat of the water is communicated directly through the sand to the cutting or seeds which will germinate in a few days.

All cultivators need to know that for propagating purposes, there is needed heat and moisture, and to be successful you need a greater bottom heat than surface heat, and also, still, quiet atmosphere.

If this case is used in a room where the temperature is usually quite mild, no glass covering will be needed; still if it is needed, a case like that described in the former part of this chapter may be constructed for each shelf. If pots are used in these little cases, they should be very small, not over two inches in diameter.

Fig. 20.

Such little contrivances as these render it comparatively easy for any lady to raise her own Verbenas, Pelargoniums, or other simple plants, and would undoubtedly do more to please and instruct children and visitors, by way of amusement, than the whole apparatus originally cost.

In spring, which is the time that artificial heat will be most required, the zinc reservoirs of your propagating boxes will need to be filled with water, both night and morning. In cases like our first mentioned one, not heated with the lamp, boiling water should be used, and the temperature in the closed case will vary from 60° to 75°; the silver sand as soon as it becomes a little moist, heats the soil in the pots, and the heat is retained for a long time, often 24 hours after the tank was first filled.

Another home made case is constructed out of an old tea chest; cut it down about one third, then fit into it a zinc pan 4 to 5 inches in depth to hold the water, over the top put a large pane of glass, and in such a box, large numbers of cuttings may be raised with much less trouble than a hot bed causes. It can be kept in a back room or in the attic, and filled with small pots of cuttings and seeds. The glass top may be hinged on. But the best designs are, however, thus illustrated in Figs. 17, 18, and 19.

Cold Frames.

Many plants that have grown out of doors all summer, and may be needed for blooming in the window during the winter and spring, may be safely housed in cold frames. This is a very desirable method for keeping a large quantity of plants.

A frame may be made very easily and cheap as follows: Take a sheltered location, protected from the north wind, and well drained, dig down four feet by eight—or four by twelve is a convenient size.

Insert at each corner scantling posts, rising six inches above the surface in front, and eighteen inches above at the rear; nail boards to the inside of these posts, leaving about six inches space between them and the earth to be filled with manure or tan.

Outside the posts nail boards above the ground, leaving a space to be filled up with tan, etc.

Cover the top with double sashes. Fill in the bottom of the pit with small stones, or bits of charcoal, and throw in a foot or more of tan in which to sink the pots. Coal ashes will do as well as tan; they are required to secure dryness, warmth and ventilation.

When the cold weather comes on, cover the sashes with straw mats or carpeting—and bank up the pit with tan or manure—put a good embankment about the whole pit.

Place the plants in the pit, in the autumn, and let them have as much air as possible in mild days, covering closely, in cold nights.

The chief care is to give fresh air in sufficient quantities, and to protect in severe weather from frosts.

Roses, Geraniums, Salvias, Fuchsias, Heliotropes, etc. can be kept quite safely in such a pit, and be ready to force in the windows or conservatory by March.

When warm days occur the sashes can be uncovered, and the sun allowed to shine through the glass on to the plants, but until February it is better to keep them in darkness, and not admit fresh air oftener than once in two or three weeks. Do it when the air is most genial, and raise the sashes only long enough to inspect the plants, and if very dry give a little water.

CHAPTER VIII.

WINDOW POTS, BOXES, JARDINIERES, AND PLANT STANDS.

Glazed pots are not as good to grow plants in as the real pottery, on account of their want of porosity, which is a great help in watering, evaporation and aeration; likewise their saucers are sometimes fastened to them, and are liable to fill with earth, clog up the outlets, and are not easily cleaned.

Fig. 21.

The earthen pots are easily cleaned and plants thrive much better in them, than in fancy china or glass ones. Still these last are often desirable for room decoration, and many very handsome ones are made, which can be used by simply setting the other common pot in-side, and if there is any vacant space between, it may be filled up with moss.

The size of the pot should be in unison with the size of the plant; the most con-venient ones to handle, may measure from five to seven or eight inches across top. Yet if any have extensive window gardens, they will need all sizes. from 3, 4, 5, and 6 inches diameter, up to eight inches—some for propagating pur-poses, others for shifting into, from smaller sizes. Saucers of course, of the proper sizes, should fit each pot.

A new pot should be placed in a pail of water to soak, and expel the dry air from the pores, and an old pot should be carefully washed both inside and out before use. Pieces of charcoal broken up fine should be put into the bottom of each pot to the depth of about two or three inches; less of course in the smaller sized pots.

Fig. 22.

As the pots become filled with roots, the plants must be shifted into a size larger, and when these are filled, again repotted into others.

Fig. 23.

Fig. 24.

It is easy to find when to repot the plants, by running a broad bladed table knife around the inner edge of the pot, and turning it bottom side upwards over the hand ; the ball of earth readily slips out, and the roots are disclosed to view. If you suspect there are worms in the soil, their presence can be detected, by the fact that they soon come to the surface to know the cause of the disturbance, and then they can be destroyed.

The soil should be frequently stirred about the surface of the pots, and for this purpose a good sized hair pin or two-tined fork are good instruments. The for-

Fig. 25.   Fig. 26.

mer is best as its prongs are so small, raking up the earth without disturbing greatly the tiny rootlets.

In potting or repotting it is needful sometimes to cut back the plants, and when it is done, due deference must be paid to their shape, thinning out the branches so that they will be in good form, for the beauty of the plant is greatly dependent upon this.

Figs. 21 & 22 are very neat pots made of pottery ware nearly white, glazed on the outside, and intended to hold inside the common pots of earthen ware. Most of the florists have them as they are quite ornamental and are becoming popular. Their price is from $1.50 to $2.50.

An objection has been raised to the common pots, that they soon become dirty and covered with mould and rust, and need considerable care to keep clean. The only remedy is constant scrubbing. And it is impossible to have a thoroughly porous well drained pot, without its sides becoming in time old and sour; attempts have been made to paint them with ochre, or red whitewash, but it soon rubs off and is disagreeable. To combine ornament with use, the one must be placed inside the other.

There is a style of mountable flower pot, now used somewhat by English florists, made of separate slabs of wood joined together with flexible hinges. (See Fig. 23.) The advantages claimed for it, are that it can be taken to pieces and adjusted, that plants can be easily transplanted without disturbing the soil or injuring the roots. With small window gardens it would not be needed; but in the case of very large conservatory plants, where a diameter of two feet

Fig. 27.

Fig. 28.

is required it might be found useful, as the plant might need examination to perfect the drainage, or remove the soil and replace with fresh compost. The wires, as shown in the engraving, are moved down or up for tightening or loosening, so that any one can make them. There are several styles of pots, square, and made of prettily ornamented pieces of wood, (Figs. 25 & 26,) so simple that they need no explanation. The same designs have been copied in glazed ware with various colors and are accessible to any one who will visit the horticultural stores, or those places where the most tasteful pottery and household ware is kept for sale.

Fig. 29.

Fig. 30.

Fig. 31.

Fig. 32.

An exceedingly ornamental design for a flower pot for a drawing room is shown in (Fig. 27,) made of Minton tile, the ground work of which is dark blue and the flowers white. All such decorative pots impart a pleasant tasteful look to any room. We would be glad to have them multiplied and constantly improved. Fig. 28, is of the same material, but of various shades of white, red and green.

Jardinieres.

These are fanciful, single or double boxes, of more artistic construction than the common pot, and intended to be used for decoration purposes entirely. Many are constructed and filled with entirely artificial moss, and imitation plants with highly colored leaves, are set therein. Of course little or no interest is felt in them after they have been placed in their position, while if they had been natural living plants, the very care they daily required would have developed far more love and appreciation than the former; still we would not omit either, all do well in their proper place.

Fig. 33.   Fig. 34.

Figs. 28 to 34, are rare ornaments of beauty, especially 29, 30, 32, which are exquisite in their rich coloring and material. They are constructed of glass mosaics, and intended to contain pots of choice plants, hidden with moss, and thus prepared to adorn the window of the drawing room or library. The glass mosaic is arranged in designs of richest colors, set into cement of pure white color, and the whole hardened and polished to one glistening surface. Some of the designs are imitations of snow crystals, and of course are the perfection of art. The interior of these pots is lined with zinc, and they may at will hold either plants with earth, or be filled with moss and hold cut flowers. The illustrations are taken from originals exhibited at one of the Crystal Palace exhibitions in London.

Figs. 31, 33, & 34, are sketches of other designs of rustic stands and boxes, with the Dracaena, which is a favorite with all fond of the plant decorations of

Fig. 35.

rooms. No. 34, is a rustic Tile Jardinet, hexagon shaped, and 11 to 16 inches in diameter. No. 31, is the same mounted upon a rustic cedar wood stand. No. 33, is a china flower vase with fence pattern, made entirely round, and from 6 to 14 inches in diameter. No. 35, is a pretty little idea of a sea shell, fitted to a rustic frame; the interior of the shell is filled with compost or moss, and from it grows a feathery fern. No. 36, is a rustic wood basket, made by any one with a taste for mechanical construction and very simply put together. It is suitable for any house, and adapted to any position out doors or in doors. Will look best if filled with ferns, but when bulbs are in season, fill it with good selection of Hyacinths, Tulips or Crocuses, according to the fancy of the fair gardener. No. 37, is a rustic vase of circular outline, intended especially for indoor decoration. They are very cheap; both should be lined with zinc, or else the presence of the damp earth will cause them to rot. When bulbs are past their spring blooming, then take Ferns or Dracaena, or any plant provided it is not of too great height, and must have an agreeable shading of color, with appropriate form and contour.

Fig. 36.   Fig. 37.

A large number of vari-colored floral pots and jardinieres, made of lava, and now imported from Europe, can be found of various prices from $1.50 to $5.00, in any of our fancy china ware and porcelain stores. They are of beautiful finish, and usually very cheap.

Some American manufacturers are now producing designs in terra cotta which are pleasing. Fig. 40, is used both as a hyacinth or bulb pot, or as a bouquet holder, the interior being previously filled with sand. The sizes vary from twelve to eighteen inches high, and consist of from three to five apertures for placing the bulb. They are usually well drained beneath.

Fig. 39, is a rustic pot of about nine inches high, resting upon a dolphin base six inches high. The sides of the pot are ornamented with a grape vine running around, and clusters of leaves and fruit.

Fig. 38, is a wall ivy basket about eight inches high, and proportionate height, intended to hold earth and a plant of Ivy, which will grow and clamber up either the sides of the room, or over the door if the pot is hung near. Two pots of the same design, might be very appropriately hung, one on each side of a window out doors, and the Ivy as it grew, be trained gracefully over the sides and top or the front of the house.

Fig. 38

Window Boxes.

If the window should happen to be in a recess, the sills may be occupied with boxes. Almost anything will do if clean. A wooden trough lined with lead or zinc, may be constructed to hold a considerable quantity of earth, and here climbing plants may grow and root, and be trained in profusion over the entire window. The Cobœa is often used for this purpose, and after it has

Fig. 39.

Fig. 40.

grown enough to fill the whole window, it may be allowed to hang down in fes-toons, forming a natural and graceful screen in any sunny window. Climbing vines need considerable care and examination, for they are apt to harbor spiders and insects of various descriptions. Likewise, they drop their dead leaves and flowers, necessitating constant cleanliness. Nothing is so clean and satisfactory as the Ivy. Everything in these pots must be regularly watered, and like all other pots, precaution must be had as to drainage; all troughs or boxes without exception should be lined with zinc.

Fig. 41.

Fig. 41 is a design of a window box, constructed by an ordinary carpenter. Two boards of common timber eight inches wide, half an inch thick, and three and a half feet long, form the side of the box; the ends are twelve inches wide, eight inches high, six and a half inches broad. The bottom board is twelve inches wide, one inch thick, three and a half feet long, and projects about an inch beyond the side all around. A tray or lining of zinc was made by the tin-man and fitted in. A piece of oil cloth with a pretty pattern, and some mosaic tile work was obtained at the carpet store, and tacked carefully to the sides. Mould-ings of wood were nailed all round the top, bottom and end, then all the wood work was stained by rubbing it over with burnt umber and water, and after it was dry, a coating of varnish was put on to finish it.

For filling such a box there is a great variety to choose from; at one time you may use Begonias, at another, Geraniums, with variegated foliage, such as the L'elegante. Then at your pleasure you may, in cool weather, change to young evergreens, of which Arbor Vitaes, twelve inches high, make the most cheerful appearance. During the winter time if you have it in a reasonably warm room, you can place several Dracaenas, the *D. Terminalis* and *D. Australis* being the best.

Fig. 42.

Fig. 42 is of plain tile or glazed earthenware.

Fig. 43, is of Minton tile more highly decorated, and costing about $15.00. The third or Fig. 44, is still more elegant, and represents it as it would appear filled with Bulbs, Hyacinths, Crocuses and Tulips.

The use of these costly window tile boxes is becoming more general every

year, and tradesmen inform us that the past year alone the demand in this country for these objects of taste has completely trebled.

Boxes made of plain wood may be ornamented with acorns, as shown in Fig.
45, a design often used for green-houses or staircase windows. Take a mixture
of acorn and powdered shells, cut all the acorns in half, lengthways, cover the
box with glue, then lay the acorns flat side down along the edge and bottom
of the sides, one after the other, and in the open space between, affix them in any
fantastic plan you like; then sift the powdered shell thickly all over the box
between the acorns, and it will soon dry. If you choose, you can vary the

Fig. 43.

acorns with cone seeds, and red berries cut in half. Another style, Fig. 46,
is made in a similar way, excepting only that pine cones are used in place of
acorns, and the edges of the box and its ends, and supports at bottom, are constructed of rustic cedar wood. This pot is filled with a fine collection of Bulbs,
Hyacinths, Narcissus, Jonquils, Tulips, Crocuses, Snow Drop and Scillas, length
about three feet, and width about eight inches.

There are other very pretty rustic modes of construction. The outside of
home made boxes, may also be ornamented with white and gray lichens, wet in
water to make them pliable, then glued on, or fastened securely with thread wire,
attaching the wire to small brad nails on the inside and outer edge of the box.

Fig. 44.

When dry it will have a pleasing appearance. Sections of bark may also be used
to cover the sides, or wood mosaic introduced; take the split half of small sticks
of spruce, maple, oak and birch, arrange them in alternate diamonds, oval and
square, varying the colors with an artistic eye, and fastening the cleft sticks
with small brads, which will not be perceptible. When finished, cover with a
coat of varnish.

Gum shellac, dissolved in turpentine, or common furniture polish may be used
for varnishing. Pine cones are favorites in these box decorations, and sometimes

are used either whole or are pulled to bits and nailed in regular rows along the boards.

The preparation of these boxes for plants must be good ; place, first a layer of finely powdered charcoal an inch in thickness over the bottom. It acts not only as a preventive against mould, but also as a fertilizer, enriching the soil   Then select your compost, which has been previously described, composed of rich loam, sand and forest leaf mould, and decayed barn-yard manure, and fill up to the brim.

If you are growing bulbs leave out all manures, and use more leaf mould ; see that the bottom of the box has means of drainage by a hole, into a saucer or dish to receive surplus water.

Fig. 45.

In arranging your plants give due heed to height and coloring. The flowers which grow the tallest must have the central position, and the dwarfs occupy the edges and corners. For drooping vines select the Money-wort, it grows freely, and its bright yellow flowers are very attractive. The *Partridge Vine*, which grows so plentifully in all the woodlands, is also desirable, its coral red berries adding greatly to its beauty. The variegated and green "Coliseum Ivy," is

Fig. 46.

good for this purpose. German and English Ivies are very valuable, growing with great rapidity, the former often two or three inches a day. The Convolvulus possesses bright green foliage and exquisite flowers ; it is always a favorite in window gardening.

The *Cranberry Vine* has been overlooked, and deserves especial recommendation, both for window boxes and hanging baskets. Its prettily cut foliage, pure white flowers, and rich scarlet berries, make it very ornamental; it is easily obtainable by any one.

For a good selection to fill one box for winter blooming, we would proceed as follows:

Place in the centre a winter blooming *Fuchsia*, either *Speciosa* with its pink waxen petals, and brilliant crimson corolla, which will bloom ten months in the year, or *Serratifolia*, with its corolla and petals of two shades of crimson.

Next place on each side the *Lady Cullum*, a variegated Geranium, and the *United Italy*, with its leaves edged with silver. Both of these plants give scarlet flowers, but as they are grown principally for their leaves, you will nip off all buds. *Bouvardia Elegans*, with its coral, trumpet-shaped flowers, should come next; on the other side, a pink *Monthly Carnation*, with its rich spicy bloom.

If the proportions of the box will admit, we would also plant *Tom Thumb Geraniums*, white and scarlet. Then at the four corners, add in the corners some of the different varieties of the *Chinese Primroses*, which bloom almost ceaselessly, sometimes eleven months in the twelve; then bring in an Alternanthera, with its brightly veined lance-shaped leaves, and a variegated *Sweet Alyssum* with its white cluster of minute flowers. Bulbs of the *Duc Van Thol Tulips*, or Crocuses or Hyacinths, may be added, taking care to sprinkle the holes made for their reception with sand, and to cover them with it. Shroud them in fresh green moss, so that the leaf buds may not start before they have taken deep root, which will enable them to support and nourish the gorgeous flowers which lie embedded in their bosoms. Thus shaded, all will grow, and soon delight you with their fragrance.

One great advantage of these window boxes consists in the ease with which they are watered and cared for; there is no shifting of pots, or other manipulations. With a good moist temperature, and protection from frost at night, these box gardens will be a constant succession of bloom from early winter to leafy spring.

If proper fastenings are provided, these boxes may be placed out doors, just on the window sill, or may have temporary staging erected for the purpose, and there be tended and sprinkled without fear of damage to either window or furniture. Here, in the open air and balmy days of spring and summer, can be grown Verbenas, Heliotropes, Fever Fews, Geraniums and trailing vines, like *Tradescantia, Moneywort,* &c., and there will always be flowers for a bouquet or a button-hole.

In an eastern or north-eastern window, *Fuchsias, Mignonette and Pansies,* which shun the heat, can be grown to advantage.

Plant Stands.

Here again we meet with an endless variety of designs and forms of construction. Every conceivable form of taste, has been devised and executed, and we are at no lack of convenience, but rather in a quandary, what to chose from so many things that are so good.

Fig. 47.—Design for Plant Stand.

Fig. 49 is a very pretty little flower basket, made of wire work, painted green. It is supported underneath by a frame work of wood, either oak or pine, neatly decorated, and having castors attached by the legs, for ready removal.

A zinc tray of perhaps four inches depth, is fitted inside the wire which **holds** all the earth and water, (which all other baskets of this construction should have,) a small aperture for the withdrawal of the water, and fitted with a small stop cock which should be hidden from sight. The plants kept in here, are to be packed in moss and will, with occasional watering, keep fresh and green upon the surface.

Fig. 48.

Figs. 50 and 51 are simple stands to be used for the same purpose, or can be adapted to the keeping of cut flowers. The top of No. 51, is covered with a small movable brass wire grating, the meshes being half an inch square, to support the flowers, and keep them in an upright position.

Fig. 50 is more convenient for preserving small plants, just in bloom, packed in with moss. This is, also, covered with wire work of brass.

Fig. 52 is a plant table, made of any style of wood, the heavier the better. It is of considerable depth, and will hold a large quantity of earth, is also lined

with zinc or copper, and provided with a waste pipe.   Around the top is a basket work of brass, usually four to six inches in depth.   The pots placed inside
are supposed to be deep enough to reach only to the lower edge of the brass work,
and covered with moss.   Cut flowers, Dahlias, Pinks and Carnations, may be
placed in here, half of the box having previously been filled with moss, and

Fig. 49.   Fig. 50.

the rest with sand, into which their stems are pressed.   If the flowers are tastefully arranged according to harmony of colors, they will give a pretty effect, and
the flowers will last several days.

If it is possible, it will be well to provide all stands used for cut flowers, with
glass shades which can be removed during the day time, but at nightfall be placed
over them, both to secure from too cool temperature, and to protect against dust
which comes from the morning's sweepings.   Flowers will also keep fresh longer
if preserved in moistened sand, than if kept in water alone.

Fig. 51.   Fig. 52.

Fig. 48 is a plant stand for household use and ornament of more than customary spaciousness.   It is constructed either in a full circular form or semi-circle
to suit the fancy, and will usually fit into the recess of any bow-window.   It is
built of a wire frame, principally with wooden legs and supports.   Has the usual
zinc tray inside, well filled with growing plants.   Its size is about four and a

Fig. 53

Fig. 54.

Fig. 55.

Fig. 56.

Fig. 57

half feet in diameter, and stands two and a half feet from the floor.   The illustration represents a great variety of plants within, fully 50 varieties, from Roses

Fig. 58.   Fig. 59.

Fig. 60.   Fig. 61.

and Fuchsias, to Ferns, Coleus, Bulbs and Primulas. It is a happy gathering
of floral treasures.

Figs. 60 and 61 are two exquisite flower stands, very suitable for setting in the parlor window, just under the drooping lace curtains.

Fig. 61 is constructed of iron, but has a basin above filled with sand, in which may be grown either bulb or cut flowers, placed in moist sand.

Fig. 60 is a lovely basket of rustic work, principally of the same material as that from which our cane chairs are constructed. It is filled with ferns, drooping plants, Smilax, and has a great variety of other plants too numerous to mention in detail. Such a basket can be easily obtained or constructed at any furniture store, and filled by any florist.

Fig. 62 is of Terra Cotta, delicately moulded in the form of vase rather than a plant stand, and filled with a profusion of charming plants from Tulip to Achyranthus, and Snow Drop to Fuchsia.

Every one who wishes to learn the best plants for such purposes will find full descriptions in Part Two.

Figs. 53 to 59 need little explanation. Every one has necessity for some plant stands for the pots before the window. All these designs are

Fig. 62.

constructed of iron or made of wire and in countless patterns and devices. The cost is but very moderate ranging from $5.00 to $25.00. All are easily movable and light.

Fig. 63.

Fig. 64.

Ornamental Parlor Stand.

Fig. 65.—Design for a Conservatory.

CHAPTER IX.

CONSERVATORIES AND GREENHOUSES.

These are costly and mainly afforded only by the wealthy. As an ornament of architectural value, no villa is complete without them, and even the owner of the city mansion does not seem well satisfied till he has added one of these elegancies to assist the look and feeling of taste.

Usually they are quite costly, and both interior and exterior are highly decorated, and as objects of effect on the lawn, or among the shrubbery, they are worth all their value in their embellishment of rural art.

Still, even the person of moderate purse, may have one not very showy, yet very convenient, and well adapted to this purpose, viz: The keeping of plants in larger quantities than the ordinary space of the window, or parlor garden, and also in a better and more successful atmosphere than that of the living room.

It would take a volume alone to point out all technical details necessary to any one about to build one. For an extensive design, the advice of a horticultural architect is indispensable, but for home purposes, a design such as any carpenter can erect is seen in one of our succeeding plans.

Conservatories and green-houses are also somewhat distinct in their uses. The one is mainly devoted to ornamental purposes, and the exhibition of plants in full beauty of growth and bloom, while in the humbler green-house, propagating boxes are the chief furniture used by the gardener, for the production and forcing of his young plants. Still either term is appropriate, and the term greenhouse includes both.

Costly conservatories are built of iron and glass, more moderate ones of wood and glass. In building them, due heed must be given to ventilation. If in small home conservatories, they are not well heated, it would be well to have heavy outside shutters, so as to be rolled down at night, or double window panes of glass; usually a flue from the furnace which warms the house will, in most latitudes, give sufficient warmth, provided the furnace will keep up a uniform degree all night. This, after all, is not regular in large conservatories; and then the only satisfactory mode of heating is by pipes of hot water from a furnace specially constructed for the purpose.

If there is danger of frost, and it is feared that the heating arrangements are not sufficient, turn all the heat of the furnace into the conservatory. Yet there is on the other hand considerable trouble from having too much heat or light in the evening, especially if the conservatory is entered immediately from the drawing room.

Houses that are warmed by water pipes, branches of which are allowed to run through the conservatory, not only keep up a more steady heat, but afford considerable moisture to the atmosphere, and are of decided advantage.

Every Autumn, apply a coat of paint, not only to render it fresh and clear, but to fill up all hiding places for insects, and clear them out if perchance they have obtained possession, and in September early, put the pots and plants in their proper places. It is not desirable that they should remain out later than that.

Fig. 66.   Fig. 67.   Fig. 68.   Fig. 69.

For hanging pots up against the side of the house or wall, the *floreteen* is a convenient little utensil, constructed of double iron hoop, bent in the middle at an angle of 90° and reversible. Cost is very trifling and made by any blacksmith.

When filling your house with plants, clean the pots well, and turn out the balls of earth to see that the roots have sufficient room, and are in a healthy state.

It is well, also, to scrape away the surface soil, and supply fresh compost.

Give your plants plenty of room, not crowding too thickly, allowing free circulation of the air, for then it is easier too keep them perfectly clean and healthy.

Heliotropes, Verbenas, Geraniums, and indeed all herbaceous plants should be placed as near the glass as possible, as they require much sunlight, while variegated leaved plants Mignionette, Camellias, Primulas, &c., will not flourish luxuriantly, if the hot sun shines on them at noon day.

Fig. 70 is a design of a small home conservatory attached to the side of a village residence and entered from the parlor. Its length is about eighteen feet and width twelve to fifteen, affording all necessary room for a good home plant conservatory.

Such a house is heated either by a flue from the furnace, supposed to be placed in the basement of the house, or there may be a stove placed in depression of the floor at one end, of the conservatory and with pipes running from a drum lengthway each side to the other end, and returning to it again, may heat the room sufficiently; but there would be nothing to prevent a low temperature at night, unless some one could see that the fire was kept steadily burning. The most steady heat would come from the flue of the same furnace which heats the house. There are stands running around each side of the conservatory and a large square one in the middle.

The cost made by any carpenter, if constructed of wood, will be from $250 to $400, and if he has taste may be richly decorated and painted for that sum. A good conservatory could not well be built for a less price.

For a more elegant design still, we commend Fig. No. 65 of a beautiful form of architecture, lofty enough to admit of palms or tall ferns; large enough for abundance of fresh air, not close or stifling, and of a character highly ornamental for any situation. It is constructed of iron, yet nothing prevents it from being made of wood. The glass is in long lengths corresponding to the general style of construction. Ventilators in the top are easily opened or closed by pulleys.

Fig. 70.—A Village House with Small Conservatory.

There is a door for entering to the drawing room, also, one opening upon the lawn, with ornamental flower beds laid out along its side; it forms a design of rare and pleasing taste.

For out door plant houses separated from the dwelling we show designs of two styles.

Fig. 73 is still more artistic than the other, elevated upon a parterre embankment and surrounded with evidences of garden embellishments. This, also, is of iron, still it may be constructed of wood; is about twenty feet wide and from forty to fifty feet long; cost not less than $5,000. Most of the green houses in this country are now built upon the plan of low curved roofs, which afford great economy of space and heat, yet we believe variety and taste will admit the use of other styles. Such a one as this is a novelty in this country.

Fig. 71.—Interior of the Government Conservatory at Washington, D. C.

Rarely have we seen any thing like it, presenting as it does a decided look of richness and elegance in the rural grounds of any wealthy villa proprietor. It is worth adoption.

Fig. 72 is intended purely for ornamental purposes suitable for the grounds of those of humbler means than those who can afford such rich designs as our last.

It is a straight roofed span conservatory with cast iron fronts; sides about four feet six inches high with top and bottom ventilation, glazed with twenty-six ounce sheet glass, enamel painted throughout with ornamental finish, crestings, &c. This style of conservatory is set upon a foundation of white stone or granite, which gives a fine contrast with the green and shrubbery.

In general the handsomest, lightest, strongest and most serviceable conservatories are constructed of iron frames, yet few or none are made in this country and no one offers them as a specialty. We find nearly all the best styles and designs of this character offered only by English horticultural manufacturers.

In England, nearly every one has either its Window Garden or its green house, and scarcely any family of intelligence but knows something of culture and propagation of indoor plants.

Fig. 72.—A Small Greenhouse.

Here we love these delicate treasures dearly and our taste is rapidly developing in this branch of rural pleasures, yet the green house is still to many a mystery, and seems an enormous expense. If good and suitable designs could be built for $100 to $500, their number would be quadrupled every year, and their general use be considered a desirable fashion.

An important consideration in the management of greenhouses is an abundance of light. It is quite essential that the conservatory should be placed on the sunny side of the house, and that its windows or door should open into the parlor or dining-room, and, if possible, avoid planting trees too near to cover it with their shade. If the location is southwestern or northerly, much more heat will be required; and both for economy and enjoyment, only one position is desirable, and that is southerly.

Fig. 73.—An Ornamental Lawn Conservatory.

Ventilation should be arranged so that the air will circulate *over* the tops of plants, and not upon the surface of the pots.

The slope of the roof should be at an angle of 45°, as this has been proved to afford the greatest amount of heat from the sun's rays.

A low staging upon which the pots are to be placed, should run all around the conservatory, and if it joins the wall, climbing vines may be planted which will clamber over it, or brackets may be put up, which will hold pots of drooping plants. If tastefully constructed, the floor should be made of tiles with pretty patterns, and even various plant boxes may be made of them.

The plants would flourish better if they were sunk in beds of sand, mould or moss, instead of separate pots upon a staging.

A thermometer is needed in every green-house, in order to regulate the temperature, and it should hang where it cannot be affected by the rays of the sun. The temperature should not exceed 66° by day, nor fall below 45° at night.

Watering.—Water the plants as soon as the ball of roots begins to dry. This will be visible on the surface, or by knocking against the pot. If a full, deep sound is heard, there is sufficient water; if a clear, hollow sound, water is needed. All plants of a rapid growth, luxuriant leaves, and masses of flowers, require more watering than others of a delicate habit. Ferns and tropical plants must have plenty of water; succulent plants require less water.

Watering may be done by a sprinkler or syringe, and care must be taken to give water to the soil and roots, as well as to the leaves, which, if watered from overhead, may often shed it and prevent any from reaching the pots.

Apply the water either at night, or so early in the morning that the heat of the sun will not injure the plants. Let the water stand or drip awhile before wiping up, permitting the moisture to permeate the atmosphere; after two or three hours the remaining water can be cleared away.

Steps or a ladder are necessary also, to use in removing plants from the staging, and also to assist in watering. Standing upon them a person with a watering pot can produce a miniature rain, which will tend to keep away all insects, and also wash the leaves effectually.

Once a week give in your waterings a stimulant such as has been mentioned in previous chapters.

The plants should also be frequently turned around so as to keep them in good shape, and by frequent changing of position all have a chance at the best places.

All the directions minutely given in former chapters as to culture, propagation, potting, repotting, will apply as well to conservatories as to ordinary window gardening.

Plants.

For the greater convenience and accommodation of private citizens, lovers of plants, or, perhaps, not well instructed gardeners, we give a list of decorative plants for greenhouses and conservatories, which are distinguished by masses of flowers, fine leaves, interesting habits, and easy cultivation. We do not use for this list any catalogues of nurserymen, nor do we make a collection from books or advertisements. We have carefully selected only such plants as are recommended by long experience in cultivating plants, and thorough botanical knowledge. Every plant which this list contains is for sale in this country.

Avoid an unfit composition of every possible or heterogeneous plants; the effect will be very poor. For instance, tropical plants do not mix well with plants taken from colder climates. Plants with expanded branches or like habits, are suitable mainly for standards, for vases, stands, etc.

Plants of a fine and graceful habit should have a free and light position. Put *Camellias, Azaleas, Rododendrons, Magnolia grandiflora, Viburnum tinus, Eugenia australis,* etc., as soon as they leave off blooming in the background, and move in the front row the following: *Acacias, Polygala, Metrosideros, Leptospermum, Franciscea, Melaleuca, Edwardsia microphylla, Diosma,* and *Erica.*

For *groups of plants* which have a *tropical character,* place so that they may show well: *Begonia, Ferns, Lycopodia, Amaryllis, Eucharis, Peperomias,* besides all plants with variegated leaves or thick foliage. For the background may be mentioned: *Ficus elastica, Cooperi australis, Gardenia, Fortuni, Musa, Heliconia, Bambusa, Eugenia Iambos, Justicia carnea, cristata, Porteana, speciosa,* etc. He who prefers succulent plants, and intends to keep his greenhouse filled with them, will not have much difficulty in arranging them, as they can be easily put in little groups, according to size and habit.

I. LIST OF PLANTS FOR A SMALL CONSERVATORY, GREENHOUSE, OR FLOWER-PARLOR, which is frequently visited by the family or visitors. The temperature of the house is to be temperate at night; in the day time thermometer may go up a little higher, as this will be the case when the sun is out. The situation of the greenhouse may be in a southern, eastern, or western direction.

a. PLANTS FOR STANDARDS, CENTRE OF GROUPS, STANDS, COLUMNS, ETC.:

Araucaria excelsa, imbricata, brasiliensis; Aralia leptophylla, Sieboldii papyrifera; Chamærops excelsa, humilis, tomentosa, and stauracantha.

Rhapis flabelliformis; Sabel minor, Seaforthia elegans, Chamædorea lunata, Schiedeana, gracilis, desmoncoides: Latania borbonica; Corypha australis: Dracæna Draco, brasiliensis, terminalis, ferrea, Cooperi, stricta, rubra, congesta, australis, indivisa, and *Veitchii; Yucca gloriosa, aloifolia fol. var, flaccida,* and *quadricolor; Uhdea pinnatifida, Senecio Giesbrechtii, Melianthus major; Solanum Warscewitzii; Alocasia cucullata, odorata,* (*arborea,*) *macrorrhiza fol. var, Caladium cupreum,* (*porphyroneurum,*) *pictum.*

b. PLANTS FOR DECORATION IN GENERAL:

Azalea indica, best new varieties; *Camelias,* best imbricate varieties; *Rhododendra, arborea,* and *hybrida; Acalypha tricolor; Andromeda floribunda; Trimalium fragrans; Leucopogon Cunninghami; Allamanda neriifolia; Aphelandra aurantiaca, pulcherrima carnea superba, Porteana cristata, Leopoldii; Justicia speciosa; Ruellia varians; Eranthemum pulchellum, Cooperi, tubercu-*

latum ; Ardisia crenulata, Brexia madagascariensis, chrysophylla, serrata ;
Brugmansia sanguinea, floribunda; Comaclinium ianthinum; Croton pictum,
variegatum; Cyperus alternifolius: Panicum plicatum, fol. var.; Curculigo
recurvata; Aspidistra lurida, fol. var. (Plectogynæ) ; Eucharis candida; Var-
lota purpurea; Amaryllis vittata varietas; Ficus elastica, Cooperi and austra-
lis; Franciscea latifolia, eximia hydrangæformis; Maranta sanguinea, ze-
brina, vittata; Gardenia citriodora, radicans ; fortunei and florida grandi-
flora; Mahernia odorata; Hibiscus rosa sinensis var., double kinds ; *Cooperi,*
splendens; Inga pulcherrima; Edwardsia microphylla; Jasminum Sambac,
Duchesse d'Orleans, gracile; Lasiandra, splendens, macrantha; Psidium catt-
leyanum; Magnolia fuscata; Olea fragrans, ilicifolia; Myoporum parvifolium,
crystallinum; Eriostemon buxifolius, scabrum, neriifolium, intermedium;
Medinilla magnifica; Meyenia erecta; Plumbago cærulea; Calla Æthiopica
minor ; Tecoma Capensis ; Solanum capsicum, fol. var. ; *Vinca rosea* and
rosea alba; Abutilon Thompsonii; venosum floribundum, vexillarum, fol. var.;
Acacia armata, paradoxa, dealbata, lophanta, pulchella magna, floribunda, mela-
noxylon, glaucescens, mollisssima, lineata verticillata, vestita; Agapanthus um-
bellatus; Bambusa Fortunei var. Bouvardia Leyantha, splendens, jasminoides;
Cassia floribunda; Centaurea candidissima, plumosa, gymnocarpa; Cestrum
aurantiacum; Iochroma tubulosa, Warcsewitzii; Linum trigynum; Chorozema
ilicifolia, varia; Citrus sinensis, myrtifolius, aurantium mobile (Mandarin);
Clethra arborea; Sparmannia Africana; Clivia nobilis; Cyclamen persicum,
Coum, repandum; Cytisus Atleyamus, racemosus; Genista canariensis; Daphne
indica rubra; Diosma alba, ambigua, ciliata; Echeveria secunda glauca, metal-
lica grandiflora, sanguinea, racemosa gibbiflora; Cotyledon cristatum, orbicu
lare, rhomboideum: Crassula coccinea, var. kinds ; *Rochea falcata; Sempervi-*
vum arboreum fol. var., tabulæforme, canariense, orbicum; Sedum Fabaria, tele-
phium fol. var. Sieboldii variegata, dasyphyllum; Mesembryanthemum spectabile,
coccineum, aureum, deltoideum, echinatum; Kleinia repens, ficoidea; Eugenia
australis; Habrothamnus elegans, fascicularis, Indigofera australis, decora;
Laurus Camphora, Melaleuca alba, hypericifolia, decussata, ericæfolia, foliosa,
lucidula, squarrosa, thymifolia, ovata, linearifolia, speciosa; Phormium tenax;
Pittosporum Tobira; Polygala Dalmaysiana, grandis, speciosa; Rhododendron
Gibsonii, jasminiflorum, Princess Royale, Veitchianum; Rhopala corcovadensis,
Schizostylis coccinea; Statice arborea, Halfordii, macrophylla; Veronica An-
dersoni, imperialis, salicifolia, speciosa floribunda; Libonia floribunda, Centra-
denia floribunda, grandifolia ; Clerodendron infortunatum, fallax, Balfouri,
Kaempferi; Coleus, var. kinds ; *Heliotropium,* var kinds ; *Poinsettia pulcher-*
rima; Nandina domestica; Rogiera cordata; Rondeletia speciosa; Russelia jun-
cea; Sanchezia nobilis; Scutellaria mociniana; Solandra grandiflora; Aloe
fimbriata Tabernæmontana coronaria fl. pl., Crowea saligna; Diplacus puni-
ceus floribundus ; Farfugium grande; Ligularia Kaempferi fol. var. ; Callis-
temon semperflorens; Begonia ricinifolia, ricinifolia maculata, heracleifolia, ma-
crophylla, Huegelii, Hernandiæfolia, grandis, Dregei, peltata, Pierscei, manicata,

hydrocotyledes Warszewitzii, coccinea, sanguinea, incarnata, odorata, argyrostigma, stigmosa, smaragdina, Rex var. hybrides, Sedenii, Weltoniensis boliviensis.

c. PLANTS FOR HANGING BASKETS, FLOWER STANDS, LAMPS AND CANSOLES, ETC. :

Leucophyta Brownii, Vinca major fol. var. ; Mesembryanthemum cordifolium fol. var. ; Crassula spatulata ; Sedum carneum variegatum ; Cerastium tomentosum, Biebersteinii ; Tropœolum majus fl. pl. ; Clematis azurea grandiflora, lanuginosa, Jackmanni ; Ficus stipularis (repens) ; Gelsemium nitidum ; Æschinanthus zebrinus, grandiflorus ; Tradescantia zebrina, Warscewitzii ; Saxifraga sarmentosa, Sieboldii fol. var. ; Clorophyton Sternbergianum ; Lonicera Brachipoda aureo-reticulata ; Solanum jasminoides ; Isolepis elegans ; Fragaria indica ; Euonymus radicans ; Ajuga reptans fol. var. ; Glechoma hede racea fol. var. ; and var. species of Selaginella.

d. PLANTS FOR FESTOONS, COLUMNS, AND FOR DECORATING WALLS, ETC.

Passiflora actinea, cærulea, racemosa, edulis, insignis, quadrangularis, kermesina, Loudonii, trifasciata, princeps ; Tacsonia splendens, Van Volxemii ; Rhynchospermum jasminoides, obtusifolium variegatum ; Cobæa scandens fol. var; Akebia quinata ; Stephanotis floribunda ; Pilogyne suavis ; Bignonia venusta, speciosa, australis, Latrobea ; Tecoma jasminoides rosea ; Mandevillea suaveolens ; Phaseolus caracalla ; Physianthus albus ; Thunbergia laurifolia, gran. diflora ; Mikania scandens (Senecio micanoides) ; Tropæolum pentaphyllum, tricolorum, speciosum ; Pharbitis Learii, ficifolia, insignis, palmata ; Maurandia ; Lophospermum ; Rhodochyton volubile.

e. FERNS FOR GENERAL DECORATION WHICH REQUIRE A MODERATE TEMPERATURE :

Acrostichum alcicorne (Platycerum) ; Adiantum tenerum, concinnum, cuneatum, formosum, pubescens, trapeziforme ; Anemia villosa ; Aspidium molle, violascens, Kaulfussia ; Asplenium flabellifolium, palmatum ; Blechnum australe, brasiliense ; Cyathea medullaris, australis ; Cyrtomium falcatum ; Davallia canariensis ; pixidata ; Dicksonia australis, antarctica, umbrosa ; Doodia caudata ; Doryopteris palmata ; Polypodium aureum ; Gymnogramma chrysophylla, peruviana ; Lastræa elegans ; Lomaria Gibba, latifolia ; Nephrolepis exaltata, tuberosa ; Oleandra neriifolia, Pteris, longifolia, serrulata stricta.

II.—PLANTS FOR GREENHOUSES, CONSERVATORIES AND FLOWER SALOONS, WHICH REQUIRE DURING THE WINTER ONLY A LOW TEMPERATURE, OR HAVE A NORTHERN EXPOSURE :

a. PLANTS FOR THE GENERAL DECORATION :

Rhododendron hybridum, var. kinds ; *Azalea indica,* var. kinds ; *Azalea amoena ; Kalmia latifolia ; Photinia serrulata ; Aucuba japonica,* new var. ;

Ilex aquifolium, fol. var. ; *Mespilus pyracantha* ; *Eucalyptus*, var. kinds; *Andromeda floribunda* ; *Kassandra canaliculata, speciosa, pulverulenta,* etc. ; *Erica arborea, mediterranea, hibernica, strigosa, herbacea, multiflora* ; *Cryptomeria japonica, elegans, araucaroides* ; *Cedrus argentea (africana)* ; *Cupressus sempervirens, funebris* ; *(Thuja) Biota filiformis* ; *Retinospora*, var. kinds ; *Fagus antarctica, Cunninghami* ; *Laurus regalis, nobilis* ; *Nerium Oleander* ; *Olea europæa* ; *Viburnum tinus, macrocephalus, suspensus* ; *Magnolia grandiflora* ; *Bambusa Metake, falcata* ; *Polygala Chamæbuxis* ; *Rhuscus androgynus, racemosus, hypoglossum, hypophyllum, aculeatus* ; *Abelia floribunda* ; *Arbutus Unedo, Andrachne* ; *Podocarpus elongatus, neriifolius, latifolius, elegans; Berberis Darwinii, dealbata, Fortunei, ilicifolia, macrophylla, japonica : Budleya globosa* ; *Ceanothus azureus* ; *Melia Azedarach, Pistacia lentiscus* ; *Vitex agnus-castus* ; *Cerasus Lauro Cerasus* ; *Ceratonia siliqua* ; *Cistus roseus*; *formosus, ladaniferus, Lusitanicus, grandiflorus* ; *Leicesteria formosa* ; *Coronilla glauca, fol. var* ; *Daphne Fortunei, Laureola, alpina, collina, Cneorum* ; *Elæagnus reflexa* ; *Escallonia floribunda, grandiflora* ; *Eurya japonica, fol. var.* ; *Skimmia japonica* ; *Ophiopogon japonicus, spicatum, Jaburan; Euonymus japonicus, fol. var.* ; *Juniperus bermudiana; Rhamnus alaternus, fol. var.* ; *Phormium tenax* ; *Genista tinctoria, fl. pl.* ; *Helianthemum*, var. kinds ; *Hypericum calycinum* ; *Jasminum revolutum, lucidum, Wallichianum* ; *Ligustrum lucidum, fol. var., japonicum, fol. var.* ; *Mahonia japonica* ; *Myrica Californica* ; *Osmanthus fimbriatus* ; *Ulex europæus* ; *Yucca* and *Agave*, var. kinds ; *Pinus lanceolatus* ; *Pernettya floribanda* ; *Stuartia pentagyna* ; *Libocedrus Chilensis, nuciferus, californicus* ; *Magnolia conspicua.*

b. The following Plants may serve for heightening the effect of Flowers in the Winter-time and Spring :

Polygonatum stellatum, verticillatum, multiflorum ; *Doronicum Caucasicum* ; *Adonis vernalis, Dicentra spectabilis, Corydalis aurea, nobilis* ; *Lindelophia spectabilis* ; *Omphalodes verna* ; *Cyclamen æuropæum* ; *Anthericum Liliago* ; *Dodecatheon Meadia, Jeffreyi* ; *Dianthus*, var. kinds; *Nardosmia fragrans,* (*Tussilago*) ; *Funkia, fol. var.* ; *Gentiana acaulis* ; *Primula cortusoides* ; *Helleborus niger* ; *Hepatica triloba, angulosa* ; *Iberis sempervirens* ; *Iris*, var. kinds ; Hyacinths ; Narcissus ; Crocus ; Tulips ; Muscari ; Galanthus ; Colchicum ; Leucojum vernum ; *Trillium grandiflorum* ; *Orobus vernus* ; *Pæonia tenuifolia* ; *Pulmonaria virginica, saccharata* ; *Ramondie Pyrenaica* ; *Erinus alpinus* ; *Soldanella alpina, minima* ; *Rhexia Virginica* ; *Sanguinaria canadensis* ; *Saxifraga ligulata, sibirica, crassifolia, cordifolia* ; *Spigelia Marylandica* ; *Primula acaulis, fl. pl.* ; *Viola*, var. kinds ; *Lychnis Haageana, Sieboldii.*

c. Climbing and Hanging Plants for a house with a low temperature :

Adlumia cirrhosa ; *Tropæolum pentaphyllum* ; *Akebia quinata* ; Various kinds of *Clematis* ; *Ampelopsis Veitchii* ; *Bignonia capreolata* ; *Hedera (Ivy)* var.

kinds ; *Lonicera japonica, grata, semperfllorens, Brachypoda aureo-reticulata; Cissus antarctica ; Rubus rosæflorus, fl. pl. ; Rosa sempervivens, Banksia, Thea, Noisette, multiflora, Fortunei ; Gaultheria procumbens ; Vinca minor,* var. kinds ; *Phlox verna, repens, setacea, Lysimachia nummularia ; Linnea borealis.*

d. FERNS WHICH CAN HAVE A LOW TEMPERATURE :

Adiantum Capillus Veneris, pedatum ; Asplenium fontanum, marinum, rutamuraria, viride ; Aethyrium filix-fœmina, flexuosum, laciniatum, plumosum ; Blechnum boreale (occidentale), spicant (Lomaria) ; Cystopteris bulbifera ; Onoclea sensibilis ; Lastræa filix-mas, rigida, dilatata, Goldiana ; Lomaria Magellanica, alpina ; Osmunda regalis, cinnamomea ; Polypodium vulgare, alpestre ; Polystichium aculeatum, angulare, acrostichoides ; Scolopendrium officinarum (vulgare) ; Struthiopteris germanica ; Cyrtomium falcatum.

e. Finally, we add a small list of *Orchids, or air-plants,* for amateurs, who may cultivate them in a green house or flower saloon of a moderate temperature. The following species are free bloomers, not very tender, and easily cultivated :

Dendrobium nobile ; Cattleya Mossiœ, labiata, Skinneri, guttata, Perrinii ; Laelia majalis, autumnalis, superbiens ; Calanthe veratrifolia, vestita rosea; Cypripedium barbatum, insigne, venustum ; Epidendrum ciliare, fragrans ; Gongora maculata ; Maxillaria tenuifolia, Harrissoniæ, picta ; Oncidium pupilio, roseum, picturatum, ampliatum, flexuosum, luridum ; Odontoglossum grande, pulchellum, Uro-Skinneri, Insleayi ; Lycaste aromatica, Deppii, Skinneri ; Stanhopea tigrina, saccata, oculata, gutulata, insignis ; Schomburgkia crispa ; Acineta Humboldtii, longiscarpa ; Zygopetalum Mackayi, crinitum ; Phaius grandifolius (Bletia Tankervilliæ, Limodorum) ; Peristeria alata ; Miltonia candida ; Cœlogyne cristata, Trichopilia tortilis Cymbidium aloifolium, ensifolium ; Bletia hyacinthina.

PART II.

PLANTS FOR WINDOW GARDENS.

Fig. 1.—Design for Ornamental Hanging Basket.

CHAPTER X.

HANGING BASKETS.

Hanging Baskets form our simplest and also cheapest style of window ornament. They need very little care, their demands are not very exacting, and the chances of failure are very much less than plants of more sensitive nature, fit only for careful pot culture. The Hanging Basket is supposed to be a modern invention, or, at any rate, not very popularly used until late times; hence, it strikes us with feelings of curiosity to learn that, in the observance of the Jewish rural festivals hundreds of years ago, plants and cut flowers were tastefully arranged, placed in vases, and suspended from the branches forming the roof of the leaf-covered tabernacle. This was made of the branches of the oak, cedar, palm, and willow, so cut as to prevent them from withering for seven days, while the Passover was celebrated.

The directions for culture are very simple: . Choose as pots or baskets clay bowls of porous ware, which may be set inside either a wire or wooden frame, or a glazed vessel. In non-porous pots or vessels, plants will not grow to perfection; there is usually no outlet or drainage for the surplus moisture to escape, and all side ventilation or aeration is cut off. Hence, the soil becomes sodden, and the roots are liable to decay. After you have provided your baskets, then fill the bottom to the depth of an inch or two with small bits of charcoal, for the triple purpose of drainage, purification, and as a fertilizer. Charcoal dust is also desirable to mix with the soil. A coarse sponge might be put in, if the vessel is deep, to drink up the surplus moisture, and yet keep the soil moist by giving it out again when dry. You do not need a very rich soil; good garden soil is well enough; because, if too rich, your plants will grow too rapidly for grace and beauty, and run too much to stem. Climbing or drooping vines may run as much as they please; the more freely the better, as it is the very thing desired; but standard plants in baskets must not be stimulated much; they would outgrow their space.

Sand is a needed ingredient; at least one third the soil should be composed of "*scouring sand.*" Mix it well with dark loam and leaf mould. The soil from around pine trees is most excellent for your baskets; in fact, there is none better.

If the baskets become very dry from the excessive heat of the sun, it is best to place them in a dish of water for half an hour. Thus treated, the roots suck up a copious supply, and need not receive any more for two or three days.

Plants do not thrive luxuriantly in baskets, year after year, with soil or position unchanged; hence, it is well to renew them every autumn, for healthier plants will be the result.

In the summer time, when the rooms are closed against sun and flies, there is not light enough to keep the plants healthy, and then they should be hung in the shade of the porch or piazza, or under the trees.

Hanging Baskets, provided with the charcoal and the sponge in the bottom, need not have a hole for drainage, for these will supply their place.

Plants of very watery tissues, usually grown in the neighborhood of ponds or woodland streams, will do best in soil transplanted from such location; but ordinary leaf mould will answer for almost everything.

It is a good plan to keep a good reserve supply of soil at hand in a heap, ready at any time you may desire to make a new basket, fill a new pot, or change the plants in either.

When you are potting the plants into any vessel, press the soil well down around the plants, and never use wet soil; let it be well dried and friable.

Watering should be carefully administered, for few know what to give their plants, how to give, or when. An hour's neglect or forgetfulness may blight the entire beauty of your basket; or, again, an overflooding in a hot, dry room, may cause them to mould.

Whenever they are watered the whole of the soil in the pot should be well wetted, and the frequency of watering depends upon the temperature of the air; the warmer the room the more frequently will they need it. Usually once a day, in the early morning or previous evening, is sufficient, if the thermometer measures 45° to 65°; if over that, and averaging 60° to 80°, twice a day, watering moderately, will be sufficient. In winter time do not apply cold water; either use it of same degree as that of the room, or bring your dish of water in the room and let it stand an hour or two before applying. More damage than a little is done by applying too cool water, giving the tender plant a severe chill. If the surface soil cakes any, break it up frequently, and keep a good watch for insects.

Construction

The devices for making hanging baskets are nearly endless. Our florists offer a great variety of patterns; our wire manufacturers offer some pretty designs, and our pottery and tile merchants have equally attractive models of elegance and beauty. Choose anything you like, only we recommend to you not to get them too small. We would select nothing less than eleven or twelve inches in diameter, and six inches deep. Let the soil be filled in even with the edge of the rim, and then rise toward the centre like a small mound. If there are but one or two large plants in the basket, cover the surface of the soil with moss, which will retain the moisture in the soil, needing watering only at occasional intervals; the moss from trees is not as desirable as that usually found growing

Fig. 2.—Trailing Morning Glory—Convolvulus Mauritaniaus.

on the ground in some low, moist place, near a swamp. Pots of lava, or non-porous material, without a hole at the bottom for drainage, must be used only for holding other and more porous pots inside, the insterstices being filled with moist moss. Very pretty wire baskets are found at some of our stores; and these, being open, must be filled with moss first, and then a little soil in the centre, and the plants added afterwards.

Fig. 3.

Large sea shells, (nautilus or conch,) will hold soil enough to support trailers, and are usually very tasteful window ornaments. One of the prettiest baskets ever seen was made from a singe sea shell, quite large. Holes were bored through the edge to fasten cords to hang it by ; the interior of the shell was filled with light, rich soil, and *Lycopodiums* and *Lobelias* were planted in it. The rind of the gourd, and of the scallop squash, make elegant baskets for drooping plants. Cocoanut shells, whether in their natural state or embellished, with rustic work around, are acceptable.

Home-made baskets of wooden bowls, (such as we use in our kitchens,) are very common and desirable. Four or five holes should be bored with a gimblet in the bottom or the sides of the bowl. The best sizes are 12 to 16 inches in diameter, and if there are no rustic arm supports, there must be several holes bored around the edge, in which

Fig. 4.

to fasten the cords it is supported by—three are enough. To ornament the outside of the bowl, choose the gray and white lichens of the woods, fasten them on with glue, or nail on with small brads. If the stiff mosses from the pine woods are used, they can be wet with water, which renders them pliable, and fastened on with thread copper wire, nailing nails on the inner edge of the bowl and at the bottom, around which to twist the wires. The contrast between the gray and white moss, and the rich emerald or brightly variegated vines, is very beautiful. Such a basket, if planted with nothing more than the *Tradescantia Zebrina*, and the green leaved variety of the same plant, mingled with soft hanging grasses, or the bright green of the *Moneywort*, would be very pleasing. City residents, of course, will not desire to make their own baskets, but prefer to get them filled from the most convenient florist. We introduce several very pretty designs, which deserve to be copied.

Fig. 1, is a design for a hanging basket of more than usual elegance, and is a specimen out of many favorite styles prevalent among the well-to-do classes of Berlin, Germany. The box is made of handsomely carved wood, the inside lined with zinc or clay; the basin is filled with earth, and in it are planted Begonias, Caladiums, Coleus, Geraniums, Ivy, Ornamental Grasses, Calla Lily, and quite a variety of other flowers. The size is about two feet wide by three and a half feet long. Worsted cords and tassels help out the richness of the frames, and the brilliant hues of the foliage of the plants within. Few or no hanging baskets we have seen can equal this for artistic taste.

Fig. 2, is an illustration of a large, deep basket, filled with a dense growth of the *Convolvulus Mauritanicus.* This is a highly ornamental plant, of drooping, half shrubby character, slender habit, with a profusion of elegant light blue blossoms, upward of an inch in width, forming an admirable plant for suspended vases or baskets. It continues long in bloom, and its porcelain blue blossoms are conspicuously beautiful.

Fig. 5.—Group of Ferns.

Fig. 3, is a picture of the Convolvulus drooping over the sides of a rustic carved hanging basket. The outside framework is wood, but contains a clay bowl sitting neatly within. The Convolvulus family afford many very desirable plants for baskets of this description. One lady cultivator goes so far as to say that the common Morning Glory is one of the most satisfactory plants she ever cultivated. "The vine, by house culture, becomes delicate in form, and is very thrifty. The flowers, a little smaller than the Convolvulus tri-color, appear every morning, and remain until nearly night. Seeds planted in early spring, say March, will flourish and bloom in less than six weeks." This family generally are free bloomers, very showy, and have exceedingly handsome flowers, with rich colors.

Fig. 4, is a sketch of a pretty wire basket, filled with Ivy and Ferns; branches of the partridge vine hang over the sides of the basket; the interior is filled with moss, and over them all peep out clusters of exquisite ferns. The stems of the Ivy and the partridge vine are all stuck into bottles filled with water, and hid away here and there in the moss. The ferns had all been gathered from the woods, and then pressed out smooth and clean, and arranged gracefully, their stems standing in the water of the bottles; the bottles are filled with water every two or three days. The Ivy has also grown from only two or three little slips stuck into the water, and has twined its arms around and above the cords of the basket, clear to the very top.

Fig. 5, is a group of Ferns of great variety, gathered into a wire basket of neat and simple design. In the centre of the group is one of the *Dracænas*, having leaves of a brilliantly

Fig. 6.—Flower Basket.

shaded dark crimson—a class of plants always very handsome.

Springing out of this is the *Goniophlebium Subauriculatum*, with its long primate pendulous fronds; the *Cheilanthes Spectabilis*, which delights in moisture, warmth, and shade; other Ferns, such as the *Maiden's Hair*, (Adiantum,) usually of large growth. The *Athyrium*, and many of the *Spleenworts*, (Asplenium,) are introduced here to form one of the finest styles of natural Hanging Baskets we can suggest for imitation by our readers.

Fig. 6, introduces a style of basket very suitable for bulbs. It is made of wire, and the interior is lined with zinc. There is a small vessel beneath to hold drippings from the hole for drainage. Zinc vessels are not always perma-

nent; in time they corrode, and must be renewed.   Clay or wood **are preferable**.
The plants herein are several Hyacinths, Tulips, Crocuses, Lily of the Valley,
&c.   The directions for the starting of these bulbs and their culture **has already**
been explained in the chapter on bulbs.

Fig. 7.—Ornamental Hanging Baskets.

Fig. 8, is a Conservatory Basket, of lava ware, made unusually deep.   The
plants herein placed are Dracænas, Crotons, Indian Ferns, Niphobolus pertu-
sus, and N. rupestris; also the Variegated Panicum.   Ivy droops over the
sides.

Fig. 9, is an ornamental hanging pot of lava or Majolica ware, covered with drooping vines. The most popular favorites for drooping vines are the Nasturtium, Tropæolum, Convolvulus Minor, Honeysuckle, Trailing Mesembryanthemum. The centre may also be occupied with low growing plants, like the Verbena, Heliotrope, Petunias, Nemophilas, Lobelias, Mimulus, &c.

Fig. 10 is a sketch of the *Sedum Sieboldii*, a plant of very easy growth, and does best when kept in the greenhouse or conservatory. The soil most suitable is light, yet rich. Say turfy loam, 1 part; rotten dung, 1 part; sand, 1 part;

Fig. 8.

brick broken small, 1 part. It should be always under glass exposed to the full daylight, and have abundance of water. It is naturally a trailer, and will droop gracefully over the outsides of the pot, and will bloom most profusely. It should be watered carefully, so that no water will get on the leaves. Give it fresh air frequently. The habit of growth of the Sedum Sieboldii is very

peculiar. From one central crown or stool appear a number of slender branches; at regular intervals come the leaves in groups of three, and these continue to lengthen until in the month of August, when flower buds appear at the terminals of each branch.

The average growth of good specimens is about one and a half feet long, and the flowers have a spread of nearly six inches. As described by Shirley Hibberd: "In every stage of growth the plant is a beautiful object, the leaves being

Fig. 9.

slightly concave on the upper surface, and covered with a delicate glaucous bloom. The flower-buds appear a long time in advance of the flowers, but when at last these open in September, their lively, rosy, pink hue and symmetrical disposition are remarkably beautiful, and contrast chastely and cheerfully with the peculiar tint of the leafage. After the blooms have faded the stems die down, and are immediately succeeded by a new growth from the root, and thus, if encouraged by good culture, a specimen will become larger and larger every year, and may ultimately be grown to colossal dimensions. It is one of the easiest plants to grow, and its habit is remarkably distinct and elegant."

Fig. 11 is a plant of the Variegated Ivy. This is both cheap, clean, needs little attention, grows rapidly, and is the most permanently attractive of all plants for the window. Were there no other plant than this in the window it might still be considered well furnished.

Fig. 10.—Sedum Sieboldii.

Fig. 12 is a sketch of the *Saxifraga Fortunei Tricolor*.

Fig. 13 is a sketch of a bracket, with a wooden bowl, holding a plant of the Sedum Sieboldii trailing from it. This can be easily attached to the sides of the room, fastened to the centre of the window frame. It is very suitable for the Ivy either to trail from, or it may be placed at the bottom of the window, and the vine trained upward along the window casing.

Home-Made Hanging Baskets.

Nearly every one appreciates best some basket made by their own hands.

Usually only ordinary taste is requisite to contrive some very agreeable designs, and only a few hours' labor are needed. So we will give suggestions of how to make some Home-Made Hanging Baskets of handy and inexpensive materials.

For trimming the outside of some wooden bowl the roots of the laurel are very suitable, also those of the briar rose, which grows so plentifully near the woodlands and in fence corners. They are very crooked and gnarled, but when thoroughly cleansed from soil they can be nailed upon these bowls in grotesque and picturesque forms. A coat of copal varnish laid over the whole will often

Fig. 11.

make the basket possess as handsome an appearance as those for sale by any florist.

The boughs and roots of the wild grape vine supply materials for this style of rustic ornamentation. Do not remove the bark unless it is very ragged, and then tear it away carefully, not taking more than is needful. By peeling in this way the stem will be vari-colored. If a darker hue than the natural wood is preferred, take two ounces of gum asphaltum and dissolve it in half a pint of turpentine or coal oil. Apply the stain with a common paint brush, putting on two coats if it is not dark enough at first.

A simple rustic basket may be made of three forked branches of any old tree, the more thickly bestudded with little branchlets, and the more gnarled and mossy, the better. Get those with drooping gray beard moss, if possible. The sticks should be less than an inch in diameter, and six or eight inches in length. Unite the three forks by their heads, winding them with very strong twine or pliable wire, and then, with the same material, fasten the branchlets here and there, to form a sort of lattice-work, and wind the gray moss over all fastenings. Then, in the same way, attach stout cord for handles. Set in this a common clay pot with its saucer, crowding around it plenty of moss, and you have a pretty thing complete.

Some persons take the common wire baskets, and make an improvement by surrounding them with strips of pasteboard. This is completely covered by pasting or glueing upon it gray or green lichens, with a few bits of the creeping moss, and a little of the coral or red cup moss. If none of this last can be procured, heat red sealing-wax, and with it touch the rough edges of some of the lichens.

Wire baskets are in general better suited for the conservatory than the par-

Fig. 12.

lor, because they need a good watering two or three times a week, and will drip more or less constantly.

A very queer Hanging Basket was made by a flower-lover after this fashion : A piece of board one foot long and eight inches wide was first s e l e c t e d , t h e n around the edges was nailed a lath projecting about an inch above ; in each of the corners was driven a nail, and by means of strings tied thereto the basket was hung up. In the bottom were scattered a row of stones of moderate size ; t h e n they were covered with a layer of earth ; above this was another row of smaller stones, then a layer of earth, then sand pebbles, and a final coating of earth over all, forming a mound in the centre. Here were planted very small rooted cuttings of trailing plants, such as the Morning Glory, which soon filled the basket to overflowing. Two plants only will be sufficient. The Cypress vine will be liked for the purpose. Choose five or six plants. The Madeira vine is unexcelled for such a position. Erect plants should not be chosen, although Verbenas, Abronias, and Thunbergias are not objectionable.

Where shells are used, they may be ornamented with different shades of moss, mixing the white mosses with the green as you glue them on.

The sections of large pine cones will also ornament prettily. Tack them on with brads, boring each scale with a brad-awl, so as not to split them. Alternate the scales, and varnish the whole, and you will be quite satisfied with the effect. It can be suspended with red or green curtain cord, fastened through holes, as before directed, with bows or rosettes at the top and sides. The cones of the dried burs of the Sweet Gum Tree, if strung together on wire or strong twine, as beads are arranged in fancy baskets, make a handsome basket, whose rustic appearance is very pleasing.

The simplest and prettiest of all these constructions is that made from small sticks of oak, maple, beach, or other wood, cut in lengths of eight, ten, twelve, or more inches, according to the size you desire. They must be about an inch in diameter, and a hole should be bored with a gimblet an inch from the end of each stick. They are put together in log-house fashion, one stick lopping over the other, and a wire with a loop on the upper end is passed through the holes at each corner, and bent up on the under side. A piece of board an inch thick is then fastened to the sides for a bottom, and the spaces between the sticks should be filled up with moss. Small iron chains suspend such baskets, and rich soil from the woods is the best to grow the plants that will twine round the chains and wreath them. Ribbons can be used if desired. We have seen more than fifty of these baskets suspended from the roof of an orchid-house, and the effect was exquisitely beautiful.

A cocoanut affords a very pretty miniature basket. Leave the husk on, and

Fig. 13.

saw off about one-quarter of the nut; dig out the meat, and bore holes through three sides of it. The stem end is the part to be sawed off. Tie cords into the holes. There are many articles lying about every house that could do duty for hanging baskets. Worn out fly-covers can be lined with moss or cartridge paper, and when filled with soil and beautiful plants they produce as fine an effect as many a more picturesque affair. We saw one but recently covered with the golden flowers of the Moneywort, mingled with the bright blue of the Lobelia, and the Zebra-striped leaves of the Tradescantia, all growing luxuriantly, and making a humble cottage window a picture of grace and beauty.

Ox muzzles are within the reach of every country girl, and when painted green and lined with moss they form most desirable baskets to suspend from piazzas or trees. They will hang from the trees all winter, and in the spring the hardy vines, Moneywort and Partridge vine, (*Mitchella Repens,*) come forth in fresh beauty and gracefulness.

Miniature baskets can be made of a goose or turkey's egg, that are exceedingly pretty and attractive. Select the largest size, make a hole with a needle at each end, and blow out the yolk and white. Then dip the egg into boiling water, and while it is hot cut it in the middle, a little at a time, for fear it will crack down too far. Use a pair of small, sharp sissors. For a covering and c rds to suspend it, take scarlet, green, or blue split zephyr worsted, and either net or crochet a cover. Use a fine mesh or needle, and make an ornamental scolloped edge around the top. Crochet cords, or twist them, of the zephyr, and hang the tiny baskets with them. Three baskets can be made and sewed together, with a cord attached to the edge of each shell. A different vine can be planted in each egg shell. Use a rich, but rather sandy soil, and the vines will grow luxuriantly.

The same device can be suspended from the chandelier to hold cut flowers, or the chains can be omitted and the baskets be used as vases.

Boys or girls who possess any ingenuity can construct these pretty floral adornments in their leisure hours. Money is not always required for their manufacture, nor need those who live in the country apply to the florists for plants to fill them; for the fields and woods contain many twining vines that are very suitable for them. Almost anything will do for a basket—shells, horns, or anything that will hold earth, have been used for the purpose. Even turnips and carrots can be hollowed out and made to hold pretty little plants—so no one need be without these simple floral adornments for parlor or dining-room.

Plants for Hanging Baskets.

Our theme is now a more pleasing one, for how infinite, and yet indescribably beautiful, are some of the combinations of plants in baskets which we occasionally see.

Take, however, from us one general word of advice : Do not crowd in too many plants of upright growth. Usually one erect plant of showy, striking character, should be used—say a Begonia or a bright flowering Geranium ; then around this gather your plants, of great variety, but lower and more compact growth, and around the edge plant both your climbers and your trailers. If your basket is to hang in a northern or eastern window, where the temperature is lower than any other exposure, you will have to choose such plants as the Lycopodiums, Periwinkle, and Moneywort. They will do well here, for they require less sunlight. An Ivy will do well anywhere, so you may consider this your safest plant. As we have mentioned before, it is not best to bring your plants immediately from the outdoors to the warm air of the living room. Do it gradually, by first bringing the basket, after it is filled, into a cool room with plenty of light, but not directly from the sun. Here let the plants get well started, and after two or three weeks you may bring the basket into the parlor or living room.

In making your choice of plants avoid the costliest favorites of the greenhouse ; *i. e.,* it is better to take something which will thrive with ordinary culture. Greenhouse plants need more care than the window-gardener can usually give. A healthy flowering Geranium is more popular with nine out of ten than a Camellia, and is in proportion as much easier to grow.

A great trouble among amateurs is too great a fancy for seed-grown plants ; *i. e.,* they purchase florists seeds, and aim to grow their own plants by sowing the seed in the basket. It is hardly necessary to say failure is the general rule, except in the case of a few climbing plants, which will grow well anywhere. If the amateur does not know enough about propagation to grow his own plants, it is much better to buy them already started from a good florist.

The list of plants may be arranged in several very distinct classes, as follows :
1. Climbing Vines—

The *Tropæolum Lobbianum,* flowers plentifully in winter, and its brilliant red flowers are very attractive.

The *Morning Glory* will grow readily in a sunny window, and its flowers are indeed a glory. A small vase can be used to plant the seeds, and it can be suspended with ribbons.

The vine of the *Sweet Potato* is very graceful. Quite a good many who have admired a basket covered with its leaves have felt a little chagrined to find it was nothing after all but a Sweet Potato vine. The tubers can be set into a glass small enough to keep the root three or four inches from the bottom. Fill the glass with water, and place it in a warm room ; give it two or three hours of sunshine each day, and in two or three weeks it will begin to grow. All through the winter it will continue to develop its glossy green leaves in profusion. The *Discorea Batatas* is the best species for home culture.

Among other climbing plants are *Senecio Scandens,* (German Ivy,) a very free grower; *Lonicera Aurea Reticulata,* with fine yellow variegated foliage.

There are no finer plants in general to be used than the Coboœas, Maurandias, Lophospermums, and Tropæolum. The Variegated Leaved Cobæa is a great favorite, either to dangle from a basket or clothe a trellis.

For Drooping or Trailing Plants the list is quite extensive. *Lysimachia,* or *Moneywort*—old, and hardly yet superseded.

Saxifragas,	*Sedums,*
Linarias,	*Lobelia,*
Yellow Flowering Gazanias,	*Tradescantia,*
Mimulus Moschatus,	*Nierembergia,*
Mimulus Tigrinoides,	*Verbenas,*
Ice Plant,	*Mesembryanthemums,*
The Partridge Vine,	*Dew Plant.*

The *Strawberry Vine* is a rapid runner, with leaves shaped like the strawberry, but much smaller. Its flowers are white, and its seed-pods are formed of bright, cherry-red berries, which render the plant very ornamental.

The *Cranberry Vine* has been used for basket purposes with great success ; its glossy, bright leaves, pure white flowers, and bright, coral-hued berries making it quite an acquisition to the list of trailing vines.

The *Coliseum Ivy* and *Smilax* are used perhaps more universally than any-thing else. They are grown from seed readily.

The *Gazania Splendens* makes a hanging basket exquisite in beauty ; reaching down one to two feet from the basket, and blooming ten times better than it does in the open ground.

Among other good trailers are the Ivy-Leaved Geranium, Linaria Cymbalaria, or common toadflax, Lysimachia, Nummularia Folea, the common Moneywort, single Petunias of free habit, Tradescantia bicolor, or zebrina, the purple and bronze leaves of which are admirable to mix with the trailing stems of *Vinca Elegantissima* and the variegated Ivies.

Of the Ivies, *Hedera Latifolia Maculata* is really superb if grown in a poor soil, in moderate shade, and abundantly supplied with water all the summer.

Mesembryanthemums do far better in hanging baskets than in pots, but are truly splendid plants when planted in a rich, sandy soil, with plenty of drain-age, and fully exposed to the blaze of summer sunshine. A hot, sunny conser-vatory is a good place for them.

Mikania Scandens will clothe a basket in a few weeks with its most elegant foliage of light green hue, and rich glistening surface. , It should be moderately shaded, and kept in a cool atmosphere.

The *Polygonum Suaves*, somewhat like the Dioscorea, is a free growing trailer of very neat habit, producing hundreds of little flowers, which emit a powerful perfume.

The *Sedum Sieboldii* is unsuitable in the open air. When placed in baskets and grown under glass, or in the conservatory, it will spread rapidly, bearing an abundance of its chocolate-colored flowers, while the glaucous hue of its succu-lent leaves presents a most striking appearance.

Plants of Upright Growth.

Here you have a large list to choose from. Usually only one plant should be chosen if the basket is of moderate size. If the basket is very capacious, and you are bound to have a magnificent collection, you may combine all three classes, climbing or trailing plants, or those of upright standard growth.

You may select any of the numerous varieties of the Fuchsia, with their grace-ful, bending drops of bloom. *Petunias,* single or double. *Heliotrope,* always agreeable for their fragrance. *Carnations,* sweetly scented, blooming freely every month. The *Neapolitan Violet,* or the modest yet lovely little *Chinese Primrose.* The *Cyclamen Persicum*, with its curious flowers and valuable foliage, the popular Geranium. The *Daphne Odorata*, which will fill your room with its sweet odor ; or you may arrange around the edges of the vessel some Hyacinths, Crocuses or other bulbs. If you want plants of ornamental foliage, you will naturally turn to some of the numerous varieties of graceful Ferns or *Lycopodiums.* The Dragon plant *Dracœna Terminalis*, has blood red foliage, and seems to be used more often than any other as a single plant. The *Begonias* and *Gesnerias* have rich velvety leaves. For curiosity you may want a *Cactus*, or a horseshoe *Geranium ;* for scent, the Lemon or Rose Geranium, or the well known scented Verbena, or the Musk plant. The little Cigar plant (*Cuphea*), is not very showy, but is esteemed for its constant blooming qualities.

Many use the Coleus and Achyranthes, when young, and possessing rich, delicate shades, they contrast well with their crimson or purple against the green of other plants, producing a good effect ; but they soon grow too tall and look out of place. They can, however, be kept pinched back. This combination of color, either by contrast or harmony, is an excellent idea, and will not only give each plant an opportunity to display its peculiar habit of growth, but a novelty of color, likely to be appreciated by everyone.

Cissus Discolor, leaves silvery white, shaded with purple.

Ficus Repens.

Isolepis Junciodes, ornamental grass.

Panicum Variegatum, variegated grass, leaves green, striped with white and rose color.

Poa Trivialis Argenta, a new dwarf grass, variegated.

Tradescantia Zebrina and *Virides.*

Vinca Elegantissima, variegata.

Selaginella variegata.

The *Ivy Leaved Geraniums* are very desirable, and L'Elegante with its light green leaves margined with white and pink, and its snowy white flowers, would be a gem for any window. This class of Geraniums are all of a low spreading or trailing habit, hanging down and flowering freely.

Myosporum Parvifolium, a very neat trailer, bearing small white flowers in autumn, winter, or spring.

Monochaetum, is a beautiful winter flowering plant, but will require tying down at first, and then will trail nicely over the basket.

Ferns.—These form plants of permanent growth and habit, very suitable for hanging baskets. The soil needed for them to grow in, is equal parts of peat, loam, and sand, with some broken crockery mixed with it. One of the finest ferns for the basket is the *Polypodium Vulgare,* or common *Polypody.* This may be grown, if desired, in nearly all moss, with the addition of only a very slight portion of soil.

The *Asplenium Flaccidum,* is esteemed one of the handsomest, having a beautiful drooping habit, and yet producing little young ferns all over the old fronds. Place this in the centre of the basket, and display it so that its branches will show over the sides, with their bright lively green, and they will look extremely beautiful, fully justifying this as one of the best in cultivation.

Pteris Serrulata, and *P. Rotundifolia,* are easily grown, have a good habit, and prove to be very good Ferns for the basket.

The true *Maiden's Hair Fern, (Adiantum Capillus Veneris)*, by spreading at the roots will soon cover the surface of a basket.

The *Asplenium Lanceolatun* and *A. Marinum*, are also spreaders.

Ferns will always be beautiful plants for window culture on account of their delicate outline and tasteful droop of their branches.   Every amateur, however, will do well to begin with two or three at first, and then study the rest gradually until he becomes familiar with their general characteristics.   In watering Ferns, use warm water only, they will require it frequently also, for Ferns are natives of moist situations and latitudes; to most of them the dry air of a warm room is often injurious; closed cases are best.

The following trailing Ferns are suited for hanging baskets: *Nothoclaena-tenera, Davallia pentaphylla, Fadyema, prolifera, Adiantum Cordatum.*

The list of plants for baskets is endless; you are never at lack what to choose. You may begin with one plant, but as you become more acquainted with the nature of each plant, and learn their habits, you will love them so dearly as to sigh because you *have not room for more.*

How to arrange Plants in the Baskets.

We offer several plans of how to fill a number of baskets easily :

No. 1.—A fine low standard for a small hanging basket is the Primula Sinensis (Chinese Primrose), bearing white or crimson flowers.   Soil—two parts garden mould and one part sand.   Water often, but slightly.   Raise from seed or division of the root, in sandy soil.   Take offsets from old roots in May, re-set them in fresh soil and keep the pots in the shade until September.   Gloxinias— flowers of rose color or crimson—make a fine display in similar pots.   They need the same soil as the Primula.   Water scantily, except when in bloom. Propagate by division of the roots, or a single leaf set in damp sand.   Just within the edge of the pot set Lysimachia nummularia (Moneywort), Nepeta Glecoma (Ground Ivy or Gill run over the ground), or Coliseum vines. These have yellow, blue, white flowers.   They will throw out trailers three or four feet long.   Twine some of these around the chains or cords that sustain the basket.

No. 2.—In the same sort of pots and soil, with the same drooping plant, Cyclamen punctatum, or C. persicum—flowers white, pink or purplish—are very pretty.   Or a root or offshoot of Mesembryanthemum crystallinum (Ice-plant), whose stems and leaves, when the sun shines upon them, glitter as if covered with pearls and diamonds.   One of these plants will soon spread over the surface and hang prettily around the basket.   The flowers are small—pale crimson or white.   Or two or three Verbenas—white, scarlet and maroon, or white, pink, and purple—spreading and drooping, and creeping and climbing as they choose; they flourish much better thus than when trained and trimmed.   Start new plants from seed, or small branches, every June.   Keep them rather dry and shaded, till September, then give them plenty of sunshine and increase the water, but never water them very freely.

No. 3.—In baskets of the same size—six inches; but in good garden soil only—set a Nierembergia gracilis, with its slender stems and fine foliage and pretty white or lilac flowers, together with a Mahernia odorata, of similar habits and foliage, with blossoms of pale yellow, very fragrant; and a Lobelia cœlestina, or L. Gracilis, with its tiny leaves and delicate white or blue flowers, that will droop over the basket's rim. Start these plants and treat them like Verbenas, or Petunias of various shades, giving them the same treatment and allowing them to grow as they choose, like Verbenas. Or three or four bulbs of Oxalis, which, if started in August, after three months of complete rest in a dry state, will fill and cover the whole basket with their foliage and flowers from November till April or May. The varieties bearing white, scarlet and yellow, make a pretty group, or pink and white, and purple.

No. 4.—Baskets a foot in diameter, filled with the same soil, may hold a Zonale geranium—Tom Thumb, Fire King, or Mrs. Pollock; or Mountain of Snow, with its white-bordered leaves—and an Ivy-leaved geranium to climb up the handles; with a Maurandia, a Solanum, or two or three Vincas to trail around the brim and about the basket. Raise these all from branches rooted in sand under glass in May. Water frequently, but sparingly, till in bud, then give the fertilizer mentioned in a previous chapter, and plenty of water.

No. 5.—"A happy family," to fill a very large basket of good garden soil, should have one of the geraniums above mentioned for its centre; a Euphorbia, with silvery foliage; Coleus, maroon or bronze; a Bouvardia, scarlet flowers; a Sanguinaria, white flowers, and mignonette and alyssum, with moneywort, ground ivy, Irish ivy, Madeira vine, Solanum and Maurandia for climbers and trailers. Raise the standard plants from slips or branches rooted in wet sand, under glass, in May or June. Transfer them to the basket in September, and at the same time set with them cuttings of the vines. Keep the basket in the shade, and water it scantily for a month; then give it the full sunshine and water enough to keep the soil from crumbling. When buds appear on any of the plants, give it the fertilizer once a week for two months. Be sure that the air of the room in which it hangs is moist by the evaporation of water upon the stove or furnace, and open the window near by twice a week for a quarter of an hour, shielding the plants from the draught by newspapers pinned into cone shape around the basket. With this management the "happy family" will be your pride and delight.

Iron Frame for an Ivied Garden or Conservatory Seat.

CHAPTER XI.

The Ivy for Decorative Purposes.

The Ivy might be called the poor man's vine, for, like the Wilson Strawberry, it will grow for almost every one. It is the easiest of all the vines for indoor use, both in growing and for training, and not a little of its merits as a favorite window plant are its permanency, for it will live long in one pot without change of soil or position. It accommodates itself to all temperatures save that below freezing, and when in full growth it adds more grace to the window than any plant yet used.

The English Ivy (Hedera helix) is what is styled a *rooted climber*, as from every little joint roots will spring out and take hold of any support. This is one great advantage of value over other climbing vines which must be trained.

It is hardly adapted to our severe wintry climate, and will not live out of doors unless covered with straw. This renders its use for windows a necessity, and who that has ever gazed upon its glossy green leaves, drooping with long garlands of graceful verdure, but has felt it well deserved to be named the most beautiful of all drawing-room plant decorations. A writer speaks of the affection with which it is esteemed in German houses: "It becomes as one of the family. Sometimes the whole side of a parlor is covered with it, and twining around over picture frames, or looped about brackets, drooped over statuettes, the portraits of father, mother, and cherished friend, look forth smiling from the leafy environment. Small articles of *vertu* gleam here and there, touched with it, framed about mirrors or doors, each heart-shaped dark evergreen leaf, instinct with loveliness, adds to them all increased beauty. Wherever it goes it makes a green, perpetual summer of indoor life."

Another writer, viewing it in a poetic view, says: "A single root has been known to wreathe a bow window with thick garlands, and then strike off into lovely, independent paths along picture cords and above cornices, till the room seemed all a-bud, like Aaron's rod. It will cover a screen of wire, curtain a curtainless window, festoon a pillar, frame a favorite picture, (and what more graceful or delicate frame could be desired?) arch a door, climb and twist about a window-sill, and swing in long-looped tendrils from a bracket. There is no end to its beautiful uses.

"Tickle it with a little guano, and how it frolics. Nip off the terminal shoots, and lo, two bright, persistent tendrils shoot forth, and curl and twine about your very fingers. Wash its dusty leaves, and no child could look more gratefully in your face. It harbors no vermin, encourages no blight, but steadily and sweetly keeps its daily course. It is a decorative artist of high ability; a companion, a friend."

Notwithstanding this poetic imagery, it must be admitted its presence, with

Fig. 14.—An Ivied Staircase.

its entwining, luxuriant foliage, gives a refreshing and pleasant look to every apartment; of uncounted worth is it in homes where garden facilities are few or none, and a sprig of green is considered equal to the nobleman's wide, rural estate.

The Ivy requires rich soil in which to grow, and must have strong food.

"Of right choice food are its meals, I ween."

You must therefore select for it the best soil which your garden can afford; add to it one-half each of well-decayed manure and leaf mould rubbed together; then set the pan of compost in the oven and bake it, if you wish to kill all larvæ of worms and white ants.

Plant the roots in large, well-drained pots, with an inch or two of bits of charcoal at the bottom, and as the roots increase transfer them to larger-sized pots or buckets. The Ivy will grow in wood vessels as well as pottery, and pails or buckets painted green can be made to do duty for the pots.

Should the roots appear to be too thickly crowded in too small a pot, run a knife around the edge of the soil and turn over the ball of earth. If this is so, cut off a few of the outer ones, and then repot in rich soil in a little larger vessel.

The Ivy seems to be the least sensitive to changes of light of any plant we have; neither does it require much heat, thus being exceedingly well adapted to situations in halls or balconies, or rooms not very well heated. Figure 14 shows how it may be of great service in decorating a hall, the brackets holding the pots being fastened to the side of the wall, and the ivy permitted to climb up both wall and porch.

If planted in pots and trained to stakes, they can be readily moved from one window to another, or from one room to another; it is much the most convenient method to have the Ivy in some portable form.

Like all other plants, however, it must have a uniform temperature, and though it will bear a little chilling without much injury, yet it should be kept where there is some degree of warmth.

It delights in considerable moisture, and if neglected or permitted to dry up, its luxuriance soon suffers; hence, a saucer or pan should be kept full of water, ready at any time for its use.

During the spring and summer months the pots of Ivy are often carried to the outer air, and placed on the balcony or under a tree in the lawn or garden. Here they might be neglected; so we again repeat our caution: do not forget the water.

When brought into the house the leaves should be carefully washed with soap-suds and water; all unsightly branches and torn leaves removed.

Ivies for the house should be brought in before November, or even before it is time to build the fire. Place first in a cool room, and then bring gradually into the warmer room.

When placed where they are to stand, the vines should be gracefully arranged, and secured by small strings to the wood-work, or to the curtain by bits of green worsted braid. The green creeping foliage is a fine contrast to the whiteness of the delicate lace curtain.

Vines can be grown by immersing the stems in small vials of water, and fastening them to the backs of picture frames they are desired to ornament. With a number of vials quite a luxuriant growth can be imitated, but care must be had to keep the vials filled with water. At intervals, two or three bits of charcoal may be added to sweeten and purify.

Fig. 15.—An Ivied Picture Frame.

A good illustration of how a picture frame may thus be decorated is afforded in figure 15, showing a looking-glass with rustic frame, and the Ivy twining around it. In this case no vials are used, but a very unique and convenient receptacle, shown in figure 16. Usually all our frames hang forward a little at the top from the wall, and leave an open space. This receptacle fits into this open space at the back of the top of the frame, and is very neatly concealed. To make this successful the frame should be of good size. The receptacle is wedge-shaped, and made of zinc by any tinsmith, and of the right length and diameter to fit in behind. After filling with earth plant the Ivy, and let its leaves ramble over and down the frame.

Such a frame should not be hung near a fireplace, for the heat and dust would hinder the growth of the plant very materially. If it can face a north or east window it is best situated. Water should be given daily at the same time the other plants usually receive this attention—by night or early morning. Note one thing, in filling this pan, to remember to place a few bits of crockery at the bottom, to secure efficient drainage. Avoid giving a surfeit of water.

A very novel style of ornament is afforded in Fig. 17, designed for a portable screen of Ivy. This is a box made very similar to those for the window, of a length varying from three to six feet, and one to two feet wide, mounted on castors. A number of laths of wood, neatly and smoothly planed, are nailed crossways, and fastened upright at the back of the box. Usually the height is about four to four and a half feet. The entire box and lattice-work should be painted green; then when dried fill the box

Fig. 16.—Receptacle for Ivy.

with mould, and set in the Ivy plants, which, when well started, will soon cover the trellis completely.

If desired, the front of the box may be ornamented by planting thickly Lily of the Valley or Primulas, or Mignionette, sown in the summer. Other climbing vines may be introduced either with the Ivy, or in place of it, such as the Morning Glory, Woodbine, Clematis. The box is an ornament in any position where placed, either before the window, or across the corner of the room, and the capacity of the box also affords opportunity for growing many choice standard parlor plants, Fuchsias, Geraniums, &c. Mr. Robinson states that such screens are used to a great extent in Parisian saloons and drawing-rooms, and in one instance saw them in quite a row, beautifully used to embellish crystal partitions between large apartments.

Fig. 17.—Ornamental Screen of Ivy.

One day in his rambles he came upon a wine shop in an obscure part of Paris, where the window was decorated with the Ivy; on going in, he found it planted in a rough box against the wall, up which it had crept, and was growing above as carelessly as if in a wood. At another time, at the Court of Versailles, in the porter's lodge, he witnessed the deep interest which the fat porter and his wife took in Cacti, &c., and their nice collection of other things, but more particularly at the sumptuous display of Ivy, which hung from over the mantelpiece. It was planted in a deep recess, and tumbled out its abundant tresses almost as if depending from a Kerry rock in its native home.

But its most successful use is in the hanging basket. Here at home it climbs, and swings, and droops at will, thriving and twining until the arms of the basket are hidden in the dense verdure. Probably no cheaper style of hanging baskets can be obtained than this, and surely none will last as long.

Another charming use to which the Ivy can be put is to twine it around an Easel in the parlor. Take a small rustic jardinet, such as are figured in one of the chapters of Part I, fill with earth, plant in it a good strong root of the Ivy, and then twine its long tendrils around the edges of the Easel, and let it droop from the top over the picture placed on the rest beneath. It forms one of the finest of draperies and borders for any art engraving, portrait or painting. Little brackets of it may be filled like Fig. 13, in chapter 10, and fastened in the centre of the side of any room, and while the Ivy itself may droop, there may be placed ferns or pressed autumn leaves above to help the effect with their gay colors.

Those cuttings which have rooted in water during the winter will need more plant food than this will supply. So in the spring, either plant them in the open border, or place them in pots, with soil, and they will soon become large plants.

Eight to ten large pots of Ivy trained over stakes and trellises, are at times used by some to ornament a single room.

Hanging baskets are sometimes constructed entirely without soil—holding only moss. A quantity of vials are filled with water and placed therein so as to be well concealed; slips of Ivy are inserted in some of these vials; Ferns are interspersed in other bottles, and cut flowers added to others; brilliant autumn leaves pressed and varnished are added here and there. All combined make a very choice parlor ornament. The only care needed is to keep the water replenished as long as it will last.

In the previous chapter on hanging baskets may be seen a design of a very handsome combination of Ferns and climbing Ivy, in Fig. 4, and in Fig. 11, is a sketch of the Ivy as we see it in its most familiar habits of growth. The bowl is an earthen one, such as now are imported and found on sale at most floral stores. A single cutting has been placed in here, and now it is branching outward vigorously.

The directions for propagating Ivy from slips or cuttings, are very simple. Take a young, tender branchlet, cut about three inches in length, and insert half an inch of its stem in wet sand, or soil, under a bell glass or tumbler. Keep the soil well moistened, and yet warm, by placing it in the sunshine for fully a week. Then loosen the sand, withdraw the stem, and if rootlets have started, put immediately in a pot of good garden earth, mixed with one-third its quantity of sand. Press the soil firmly about this young plant, to the same height as the sand reached before, cover with the bell glass again, and set in the *shade* for a week, then set the glass aside and bring to the sunshine. It should be watered frequently, but only just enough to keep it from wilting. Early in June, if it has grown too long, trim off the large branches, set it out doors in the garden, then in September, again put it in a large pot with newer soil, bring to a cool and shady room at first, then gradually bring it to the heat.

There are several varieties of the Ivy, commonly grown by all gardeners. The *Hedera helix* is the English Ivy, the common outdoor climbing variety, found in all parts of Europe. It is of slow growth, two feet a year out doors being considered good progress. It needs water more freely than any of the other sorts, for drouth is death to it. It may be propagated by first cutting slips, then rooting them in bottles of water, and afterward transferring with sand.

The *Hedera Canariensis*, is the Irish Ivy, slightly larger than the others; leaves five lobed. Will thrive in a cool, shady, and close room. Too great exposure to the heat of the sun will cause the leaves to turn purple, or ripen too quickly; yet it will seldom blossom without sunshine. The flower is very ordinary, and it is more to be prized for its elegant light green foliage, which are thrown out from its luxuriant shoots.

The German Ivy is not properly of this family, but its botanical name is *Senecio Scandens.* This grows much more rapidly than either of the above, has lighter green leaves, and is entirely free from troublesome insects. Its branches trail in long festoons. Whether grown in the hanging basket, or over the window, it will soon wreath it with its leafy canopy. It may be trained as a pyramid by inserting stakes in the pots, and then letting the vine curve around toward the top, or it may be trained as an umbrella, or bushes, or on a semicircle, or any form that the frame is made to take. Its easy propagation—for every slip will take root—a quick growth, have made it a favorite with everyone.

Another variety called the Coliseum Ivy, (*Linaria Cymbalaria,*) is also popular. It grows in slender purplish stems, having small green leaves with purple linings, and its flowers are like those of the Antirrhinum, but are very minute, being of lilac, white and yellow tints, mingled together. It grows in cracks or crevices of old buildings, and the roof of the grand Cathedral at Milan, is thickly overgrown with it in patches. It seeds plentifully, sows itself, and is also most easily propagated by cuttings. The soil most suitable for it is light sandy loam, yet it does not endure much moisture or dampness.

There are still a dozen or fifteen other varieties to be obtained in this country, each peculiar in itself, yet, the variegated varieties, *Marginata, Argentea,* &c., are the most desirable. They exist in many different forms, all variously margined with creamy, silver, or yellow colors—on the leaves. They are used either for climbers on the walls, or in beds, as margins. They do best when fully exposed to the sunshine, and in a comparatively poor soil. Under the name of Silver Edge Ivy, the *Argentea* has been used for edging flower beds and for terrace gardens, having a broad margin of silvery white,—other varieties have three colors, white, green, and rose, or yellow.

The list of varieties exceeds fifty in number, some producing gigantic leaves of thick texture, others white or golden berries, some richly variegated, others with small leaves of deepest purple. They form a study of deepest interest, and many should be better known ; yet strange to say, in the majority of the florists Catalogues, a few only are mentioned for popular cultivation, the German the Coliseum, and the variegated *L'Elegante.*

CHAPTER XII.

Climbing Vines—Balcony Gardening.

What delicate taste and suggestive beauty seem gathered up in the associations of climbing vines.

Helps to Home Adornment we have often called them, and the fairy fingers who twine them around their parlor windows, or along the piazza, or on the rustic trellis before the cottage door, will tell you how well they appreciate their value in making home so pleasant. Climbing vines afford us an opportunity of clothing not the outside of the window alone, but its inside also, with verdure and decorations of greenery, for our imagination must now include, as part of the domain of house-gardening, the ornature of the outside of the window, piazza, or balcony, as well as the interior. Ideas of refinement, taste and beauty, are invariably suggested by the presence of climbing vines. Let the corners of our houses, or the edges of our windows, be hid under the delicate foliage or brilliant flowers, and their natural festoons of mingled verdure and bloom will soften the most gloomy surroundings.

Our new built houses, with all their architectural finish and imposing design, still lack the last softening polish which comes only from the mellowing and genial touch of the vine. The first thing to be considered in growing vines indoors is the *soil*. Bulbous plants require light and very loose soil. Short, fibrous roots need a firm, fine soil. Long and spreading roots need a heavier and coarser soil than others. For most plants good garden loam, loosened, when necessary, by mixing with it street sand or gravel, and enriched by the application of a liquid stimulant answers very well. To make this stimulant, mix half a peck of stable manure or street sweepings, with a quart of pulverized charcoal, in a three-gallon vessel, and fill up the vessel with soft water. After it has stood a week the vessel will be ready for use. It should be clear. Water your plants with this three days consecutively, once in three weeks, during their earliest growth and blooming. It should be perfectly odorless; if not, then add more charcoal. As the liquid becomes more exhausted add more water. This quantity of fertilizing material will supply stimulant enough for two dozen large plants during six months.

If you can obtain leaf mould—the fine, dark soil from the woods—take this for a third ingredient of your soil. It will prove, also, quite as nutritive as this fertilizer. If fertilizing liquids are used, they must be applied directly to the soil; but when water only is used, the whole plant should be showered with it, if possible.

In selecting our list we have regard naturally to those which are most rapid growers.

First on the list is *Coboea Scandens.* It is an old favorite, and it is worthy of remark, that but few of the novelties introduced of late years can equal some of the *"old favorites"* which we have long been accustomed to grow.

The vine is named from Cobo, a Spanish priest, who first cultivated it in Mexico, where he found it growing wild, and rambling in full luxuriance and beauty. A new variety of this vine, (Coboea Scandens folius variegata) is much the most suitable for in-door culture.

The growth of the vine is very rapid, and it is equally easy of cultivation; the only essentials to success being warmth, a rich, though light soil, and sufficient water. If allowed to become very dry it will wither away. It requires sun and a warm room for it to grow in perfection; yet it is not a tender plant; *i. e.*, it will live anywhere, provided the frost does not touch it, and is one of the few plants which will flourish luxuriantly in parlors lighted with gas and kept at almost fever heat.

If grown in a hanging basket or pot, it must be large, and the roots allowed plenty of room to spread out in. In the summer the pots can be removed from the interior room to a balcony or piazza, or plunged into the ground until they are again wanted. Then clip off the growth of branches and leaves; place the pot back again in a sunny window, where it will soon start forth afresh, with new leaves and arms to cover the window.

Its flowers are two inches long, and bell-shaped. At first their coloring is of a greenish hue, but it changes to a rich bluish-purple, and will continue in bloom for a week or more. Its calyx is large, and the long stamens seemingly grow at one side of it, giving to the flower much grace. It is easily raised from cuttings and seeds. The latter require some special care. If planted in the open ground they will generally decay; hence, pot or hot-bed culture is necessary. Usually the seeds are sown in March or April in light, rich soil, in pots, warmed with a gentle heat. After they have started, the young plants, when two inches high, are potted separately into small pots, and when they have grown about a foot high are carried to the place where they are to remain. Usually there is no difficulty in the greenhouse or conservatory, where they are produced abundantly. Amateurs who cannot propagate them will do well to buy them from the florist already started.

It is one of the best of vines for parlor decoration, as it will drape and festoon the window, and stretch forth its tendrils, running up even to the ceiling. The tendrils are so clinging in their nature that they will attach themselves to anything which comes within their reach—curtain cords, branches of other plants, brackets, &c., throwing out new branches everywhere.

Smilax.

The Smilax (Medeola asparagoides) is now seen in almost every window basket, cultivated extensively for its rich, wavy, glossy foliage. For table decorations, wreaths, festoons, &c., it is very popular, and in all festive occasions where green drapery is used the Smilax occupies a prominent part—always considered indispensable. It is a bulb, a native of the Cape of Good Hope, and requires a rich but rather sandy soil to grow in perfection, also a liberal use of liquid manure, and when in a growing state must have plenty of water. Its leaves are in reality its branches; its flowers are of a whitish green, and its berries, or seed-pods, black; but it is cultivated entirely for its graceful sprays. These are often injured by their deadly enemies, the red spiders. By giving the plants a good shower of water once a week they will soon be free from the insects, or if this is not convenient, dust them with red pepper.

The Smilax does not require a very sunny location, but will thrive in a partly shaded window or on a bracket. It propagates itself by offsets from the parent bulb; yet it can also be raised from seeds. It requires some support to cling to, and will run more rapidly if a wire is fastened around the outside edge of the pot, and to this let there be attached small cords an inch or two apart. Fasten the ends of the cords together at the top of the ceiling, and on these slight supports the vines will closely twine.

In the summer give it but little water, and keep it in the shade where it will remain dormant. In September repot in fresh soil, and give occasional stimulants.

It is one of our most delicate vines for the parlor; a great favorite with every one, for its graceful leaves form a very pleasant effect when trained either around the basket, or pictures or statuary.

Tropæolums.

The varieties of this class are very numerous—all beautiful and handsome objects for either indoor or garden use. They are all rapid growers during the winter months, and are usually propagated from seeds, which produce a great variety of colors; one especial advantage being the fact of their flowering the first season so soon after planting. For ornamenting the window, or the greenhouse, or for covering the trellis, arbor, or balcony, they are admirably suited on account of their dense foliage and fine bloom.

Tropæolum Lobbianum, is better suited for window use, than the open ground. Flowers are of very bright orange and scarlet colors, and vine a very vigorous grower; propagated best from cuttings.

The *Tropæolum Tricolorum,* is a bulbous-rooted climber, and best suited for the green-house or conservatory. It should be planted in September to enable it to obtain a good start before the winter starts in. Plant the tubers, which are not unlike a potato, eye upwards, and about an inch and a half beneath the surface of the pot, which should be eight to nine inches in diameter, and filled up with a light but rich soil. Give a little water when you plant it, and set the pot in a warm but rather shady spot, not letting the soil become dry; until you see the shoots starting freely give but little water, then give water daily. When the branches appear, train them to a trellis, or archway, according to your taste. A plant of the *Tricolorum* can be placed on one side of the archway or trellis, with its crimson, orange and black blossoms to contrast with some of the other varieties, either *Lobbianum* or *Peregrinum.*

Tropaeolum pentaphyllum, a beautiful kind of Tropaeolum ; like the tri-color, but not robust in habit. This kind will come to a great perfection if planted in a large pot and placed on a balcony.

Tropaeolum trimaculatum, an annual species of more tender growth than Trop-major. It can be raised from seeds, and will give in their treatment during the summer season, a good series. Many flowers and a graceful growth is the character of this plant.

Sandy loam, with a third of decomposed manure well mixed with it, will grow the slower growing varieties to best advantage ; for those more rapid, we would not admit more than one fourth manure. When the leaves and flowers begin to fade away, and turn yellow and sere, give but very little water, and when dying down give none at all, but remove the bulbs from the pots, and keep them in sand in a cool place until another September comes around. They propagate themselves by tubers, which can be divided, and also will root easily from cuttings, which will form roots in vases of water ; if the branches are full of buds when placed in the vases, they will bloom finely, and form a very pretty ornament for the parlor or sitting-room. Put bits of charcoal into the glasses, and the water will keep sweet and pure.

Maurandia.

The *Maurandia Barclayana* is an exceedingly pretty climber for indoors. It grows readily from seed or cuttings. If from the latter, they should be started in June, so as to make a strong plant by autumn.

If grown from seed, plant in light, rich soil, in June ; water it freely, and give plenty of sun. It blossoms profusely, hanging out full of elegant white, purple, or pink bell-shaped flowers, which much resemble those of the *Foxglove.* It needs a fertilizer once a week, from the time the buds first appear till blooming is past.

It is a vine of the easiest growth and culture, winding about slender strings or supports in the window, and in two or three months' time it will cover a small trellis anywhere with its graceful branches and pretty flowers. Seeds can be obtained of most florists, which will furnish all colors of violet, white, scarlet, rose, and purple.

Thunbergia.—This is another ornamental climber, easily raised from seed. It grows in any good garden soil, and will soon cover a window frame. It is really a greenhouse perennial, and is propagated by cuttings for greenhouse use. In the open ground its seed is usually sown about the last of May; grows freely, about six feet high; has many side branches, and needs a trellis to cling to; flowers are usually a buff or white color, with a rich maroon colored throat. Other varieties have shades of orange and yellow.

The Passion Flower.

The Passion Flower, is one of our old standard varieties, much cultivated and admired, and very desirable for parlor ornament. It thrives best in light, rich soil, and needs much sunlight to bloom in profusion. It cannot bear great water-

Fig. 18.—*Passiflora Cœrulea*, Blue Passion Flower.

ing: only be sure that the leaves will not droop from dryness, and it will flourish. Plant the seed, or start cuttings in moist sand, in the greenhouse. After a plant has got a vigorous growth, it may be brought into the parlor, and remain as long as it is warm.

Passiflora Cœrulea, has flowers of a sky blue color and remarkable character ; grows finely, and is quite ornamental. It should be pruned close back to within a bud or two of the main stem every summer or autumn, as it blooms on the shoots from these buds during the next season. It can usually be had of the florist, and may be kept as a plant for the Conservatory. If planted out to ornament a veranda or trellis, it must be protected during the winter, by covering over, as it will not stand the frost. It climbs twenty feet or more, and is quite handsome. For home culture take pot plants already started ; keep in a temperature of 60° to 75°. Several other varieties are suitable also :—

Passiflora racemosa.	*Passiflora quadrangularis.*
" *permessina.*	" *princeps.*

A fine variegated variety has been produced—trifasciata ; its dark green, tricolored leaves having a broad band of deep rose color through the various centres. Its foliage is very handsome, and its flowers being of the usual color, makes it very desirable.

For training in conservatories, they are among the most effective of all ornamental climbers, producing a great profusion of blooms.

Ipomœa. The Morning Glory.

These have proved with many ladies the easiest and simplest of all vines to raise indoors. They are raised chiefly from the seeds, and will usually grow sufficiently well to bloom in four to six weeks after planting. They are very rapid climbers, and much more delicate than the Convolvulus to which they are closely allied. The principal varieties suitable for indoors are :

I. Coccinea, (Star Ipomœa,) with small scarlet flowers.

I. Limbata, white margin, bluish centre, in the form of a star.

The Ivy.

This has been mentioned in a chapter by itself. For basket purposes the *German Ivy,* or *Coliseum Ivy,* will naturally be chosen first ; but for climbing purposes, around the windows or doors of the room, choose the *Hedera Helix, English Ivy,* or the *Canariensis Irish Ivy,* which will be sure to grow in any room. Both should be frequently watered.

Cissus Discolor

Is a greenhouse climber, with finely variegated leaves, which are in great demand in the cities for the margins of baskets of flowers. It will hardly grow well in a window garden, as it needs the highest temperature of a forcing house to develope its beauties; but in a proper location it will be for a short time a great addition to a collection of plants. It will grow during the summer in the window if shaded; but will not in the winter, unless it has a great deal of heat and light.

Clerodendron Balfouri

Needs a warm temperature. Its flowers are of a bright scarlet, with a calyx of pure white, and the clusters are six inches in diameter. It blooms for many months during the winter, and is invaluable for bouquets and roses. It requires a rich soil and much sunshine, but it will grow well in a southeastern location.

The list of climbing vines is very extensive. For parlor culture it seems hardly necessary to make any addition to a list in which there are so successful and popular favorites as the Ivy, Cobœa, and Morning Glory.

Most of the climbing vines suitable for indoor growth are generally grown in the greenhouse. Often they are started in large pots or boxes, and when trained to a trellis are transferred to a warm sitting-room to stand there as objects of ornament; but few undertake to grow greenhouse climbers there for permanent use.

List of Climbing Plants most useful for the Parlor, Window, or Balcony Decoration.

a. Annual, bi-annual, or such species and varieties with tender and soft vines :
Maurandya Barclayana, Lareyana, and other varieties.
Cardiospermum Halicacaba, baloon vine.
Tropaeolum majus, and *majus fl. pleno.*
        trimaculatum.
        Lobbianum, and its hybrids.
Cyclanthera pedato, and *P. explodens.*
Adlumia cirrhosa, (*Finnaria fungosa.*)
Thunbergia alata, and *T. aurantiaca.*
Lophospermum scandens, and varieties.
Pilogyne suavis.
Ipomœa Quamoclit, and *Quamoclit alba.*
        coccinea, and *coccinea lutea.*
Obobra viridiflora.
Scyphanthus elegans.
Loasa lateritia.
Callistega pubescens flore pleno.
Manettia bicolor.
        cordifolia, (*coccinea.*)
Micania scandens, (*Senecio micanoides.*)
        b. Running plants with a more ligneous habit :
Clematis azurea grandiflora, and new hybrids.
        flammula. and *C. lanuginosa.*
Passiflora incarnata, (hardy perennial.)
        edulis fol. var.

Passiflora caerulea, and *caerulea varieties.*
      trifasciata.
      kermesina.
      princeps.
      quadrangularis.
Cobœa scandens, and *scandens fol. var.*
Thunbergia laurifolia, and *T. grandiflora*
Medeola asparagoides, (*Myrsophyllum.*)
Mikania speciosa Verschaffeltii and *Warcsewitzii.*
Akebia quinata.
Phaseolus Caracalla.
Physianthus albens.
Ipomœa digitata, (*palmata*)
      ficifolia and *insignis.*
      Hlorsfalliae.
      tyrianthina.
Stigmaphyllom ciliatum.
Solanum jasminoides.
Tecoma jasminoides.
Mimosa prostrata.
Bignonia venusta, and *speciosa.*
      argyraea—violacea and *ornata.*
Tacsonia mollissima, and *T. Van Volxemii.*
Rhyncospermum jasminoides, and *var.*
Tropæolum tri-colorum, and *T. pentaphyllum.*
Cissus discolor.
      antarcticus.
Rubus Moluccanus.
Stephanotus floribundus.
Ampelopsis Veitchii, and *quinquefol, fol. var.*
Lonicera crabhipoda aureo reticulata.

Balcony Gardening.

When the warm suns of spring and summer make the air more genial, our taste for outdoor gardening returns, and the first step after leaving the window garden is to embellish our balcony or veranda. To this spot we bring our hanging baskets and suspend them between the overhanging arches, or fasten upon one of the piazza supports a hollow bracketed vessel. Throw therein some soil, and try a trailing plant or two. In the grassy border just beneath we sow the seeds of some of our most rapid and cleanly growing hardy vines, which will cover the balcony soon with their dense shade.

To those disposed to try a little amateur gardening, and willing to undergo considerable pains and care, we recommend a series of boxes wherein may be grown plants of ornamental foliage, such as Coleus, Achyranthes, Ferns, or into which you may transfer your pot plants from inside the window. These boxes may be usually made of pine wood, painted green, and vary from six to eight inches deep, and ten to fifteen inches wide. Fill up all the interspace not occupied by the pots with sand ; also fit castors to the boxes, so that they may be easily moved from one part to the other. Into these boxes may be set trellises, and upon them may be trained the Fuchsia, Ivy, Clematis, or Morning Glory. Different boxes may be used for different classes of plants: one for Geraniums, another for Ferns, a third for Ivy, a fourth for Roses, a fifth for Evergreens, (the Arbor Vitæ being best,) another for Bulbs, (Tuberoses, Lilies, &c., being best.) The length of these boxes should not exceed four feet.

Mignionette boxes are generally made 7 inches deep, 7 inches wide, and from 1½ to 3 feet long. Mignionette looks best when the plants are grown *en masse,* and for this there must be depth of soil. It is not a bad plan to plant a few climbers in the boxes, so that when the Mignionette fades away the vines will fill up the blank space.

Tom Thumb Tropaeolums, Canary Bird Flower, Asters, Stocks, Balsams, are all very suitable for this style of box and balcony gardening.

Zonale Geraniums, Pelargoniums, of all kinds will do well. Plants of variegated foliage, like the Abutilon, need a slightly shaded locality.

Heliotropes, Salvias, Verbenas, &c., require a strong exposure to sun and air, and will bloom well in a southeastern exposure.

In a western balcony the variegated leaved Ivy Geranium, scarlet, white, and pink ; Tom Thumb Geraniums, and Mignionette, will bloom most perfectly. Ivies will twine about the frame-work, no matter what may be the exposure, but the Madeira vine likes a warm place, and the Smilax anywhere.

Fuchsias desire the shade ; hence, a northerly exposure, except when too cool, will suit them ; also the Pansies, Myrtles, and Funkia variegata do best there.

Brackets may be fitted to the sides of the window frame, and in them placed pots filled with drooping flowers, like the Colisseum Ivy and *Tradescantia Zebrina.*

At a slight expense you might construct a small hanging garden, similar to one of the designs illustrated in the chapter for hanging baskets, and suspend it at the end of the piazza. You may also introduce vases upon your veranda with good effect ; but for this you do not need tall plants. The most effective flowers are those of Pansies, Verbenas, and Petunias.

Balcony gardening in winter is of course an impossibility, unless we make exceptions in favor of a few Evergreens. These are suitable at all seasons of the year, and nothing is more neat and tasteful, requiring less care than a box of Arbor Vitæs, for these are much easier to grow than Pines or Spruces.

If the balcony is limited in space, do not attempt bushy plants, and shrubs will be out of place. Here climbing vines are the most appropriate.

But if you do have plenty of room you may introduce in the spring such shrubby plants as the *Azalea,* the *Weigela rosea,* and the *Spirea Prunifolia.* A

Fig. 19.—Design for Balcony Garden.

gay display can be made by arranging two boxes, one with the Lobelia in front, and behind it a row of scarlet Geraniums, such as the *Gen. Grant, Warrior*, or *Marie Lemoine*. For a dwarf Geranium the *Tom Thumb* is best. The *Delphinium Formosum* is good also for the balcony. Cut away the blooms as fast as they get done. In order to keep the plants in good health and growth, it would be well to see that the soil of the boxes or pots is covered with moss, and once a day, in the evening or early morning, give the plants a thorough syringing of water, for upon the dry floor of the balcony evaporation will be quite rapid in warm days. Seeds of the *Mignionette, Sweet Alysum, Phlox Drummondii*, and *Nemophila* will all do well.

Nothing is so effective as the Scarlet Sage Salvia Splendens, gorgeous with its dazzling beauty.

A good plant or two of the Dielytra will make a showy box, and then you can make room for a few Verbenas, Petunias, Larkspurs, and Heliotropes. We would not recommend any bulbs, such as the Gladiolus, except the Lilium Aurtum, which will often do well; also the Lilium Longiflorum.

If you wish to grow bulbs and make a fine display, you must remove your boxes from the balcony just before winter; fill them with appropriate soil, (such as is named in chapter on Bulbs,) sink them in the garden border, plant in it your bulbs of Hyacinths, Tulips, Crocuses, Snow Drops, &c., to remain during the winter, well covered with some mulch. In early spring take them up, replace again upon the balcony, and allow them to grow and bloom. This is a very good plan where a box of flowering bulbs is desired for the jam just outside of the window-sill. After flowering the box may be filled up again with bedding plants. Every evening give a good sprinkling of water, and once a week you may add a dose of liquid fertilizer to all your plants on the balcony. In very hot weather watering may be given twice a day, remembering the only safe rule, never to give it between the hours of 9 A. M. and 4 P. M., while the sun's rays are warmest; hence, affording the most danger. Where balconies are enclosed by glass screens upon all sides they become house conservatories, and admit of the same management which is given to plants for window or greenhouse culture. Plants of greater variety may be admitted here during all seasons of the year, but usually nearly everything is removed from them during the summer months, and placed outdoors to enjoy the fresh air and invigorating rains.

The *Aucuba Japonica* is a handsome evergreen shrub; flowers are of no value, being small, but the leaves are large, of a glossy green, blotched with a pale yellow color, tapering off to white. It must be grown in a partially shaded location, as it cannot bear the hot rays of the sun. It is hardy, and will withstand ordinary winters.

Vines for the Balcony.

In these you will find your most effective means of decoration. Most of the hardy garden favorites will grow from 30 to 50 feet in a season, and a great merit is their earliness and frequency of bloom.   The list suitable for this purpose is quite large, so we name only the best six or eight.

Fig. 20.—A Cottage Porch, with Climbing Vines at the Side.

The *Honeysuckle* might almost be called a *vine of romance*. It has been so celebrated in words of sentiment or gems of poetry. The Japan variety (Lonicera brachy poda) is much the best; leaves are large, of a bright green color; flowers of a delicate sweet fragrance. As a vine for covering arbors, pillars, trellises, balconies, &c., it is unsurpassed.

The *Trumpet Honeysuckle (Lonicera Sempervirens,)* is one of the species of the Woodbine, so well known for its beauty of flower, and high fragrance. This species is referred to by *The Agriculturist* as one of the native varieties; not as showy as some of the later varieties, has fine dark green leaves, flowers tubular, about two inches long, of a fine scarlet outside, yellow within and very brilliant. It multiplies from either layers or cuttings; will not do well north of New York, but is very suitable for the Southern States.

The *Wistaria* has the merit of permanency. Its stems, once grown and trained, do not die down yearly, but remain, and grow even more luxuriant and profuse in bloom year after year. It is quite hardy; will stand our winters without much protection. The flowers are of a light blue color, and bloom almost constantly during the summer months, although the principal period is in May; is grown from cuttings or layers. Cultivators will do best to buy a good plant already well started.

The *Scarlet Trumpet Creeper (Bignonia Grandiflora)* has much the showiest flowers of all the hardy climbing vines; flowers are of rich scarlet, produced in the greatest profusion, blooming only in July and August. It will attach itself firmly to anything it can reach, and throw out innumerable little rootlets, which do not let go their hold. It is a very rapid grower, and its appearance is very much heightened by the contrast of the flowers with the bright, glossy, deep green of the leaves.

The *Aristolochia Sipho*, or *Dutchman's Pipe*, is a very curious vine, with leaves possessing an almost tropical appearance, being of an extraordinary size, 8 to 10 inches broad. The flowers grow in the form of a small pipe, and possess little beauty. The plant is hardy, a rapid climber, and is particularly valuable for positions where a dense shade is quickly desired. Grown principally from cuttings.

The *Virginia Creeper*, or *American Ivy*, requires to be planted in rich, cool, moist soil. When well started it will grow with a rapidity unparalleled in native vines. Its foliage is its most valuable and interesting characteristic; during the summer time it is of a beautiful green, heightened in effect very materially by the festoons which swing off from the main stem, and add grace of habit to beauty of color. In the autumn the foliage, at the first advent of frost, is changed into the most brilliant of crimson colors, as if the vine were in a blaze of glory. It is best admired when seen in contrast with some other green vine close at hand, and hence, it is often twined with the Wisteria. The *Morning Glory*, (*Convolvulus Major*,) with its brilliant, purple, crimson, or white flowers, is the easiest of all to raise from the seed, and always makes a fine display.

The *Tropæolum Peregrinum*, (*Canary Bird Flower*,) is used for veranda purposes as well as for the garden or for bedding; flowers yellow; very ornamental; growth about 10 feet.

It would be best to twine a different vine around each pillar or column, and in

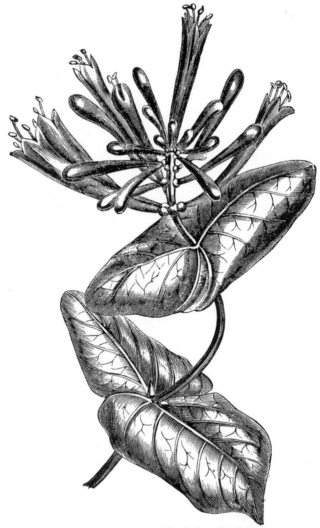

Fig. 21.—Trumpet Honeysuckle—*Lonicera Sempervirens.*

some cases, where there will be a contrast of foliage and flowers, two different vines may be twined around the same column; but it is best to keep the annuals by themselves and the permanent varieties by themselves. The Clematis, Jasmine, or Climbing Roses may be added by those who have the taste. Indeed, we would recommend for a surety at least one Prairie Rose, either the Gem of the Prairies or the Queen of the Prairies, both of which are crimson in color, the former more durable and fragrant than the latter, but not as rapid a climber.

House-top Gardening.

What a novelty! yet how reasonable the suggestion. In the German tale of the " *Old Mam'selle*," we read of its pleasures, and it is stated that in Sweden house-top gardens are not an uncommon sight, both in the country and in the villages. The roofs of some of the poorest cottages are covered with herbs, which afford a pasture for goats. In Norway they even plant trees in the turf which covers the roofs, and to such an extent is this carried that some of their hamlets or villages, seen at a distance, have quite the air of a little wood. Nothing is more common than to see rude kitchen gardens on these roofs of houses.

An English gentleman, writing to a London horticultural journal, mentions the pleasant recollections when he visited while a boy, over 50 years ago, the home of a French citizen, a Mr. Marquis, in Coleman street, London :

"This gentleman's hobby was a 'house-top garden' of the most complete and perfect character. At the lower part of the upper staircase was the root of a fine Sycamore, the foliage of which luxuriated in a 'glass house' above on the roof, amidst orange and lemon trees, with fairest flowers, tea, tobacco, and many other highly interesting specimens of vegetable life. I forget, at this distance of time, how many sorts of fruit were to be seen growing and flourishing in this 'house-top garden,' but the vine and its magnificent clusters of delicious grapes are ineffaceably engraved on memory's young tablets. Think of that, ye apathetic cockneys! hothouse grapes from Coleman street, and that not once in a day, but year after year, until the talented and spirited proprietor went to that bourne from whence no traveler returns, and then the master mind being gone the garden pined away.

"In a convenient corner of his elevated greenhouse Mr. Marquis had a lifting force-pump, with air vessel, to which a length of leather hose being attached, afforded a convenient means of watering and syringing the numerous plants collected in this unique garden."

This style of ornamental gardening is unusual here, and we remember but one instance of ever noticing an attempt to imitate it in this country. This was so successfully planned and executed that it will bear honorary mention.

In one of the principal streets of Louisville, Kentucky, may be seen a doctor's office, the roof of which is covered with a perfect mass of green plants in floral boxes. Directly in front, on the eaves just overhanging the front of the building, is a long box, about two feet wide, the same height, and extending across the entire width of the top of the house. Here were planted a perfect mass of Verbenas and Portulaccas; at the corners were set drooping vines, which, as they grew, hung their long garlands of flowers away down before the lower win-

Fig. 22.—Aristolochia Sipho, or Dutchman's Pipe.

dows. Just back of this was placed a wooden staging, with successive steps rising upward, covered with pots or boxes filled with plants of other character. Here were Fuchsias trained to a neat little trellis; Coleus in one pot; Achyranthes in another, and in one big tub had been planted a pumpkin seed, the vines from which sprawled all over the top of the staging and rustic arbor improvised overhead. Here and there, over the roof beyond, were put pots, each with a huge plant of the Ricinus fully eight feet high, and correspondingly broad. At each corner of the roof, also in the centre, and on an elevated stand near the front, were set big barrels or hogsheads full of water pumped up from below, and from holes at the bottom the water flowed through hose with sprinklers attached, and which sprinkled the plants at any time with a ready rain.

The Ricinus added vastly more than anything else to the decoration of the roof, by their stateliness and almost tropical beauty; but the trailing vines, with their garlands of bloom, helped out the symmetry and completed the grace of the whole. Scarcely a passer-by in the street but stopped long to look upon this novel scene; and the fame of the doctor's garden doubtless has been carried by strangers far beyond the borders of this lovely " *City of Flowers.*"

Not long since a lady detailed to a delighted audience, of how she, with her sister, put to good practical use the roof of a one story L building, which was used for a kitchen. The roof was nearly flat, and afforded ready means for converting into a garden. Surrounding it with a wire trellis, they placed inside as many boxes, barrels, &c., as they could find. These they filled with rich dirt, manure, and street sweepings. Here they sowed seeds of Tomatoes, Cucumbers, Squash, Melons, String Beans, and anything of quick, easy growth. They actually did cultivate this curious garden for two years, and gathered, while each growing season lasted, excellent crops of vegetables, rich flavored, large and delicious; perhaps doubly appreciated in consequence of their being the fruit of their own labor. As long as it lasted the little series of box garden was well tilled, kept well watered with liquid manure, and was eminently successful. It ran down at last, owing to a change of occupants of the building.

A very pretty plan for a Rose Garden upon the top of a house has been suggested by a landscape gardener. Let the pillars and frame-work of the house be made very strong, capable of supporting a good weight of earth, &c. Then fill into earthern cribs all the rich earth that can be obtained to the depth of 1½ feet, and cover the entire roof, except a path surrounding an oval bed in the centre. This path should be three feet wide. Here you may plant your Roses, Fuchsias, &c., in the open air, and they will, if kept well watered, bloom all the summer. The accompanying design and description, by Robert Morris Copeland, in an early number of " Hearth and Home," will explain itself:

"This little plan shows a roof 20 by 30 feet; provision must be made for a weight of 20 tons, for a cubic foot of soil weighs 100 pounds, and there are 900 cubic feet in the garden, or 600 square feet superficial area. This would crush an ordinary roof, so the weight must be lightened by taking out room for the path, and having only light weight in the centre figure.

"Surround the roof with an iron frame 6 feet high, made of iron rods, set up at intervals of 6 feet, and connected with smaller rods running entirely around the roof. Train on this fence Wistaria, Woodbine, Honeysuckle, or Running Roses.

On the fence on the north side, where the Roses would get full sun, plant Baltimore Belle, Mrs. Hovey, or Rosa Ruga, if content with single blooming Roses; or select from the Noisettes La Marque or Aimee Vibert or Madame Henrietta, and from the Teas, Safrano.

On the east fence plant the *Lonicera Halliana*, Hall's Honeysuckle, and the Golden Berried Honeysuckle—all hardy; on the south, Golden and common Ivy; on the west, Dutch Monthly Honeysuckle and one running Rose.

During the summer grow Tropæolum, Maurandia, Nierembergia, and Ipomœa among the hardy vines. In the northwest corner (*A*) set six Hybrid Perpetual Roses, then a bed of Heliotropes ; in the northeast corner six more Hybrid or other Perpetuals; *D* and *H*, occupied by roots of vines ; cover the surface with Periwinkle, Nummularia, or Lycopodium ; *E*, June Roses: *F*, Tricolor Pelargoniums, which do best out of the direct rays of the sun ; *G*, Moss Roses, single, blooming, and perpetual. In the centre bed *I* is a group of Coleus surunded by *Centauria Candidissima ; J*, *K, L, M*, are filled with China, Bengal, and Tea Roses, the surface unoccupied to be covered with Blue Lobelia ; *X* is the trap door which leads out of the roof.

Fig. 23.—Plan of a Rose Garden on the Roof of a House.

A roof garden for Roses could be planted every autumn with Bulbs, Snowdrops, Crocuses, Hyacinths, and Tulips, all of which would blossom and die before the foliage of the Roses would be large enough to do any harm.

Let there be planted for instance, four colors of Hyacinths in the beds *J*, *K, L, M ;* Crown Imperials and Tulips in *I ;* border all the beds with Snowdrops ; set Crocus in four colors inside of the Snowdrops ; fill *B, F, D, H* with mixed Tulips, and put Daffodils, Jonquils, and Polyanthus in *A, C, C, G*.

"The bed for roof gardens should be raised a few inches above the surface of the roof, the wood forming the bottom of the garden-box or crib, being perforated ; the sides of the box should be two feet high. First lay over the floor a few inches of leaves, broken bones, or coarse manure."

This idea of roof gardens may be still farther carried out, and made more permanently useful for winter as well as summer, by covering it all over with glass; then at any season of the year the flower-lover may repair here, and always be sure of finding some green things to enliven the looks, while in summer the glass may be opened to the admission of fresh air and rain.

If the amateur does not wish to go to so elaborate and expensive a construction, he may gratify his taste by the selection of large pots or boxes, fill them with soil, and then place them upon the roof, filled with appropriate plants.

Shrubs may be introduced here, such as the Dentzias, Spiraeas, or Weigelas; but usually annual plants—*i. e.,* those grown from seed—will do the best, like Verbenas, Salvias, and climbing plants. Fuchsias, Heliotropes, and Geraniums will always be appropriate.

No prettier ornament to a house-top can be devised than to erect at each corner of the roof a pretty trellis. Let there be a rod or pole running across the vacant space from one trellis to the other ; then at the bottom place a large tub of earth, and in it start a few plants of Ivy, or the Scarlet Trumpet Creeper, or the Wistaria. Keep them well watered, and their clambering tendrils, with their rich leaves, will soon festoon the arbor, and render the roof an inviting resort for all members of the family. The Ivy is much the simplest and safest ornament of this description to use, and the amateur had better not try anything else until he becomes more familiar with plant-culture and can make a good selection for himself.

CHAPTER XIII.

BULBS.

Bulbous-rooted flowering plants are so numerous, conspicuous, and exquisitely beautiful, and withal so well adapted for the conservatory, that were all other plants annihilated or forgotten, this class alone would at all times fill the draw-

ing-room with the most gorgeous as well as the most chaste and beautiful flowers, attractive not only for their delicacy, brilliancy, and variety of color, but as well for their most delightful fragrance. It is not our intention in this place to write a history of Bulbs, but merely to offer a few remarks on the adaptation and culture of the most desirable sorts, in connection with other classes of plants noticed in this work.

The Hyacinth.

Pre-eminent in this class stands the Hyacinth, which has been deservedly popular for more than three hundred years, and is to-day more sought after than any other species, simply because greater variety of color and quantity of bloom can be had with less trouble and expense than from any other. Hyacinths have a most generous nature; they will adapt themselves to almost any situation, and flower as freely and smile as sweetly in the poor man's window as in the more

Fig. 24.—" Rustic Robin" Jardinet.

costly conservatory of the wealthy. While their generosity is so marked, their gratitude for, and appreciation of, attention shown them is equally marked. No plant pays so well for good culture as this; the difference between common planting and proper growing is so great that one would scarcely think or believe the flower could come from the same bulb. Hyacinths can be grown in a variety of ways. The best, simplest, and most common, is in pots. We shall, however, describe the various ways we have grown them, and leave the reader to make his or her choice, as fancy may dictate.

First, a few words upon the selection of Bulbs are highly necessary. It may not be generally known that Hyacinths will not bloom *well* but once. In Holland, where they are only grown for market, they are not allowed to flower, except in specimen beds, from the time the setts are planted until they are large enough to sell, which is usually when they are four years old. The flower-stalk is cut away as soon as it can be without damage to the foliage. This throws the whole strength of the plant into the bulb, which is kept growing until there is danger of its breaking, which the practiced eye of the grower readily sees. Then it is sent to market, and the next season will give the finest possible bloom, after which the old bulb will "break" and several small ones form, noen of which will ever do well enough to pay for growing the second season. We do not wish to mislead; this instruction is only for those who wish none but *first rate* flowers. Bulbs planted in the open border, after having bloomed in pots, will continue to bloom a number of years, but will give small, puny spikes, with but a few bells on each.

To flower bulbs successfully they should be procured as soon as possible after their arrival from Holland, which is generally about the first of September, and immediately potted in a soil composed of equal parts of good loam, leaf mould and well rotted cow manure, which should be well mixed,

Fig. 25.—Princess Alexandra Jardinet.

after which add about one-fifth of good clean sand. No soil can be better than this for noble growth and bloom. The pots should be made on purpose; not larger than five inches across, nor less than eight inches deep; fill the pot nearly full of the compost, and press the bulb firmly in, so that the top of the bulb is about level with the top of the pot. After filling, they should be plunged in a frame or open border, and covered four inches with soil or some compost, where they should remain until the first of December. This operation is highly necessary to encourage the root growth, which must be made before the leaves shoot forth, for perfection of bloom. After the roots have reached the bottom of the pot, they may be brought into the conservatory to flower as wanted. Those brought in December 1st, will bloom by New Years. Water should be freely given them as soon as they begin to grow, but do not soak them, neither allow them to dry up. Even temperature, even watering, with plenty of fresh air, are the essentials for their well growing. As soon as the flower-stem is fully developed, one or two waterings with liquid manure is highly beneficial. The style of growth, and the size of the flowers and trusses of plants cultivated in this manner, will very much excel those grown in the ordinary way, and will amply repay the care bestowed. The same soil and treatment should be given them if planted in boxes, Jardinieres, tubs, or any device the grower may select.

Fig. 26.—"Prince of Wales" Jardinet.

Hyacinths can be and are commonly grown in glasses. One or two seasons generally satisfy the enthusiast, however, that it is not the better way. Many will every year try this method, and for such the following instructions will be most likely the ones to insure success. The ordinary Hyacinth glass will answer, but Tye's pattern is decidedly preferable. Always use rainwater; put them in the glasses about the first of October; do not fill above the bottom of the bulb. It is better not to let the water quite reach the bulb. After filling, place in a dark closet until the roots reach the bottom of the glass, which will generally be in about three weeks; be careful to keep away from frost; change the water as often as it becomes discolored, and fill up to the bottom of the bulb any time there is a vacancy between the periods of change. When they begin to grow, give them all the light possible without setting them where they will get the noonday sun. A friend once called us to see and tell him why his Hyacinths did not " do well." Upon examination we found the water hot from the sun; not merely warm, but hot enough to cook the bulb, which is not the way they should be served up. To set the glasses on the window ledge is nearly as fatal to them; the cold air coming up between the sash chills them. Plants of all kinds are as sensitive to a draft as human beings are. In order to have them near the light, put up light brackets or a narrow shelf across the window, say six inches from the glass, which will protect them both from the sun and the draft.

A very good plan for growing them in glasses is first to put the bulb in clean sand until the roots have become well grown, say six inches long; then take them out of the sand, put them in glasses, and treat as above. It is really curious to see them growing in water, and when, as you sometimes will do, you get a good spike, the satisfaction is very great.

Hyacinths will grow and bloom in moss alone, if it be kept continually wetted; but a far better way is to fill half way whatever vessel you may choose—a bowl, dish, or vase—with clean sand, place the bulb upon it, and fill the rest with good green moss. Use sufficient water to keep the sand full, but with none lying on the top. Once in three or four waterings you may use liquid manure, which may be made of half a peck of well rotted cow manure put in ten gallons of water, well stirred up, and allowed to settle, the clear liquid alone being used. This will strengthen the growth; still without such stimulant the plants will

Fig. 27.—Jardinet, with Hyacinth.

come short, strong, and well colored, if kept fully exposed to the light, and well supplied with air.

Those who grow Hyacinths in part to gratify curiosity, will be amused by taking a deep saucer or glass dish, fill it to the rim with clean, white gravel, upon which place a good, firm bulb; then treat the same as with glasses. The roots will soon fill the dish, running over and through the gravel, forming a solid mass.

SELECTION OF VARIETIES.

As a rule, we prefer the single varieties for forcing. But few of the double ones produce a fine truss, the bells being uneavenly and thinly scattered along the stem. For glasses, moss, or saucers, the single ones must be selected. With the following sorts we have generally been successful :

DOUBLE RED.—*Bouquet Royal,* large, rosy bells; a good bloomer.

Bouquet Tender, fine, deep red ; one of the best reds

Comptesse de La Costa, very fine dark rose, with good spike.

Fig. 28.—Ornamental Hyacinth Glasses.　　　Fig. 29.—Tye's Triple Hyacinth Glass.

Duke of Wellington, very fine pale rose ; the bells large and beautifully arranged, often giving two spikes.

Grootforst, pale rose ; good spike, with nicely shaped bells.

Regina Victoria, bright pink ; large bells, and fine spike.

DOUBLE WHITE—*Anna Maria,* fine, waxy white, with pink eye ; good formed bells and spike.

Jenny Lind, blush white, with purple eye ; good bells ; compact truss.

La Deese, pure white, finely-shaped bells, but thin spike.

La Vestale, lily white; small bells and spike.

Prince of Waterloo, fine, pure white; large bells; moderate spikes.

DOUBLE BLUE—*Blocksberg,* fine bright and marbled blue; very large bells and spike.

Grande Vidette, fine porcelain blue; large bells and spike.

Laurens Koster, beautiful bright indigo, large bells, and first rate form, with an immense spike.

Lord Wellington, clear blue; dark centre; good form.

Prince Frederick, fine porcelain blue; large bells and spike.

DOUBLE YELLOW—*Bouquet d' Orange,* fine citron yellow; small bells; moderate spike.

Jaunne Supreme, fine, clear yellow; good spike.

SINGLE RED—*Diebitz Sabalskansy,* bright red, moderate bells, and good spike.

Duke of Wellington, fine rose; large bells and spike.

L'Ami du Cœur, deep pink; small bells; moderate spike.

Madame Hodgson, pale pink, good bells, and finely-formed spike.

Norma, a magnificent waxy pink; immense bells and spike.

Robert Steiger, fine, deep crimson, large bells, and immense spike.

SINGLE WHITE—*Elfrida,* creamy blush; very large bells; immense spike.

Grand Vainquer, pure white; fine bells and spike; extra.

Grand Vidette, pure white, large bells, and long spike; very early.

Grand Blanche Imperiale, fine blush; moderate bells; large spike.

Fig. 30.—Ornamental Vase for Bulbs.

Fig. 31.—Ornamental Vase for Bulbs.

Fig. 32.—Tye's Single Hyacinth Glass.

Grandeur a Merville, very fine, pale blush, good bells, and immense spike.

Mont Blanc, beautiful, clear white; large bells; immense spike.

Victoria Regina, very fine, pure white, large, waxy bells, and fine spike.

Voltaire, very beautiful blush; large bells; compact spike; of immense size.

Single Blue—*Baron Van Tuyll,* fine, dark porcelain; large bells; extra fine spike.

Charles Dickens, fine, pale blue; large bells; very fine spike.

Grand Lilas, beautiful, delicate azure blue; large, perfect bells; immense spike; one of the best.

Grand Vidette, fine, pale blue, immense bells, and moderate spike.

Nimrod, beautiful, pale blue; large bells and spike.

Orandates, very fine porcelain blue, large bells, and very fine spike.

Porcelain Sceptre, very fine, pale blue; moderate bells; very fine spike.

Single Yellow—*Anna Carolina,* beautiful, clear yellow; handsome bells and spike.

Heroine, pale yellow, with green tips; large truss.

Roman White Hyacinth,

A new variety lately introduced; a most valuable acquisition for early blooming, suitable only for pots. The bells of this variety are very small, not more than half the size of the Dutch bulbs. They can be grown in three-inch pots; same soil as recommended for the other sorts. If planted in September, they can be made to bloom by the 1st of December. Flowers pure white, very fragrant, small bells, and spike; each bulb will give from three to five spikes. For early flowering it is indispensable.

We cannot leave this interesting class of plants without a word of caution to those about selecting bulbs. Do not buy cheap bulbs, neither those that are very high priced, because of their scarcity. Good bulbs cannot be had at less than three dollars per dozen; that is, such bulbs as ought to be grown in the "window." Avoid "mixed" bulbs, which are simply culls. In Holland, when the crop is harvested, the *very best* are selected and sent to England and France, where the prices are twice as much as here; the next choice is for this and other markets, sold under *Named sorts;* the next grade are put up and sold in separate colors; the balance of stock is sold at auction, to be put up in "cases" for auction in this country, or hawked about our streets by German pedlars. Go to a reliable seedsman, and if you do not know what you want, take his advice.

Tulips.

Few flowers have received the marked attention, and been so universally grown and admired, as the Tulips. But few plants are so varied in their characters, and scarcely a family so large but what has more poor relations. No class of plants has so many superb varieties. The late flowering or show varieties are among the brightest ornaments of the garden. We regret so few of the many sorts are suitable for forcing, or for early flowering in the " window." The following varieties can be successfully grown in pots, giving them the same soil and treatment as recommended for the Hyacinth. They should be planted in five-inch pots, putting five bulbs in each, one in the centre, the four equally distant about one inch from the rim. Plant as early as they can be procured in the fall. Plunge out of doors, and let them remain until the first of December, when they may be brought in. As soon as they show signs of growth, water moderately; give them plenty of light, sun, and air; a cool situation suits them best.

Fig, 33.—Pot of Tulips.

Duc Van Thol, Red and Yellow—single; the earliest variety.

    do   do double; showy and early.

S c a r l e t—very bright and showy.

White—very fine, large, and perfect flower.

Yellow—one of the best yellow sorts grown.

Crimson—large flower, but not so early.

Gold striped—early, and very showy.

Potterbakker, White and Yellow—Both are good for forcing; flowers larger than the Duc Van Tholl's, but not as early; very fine for a succession.

Tournesol, (double), Red and Yellow—a very large flower, opens wide, is a free bloomer, and very showy.

Florentine (sweet scented)—exquisite on account of its delicious fragrance.

With these varieties we advise the amateur to stop, as we think the room can be filled with plants that are better adapted to indoor culture.

The Narcissus

Is admirably adapted for window gardening; soil and general treatment same as for the Hyacinth. They should be planted in September, one in a pot, which should be not less than five inches across. Place out of doors, where they should remain until near Christmas, by which time they will be well rooted, and ready for rapid growth. After flowering, they should be left in the pots, and kept growing until they can be plunged in the garden, where they should be left (in pots) for the next season. After they have become well established they flower profusely. But few kinds of bulbs are so impatient of changes as these; they should not be taken out of the pots until the bulbs and roots have completely filled them; then take out, remove the outside bulbs, leaving the centre in a solid mass, and repot for the next season. The shifting should be done when the bulbs are at rest. The following are the most desirable for indoor culture:

Polyanthus Narcissus, (Roman,) double; white and yellow; when planted early will bloom at Christmas.

Fig. 34.—Basket of Mixed Bulbs.

Paper white; pure white, and early; very fine.

Grand Soliel d' Or, fine yellow orange; cup very handsome; comes in after the preceding.

States General, lemon yellow; orange cup; an excellent variety.

Bezelman Major, white; yellow cup; a later variety, but one of the very best.

Double Narcissus, Albo Pleno Oderato, very double; pure white; later than the Polyanthus Narcissus, and should be left out of doors until it has been frozen hard before bringing in; it will bloom about the first of March.

Single Narcissus, Porteus, a popular and well-known variety, pure white, lemon-colored cup in the centre, which is bordered with bright crimson.

Single Narcissus, Albo Simplex Oderato, pure white; very fragrant.

Jonquilles, large double and single; sweet scented; both very desirable for forcing.

In large collections, all the above varieties of Narcissus are desirable. The number of bulbs required will, of course, depend upon the space that can be spared for them. Like other kinds of bulbs, it is well to have a good supply in reserve, as they need not be in the conservatory or drawing-room more than three or four weeks; consequently, a large number will be required for from December until May, the season that the amateur's time is wholly taken up with the scores of favorites that now claim care and attention, out of doors.

Crocus.

The Crocus, which has for many ages been cultivated as an ornament to our flower gardens, can, if properly managed, be made an effective plant for the conservatory or ordinary house culture. The first thing of importance attending their culture is early planting, which should be attended to early in September. Few bulbs suffer more from being kept too long out of ground than these. The soil best adapted to them is a rich, light, sandy loam. Plant, for a good display, six to ten bulbs in a pot, colors to be arranged according to taste. A few small

Fig. 35.—Box of Bulbs growing in Sand.

pots, with but one color in each, contrasts better with other plants in the window than larger pots of mixed sorts. When planted, plunge the pots out of doors, same as Hyacinth, and let them remain until Christmas, when they may be brought in and given plenty of light and air, keeping cool until they begin to show bloom, when they may be placed in the window as wanted. With these precautions, a fine display can be had. A succession of bloom may be kept up by bringing in as wanted. Disappointment generally arises from keeping them

Fig. 36.—Tile Box filled with Bulbs.

too warm in the early stages of their growth. The following varieties are the best for pot culture, giving very large flowers of great substance, with rich and very beautiful colors:

Albion, very large white.

Albertine, white, striped violet.

Charles Dickens, large purple.

David Rizzio, deep purple.

Florence Nightingale, large, fine white purple throat.

La Majesteuse, violet-striped, on a delicately tinted ground.

La Neige, snow white.

Mont Blanc, large, pure white ; purple base.

Mammoth, very large, pure white.

New Golden Yellow—The bulbs of this variety are very large, each bulb producing from ten to fifteen flowers.

Queen Victoria, fine, pure white.

Sir Walter Scott, beautifully pencilled lilac, very large, and of great substance.

Lord Palmerston, sky blue ; very pretty.

Cloth of Gold, golden yellow, striped brown ; one of the earliest varieties.

Princess af Wales, very large, and fine, pure white.

After flowering, throw away, as they do not do well after, and the low price they are sold at enables a replenishment at less cost than the trouble of saving.

Bulbocodium, or Red Crocus,

Commonly known as Spring Colchicum, is a charming plant for pot culture, requiring the same treatment as the Crocus ; flowers of purple red, which are produced in great numbers from a single bulb. They may be brought in about the middle of December, and will flower at Christmas. They require plenty of water during flowering, after which they should be slowly dried off until the leaves dry up ; then lay away for next season's flowering.

The Snowdrop.

This ever popular and charming little flower, the first to welcome spring when planted in some snug corner where the sun loves to linger, is quite at home in the window-corner. It thrives finely in a light, sandy loam ; does not require to be particularly rich. If planted in pots alone, six can be put in a three-inch pot, which should have the same treatment as the Crocus, a little freezing being very beneficial to them. They make a lovely border to the pots or boxes of Hyacinths, the same treatment answering equally well for both. The double is larger and better for pot culture than the single ; the latter is the earlier of the two. It is of no use to plant these bulbs unless it is done in September, for they soon spoil from dry rot if left long out of ground. For house culture the better plan is to take from the open border where the bulbs have remained undisturbed a number of years. With these success is almost certain, while with newly imported bulbs failure is not uncommon.

The Winter Aconite,

Is a charming little plant, with golden blossoms, which expand simultaneously with the Snowdrop, and with which it contrasts finely. After flowering, the foliage makes a beautiful edging for pots or jardinets.

The Iris

But few plants present such rare beauty, and rich combination of color as the Iris. The name was given it by Pliny and Theophrastus, from the variety of its colors. Of the many hundred varieties, the bulbous rooted sorts are the only ones that succeed well in pots. The method of culture is simple, requiring a rich loamy soil. Only three or four bulbs should be planted in a six-inch pot, which should be filled about one quarter full with broken pots for drainage, then fill with soil, and press the bulb in so that the top of the bulb will be even with the rim of the pot. Give but very little water until they show growth ; after which it may be given more freely.

The English Iris, for brilliancy of color and vigorous foliage, takes rank among the handsomest of flowering bulbs, they grow nearly two feet high, and produce during June and July, a succession of large and beautiful flowers. This variety is too large to become popular as a window plant.

The Spanish Iris, differ materially from the English, though no less beautiful; they are not as large as the former, and bloom somewhat earlier, which makes them more desirable for pot culture.

Iris Pavonia, or Peacock Iris, is a charming little plant well adapted for pots. The bulbs are quite small—not much larger than peas. They should be planted in September or October, in a light turfy loam. Plant three or four bulbs in a four-inch pot, which should be kept in a cold frame until toward Spring when they may be brought in and watered moderately ; they will soon begin to make growth, and will flower early in April.

Iris Persica, is the best for forcing. Plant the same as I. Pavonia ; they will flower almost as soon as brought in ; the colors are white, blue, purple, and violet. They are highly prized for their delicious fragrance, which is fully equal to the violet. This sort will bloom in water like Hyacinth.

Iris Susiana, is one of those beauties that baffle description. It is one of the best for the "window," flowering freely in pots, jardinets or vases. It is the earliest sort, consequently the most desirable for winter decoration.

The Ixias, and sister cape bulbs the Sparaxis, Babianas and Tritonias, are amongst the most graceful, attractive and beautiful of cape flowering bulbs. Though differing considerably in style and habit of growth, they require the same cultural treatment. They succeed best in good turfy peat. Plant about the first of October, three or four in a four-inch pot, which should be placed in a cold frame, protected from severe frosts and heavy rains. They should be brought in about the first of March ; they will at once commence growth and flower early in April.

The color of the Ixias are of every conceivable shade, forming some of the most remarkable contrasts. The habit of the plant is most graceful, and when a quantity are in bloom, the effect of it is most pleasing. In selecting these bulbs, choose named sorts, for the same reason you would many other bulbs, viz : bulbs in mixture are apt to be bulbs of the more common sorts.

Sparaxis, are more dwarf and compact in habit than the Ixia, while their colors are as varied and beautiful. For pot culture and window decoration they cannot be too strongly recommended.

The Tritonia, in habit and form, is very similar to the Sparaxis. They are plants of rare beauty, colors principally *selfs.* For good effect about twice as many bulbs should be put in a pot as of the Ixia.

The Babiana, in habit and growth, is nearly the same as the two former, but as unlike in color as is possible for such near relatives. While the others are mostly crimson and white, with their various shades, these are nearly all purple and blue. Together, they are most desirable, and are annually becoming more extensively used for window decoration.

Ranunculus.

This family is almost endless in variety, embracing some of the most common forage plants. While the Persian and Turban varieties produce the most elegant and diversified colored flowers, that for symmetry and compactness are unequaled. When properly grown they are completely covered with flowers nearly as large and quite as desirable as roses. But little attention has been given them as pot plants; our experience with them, as such, has been most pleasing, having had more truly handsome flowers than from almost any other plant, with the same amount of trouble and expense.

For winter flowering, if possible, select roots that have been kept out of ground the previous season as they come into flower much earlier than those taken up the previous summer. The roots keep well in a dry place for two years, so that a succession of bloom can be obtained by planting at proper intervals, the whole season.

The Ranunculus, requires a strong, fresh, loamy soil, made very rich by well rotted cow manure; with such components use equal parts. For early blooming, commence potting the first of August. Use four-inch pots, into which put three roots of separate colors, selection of which to suit the taste; place the roots firmly in the mould, and cover half an inch; plunge the pot or put in a shaded frame; bring in as wanted, commencing the first of October, give them a light warm situation, and shade from the sun which completely destroys their bright colors.

For flowering the whole season, pot from August to April, and forward as wanted. The Persian varieties are the earliest, consequently should be planted first, to be followed by the Turban varieties. These two are the only varieties desirable for pot culture; but there are hundreds of named sorts, to be selected from seedsmen's catalogues that generally list the most desirable kinds. After blooming they can be dried off gradually, put in a dry place and kept for next year's flowering. The low price they are sold at does not make it an object to keep them for flowering the second year, as roots grown in the open border are generally more satisfactory.

Anemone.

Of this plant there are nearly a hundred species, each with its score of varieties, many of them present some of the finest forms of floral beauty. The double varieties are the best suited for the conservatory, and for which they are admirably adapted; the foliage is extremely beautiful, the bright green contrasting well with the dazzling brightness of the bright scarlet and purple flowers that grow in profusion. They require the same general treatment as the Ranunculus, only that a little sea sand or salt should be mixed with the soil. For a succession of bloom, plant from September until March. Those planted in September will flower in latter part of March or the first of April, while those planted in March will flower by the middle of June.

We list the following from many we have bloomed, and should recommend them for pot culture.

Feu Surperbe, bright scarlet.

Rose Surpassante, rose.

Queen of the Netherlands, white and rose, fine.

L'Ornament de la Nature, rich dark blue.

Lord Nelson, violet.

Queen Victoria, bright scarlet, a free bloomer.

Rembrandt, carmine.

Shakspeare, beautiful blue.

Von Schiller, dark brilliant blue.

The above collection includes the most striking and positive colors, and are such as bloom well. Many others might be added to the list without materially increasing the value of the collection.

The Cyclamen.

About this flower but one opinion can be entertained,—that it is the most beautiful bulbous rooted plant ever introduced for the parlor or conservatory, and its beauty is fully equaled by its adaptation for the same purpose. We are fully justified in making this assertion, by the greatly increased interest taken in it by florists, amateurs, and the lovers of flowers in general. Ease of culture is an additional feature in their character and much in their favor. The difficulty in propagation alone has prevented their becoming a florists flower. The roots or bulbs of the Cyclamen being a solid corm, they will not divide successfully; consequently the only means of propagation is from seed, which must be gathered soon as ripe, slowly dried, and planted in a green house in heat; they must be kept constantly growing until they are in full flower. This part we should advise the amateur to leave to the professional florist and depend upon such for plants for the first season.

They should be procured soon as they show flower, place in a sunny exposure and not be allowed to get chilled in winter. They are generally offered for sale about Jan. 1st. If in a warm room, even temperature, and kept well watered, they will remain in flower until the first of May; after flowering they should be plunged into a shady border, and left to care for themselves until there is danger of frost when they should be taken in, repotted in a compost of leaf mold, turfy loam and well rotted cow manure in equal parts; use pots in proportion to the size of the bulb. A pot twice the diameter of the bulb is plenty large; a pot six inches in diameter is sufficiently large for the largest bulbs. After repotting, water moderately until they commence growth, then apply as needed. We saw several bulbs last season that had not been shifted for several years; several of them gave over two hundred flowers each; more exquisite pot plants could not be had.

Scilla,

Of various kinds, have long been popular as early spring flowers; S. Siberica is of the most intense blue, and is a perfect gem, whether in the open border, in pots or any device that is used for Hyacinths, Tulip or Crocus—it can be mixed with either of them with most excellent effect, requiring the same treatment. The habit of it is exceedingly dwarf, growing but little larger than the Crocus. The flowers are borne on a slender stalk, of bell-shape, similar to a minature Hyacinth. S. Amoena, is also very beautiful as a pot plant, being a little taller and later than the Siberica—it is very useful as a succession. There are several other varieties, very beautiful for out-door cultivation but not suitable for pots.

Muscari.

M. botryoides, the Grape Hyacinth, is remarkable for its dwarf growth and neat compact heads of bloom. The three varieties, dark blue, light blue and white, make charming clumps, when planted in pots two or three of a color in each. They require but little room, a six inch pot being sufficiently large for a dozen bulbs; the same soil and treatment recommended for the Hyacinths is best suited to them. After flowering they may be allowed to ripen off slowly and they will bloom equally well for a number of years. Muscari Plumosum or Feathered Hyacinth, does not thrive well in pots generally, but should be grown in small quantities. Their remarkable plume-like appearance, so unlike any other flower, is of sufficient importance to entitle them to a place in the conservatory. Treat same as the other varieties.

Amaryllis.

This splendid and beautiful family has not as yet received the care and attention, or become as generally cultivated as their rarity and excellence deserves, containing as it does so many varieties of surpassing loveliness, beauty and grandeur. These qualifications alone should insure them a place in every "Window" Garden. Yet they have other recommendations for extensive culture, namely, that they can be made to produce their gorgeous and magnificent flowers nearly every month in the year. They are on this account invaluable for the conservatory and drawing rooms, which can be kept gay by the many truly elegant varieties as we now possess nearly the whole winter. The length of time they keep in flower, and the very pleasing variety they make, is another just claim they have for a high place among decorative plants.

The Amaryllis delight in good, light turfy loam, with the addition of a little well rotted cow manure, when planted in large pots, and all the conditions of growth are favorable, they throw up magnificent spikes of bloom. A. Johnsoni has been known to flower twice a year, a single bulb throwing up at one time four spikes, each giving four flowers. A more splendid flower than this is, it is scarcely possible to conceive. We scarcely know how to advise the amateur in the manner of treatment, but will commence with the dry bulb, which should be potted in the above compost, say in a six inch pot, fill nearly to the rim and press the bulb firmly in; one-half its diameter should be above the surface; give it a thorough watering, and place on a shelf in moderate heat; it will not require further attention until it shows signs of growth, the time of which will depend wholly upon circumstances, *i. e.*, how long it has been dry, the time of year, and whether it has been properly cared for during its rest. As a general thing the first indication of growth will be the flower stalk, which makes almost a perceptible growth, at this period. Give water freely once a week; a sprinkling of liquid manure is very beneficial; give plenty of light and moderate heat and the first flowers will be perfected in two or three weeks; large well developed bulbs will commence to throw up the second flower stalks about the time the first flowers are opened, which will make the flowering of a single bulb last from five to six weeks.

After flowering they should be immediately repotted, no matter what time of year, and given plenty of heat and water. Fully exposed to the light, they will grow most luxuriantly and the bulbs will grow in a proportionate degree, laying up strength and nutritive matter that will produce in due season another crop of magnificent flowers. When the leaves naturally show symptoms of ripeness or decay, water should be gradually withheld, and when fairly decayed the pots should be placed in a dry, airy situation away from the frost or rain; here they may remain for two months, when they should be placed in a tub of water and left an hour, then placed in a warm room for flowering again. The method of culture, as recommended here, is only to be applied to those known as Heppeastrom, which, unlike the Vallota, Belladona and other varieties, are under the florist's control and can be made to flower the whole season. An enthusiast, whose ten by fifteen green house we delight to visit, grows large quantities of Amaryllis, Johnsoni and its varieties, and gets from each bulb two crops of flowers annually. He gives each two months for flowering, two for growth, and two for rest, which he considers the best treatment, and no one that has seen the spikes of bloom that he produces can question his theory.

Vallota Purpurea,

Is one of the finest Amaryllis, and is the most easily managed. They are not at all particular as to soil, will grow in any, but prefer the same as recommended for other Amaryllis. But few plants answer as well or make as fine display for the window. Unlike most other plants, they do not require shifting but will grow from year to year in the same pot, tub or box without a change of soil, or other care than to give them plenty of water while flowering or in their growing state, and moderate watering the balance of the season. The foliage being persistent they require attention the whole year, but they can be kept under benches, in a light cellar or in any light room away from the frost during the winter, and in summer anywhere out of doors upon the piazza, the lawn, or if in pots, plunge in the border. They require but little pot room, in fact do better when root bound. The writer had a clump in a small tub last season that gave forty-one spikes of bloom; the plant was but five years from a single bulb. It is truly one of the finest, cheapest and most desirable cape bulbs.

Its season of flowering is August and September, and we have neither been able to coax or drive it into flower at any other season.

The Lily.

One of the finest flowers in every sense of the word, too well known to need description. Every one knows what a Lily is. Most every one knows how to grow it. Our only regret is that it is not better adapted for the window. All or nearly all the varieties can be grown in pots, as well as in the border. The only objection for the "Window" being the season of flowering, that is from July to September in the open border. Many kinds will not vary but a few days with any treatment we have tried. The following varities are an exception to the rule, and can be made to bloom early in April.

Lilium Candidum.

L. Candidum, or common garden Lily, more generally known than any other, and we think one of the finest. In fact, as much as we admire and love the whole family, could we have but one, it would be *this one ;* can be forced for the conservatory better perhaps than any other. It must be potted in August, soon after flowering, while at rest. Here let us remark that while many other kinds can be moved at almost any season of the year, this one cannot, only when at rest, a period of not more than four weeks duration. There has been more disappointment in buying this than all others together, as orders given for it in spring will most likely be filled by seedsmen generally; and not one that has been kept out of ground during the winter will bloom the following summer. It generally takes two years, frequently three, before they can be made to flower, when, if taken up at the proper time and planted at once, they are certain to flower. The reason is simple enough; they make the bulb in fall that is to bloom in spring, and if they are not allowed that privilege they simply bide their time at the expense of the grower's good nature.

The bulbs should be placed in six inch pots, top of the bulb even with the rim of the pot. Soon as potted plunge in the border to save trouble. Bring in before heavy frosts and place on slight bottom heat ; water freely ; give plenty of light and air and they will come into flower by Easter. They will bloom with out bottom heat in the window by giving them a warm sunny situation, but do far better with it. The best soil for them is a light turfy loam, one-third well rotted cow manure. Fresh manure must not be used in any case without a crop of disappoinments is preferable to a crop of Lilies.

Liliun Longiflorum.

Another beautiful pure white Lily, succeeds well in pots, requiring the same soil and general treatment as the Candidum. The bulbs of this variety can be obtained from November until spring. For the window they should be potted early in November, and kept moderately wet and warm until they show sign of growth, when they can be put in position for blooming. As a house plant the habit of this makes it more desirable than most any other. It is very dwarf rarely growing more than fifteen inches high.

Liliun Auratum,

The praise of which would fill a volume as its fragrance would fill a house, is another sort that succeeds well in a pot, box or any other way in which it may be planted, if we except a highly enriched soil which would be fatal to it. It will come into flower about the first of May, with the same treatment as the foregoing.

We know of no other Lilies that are well adapted for the Window Garden, not having been successful in growing others in this way. For out of door culture we most heartily beg leave to introduce the whole family from the least to the greatest to all lovers of flowers.

The Tuberose.

It is nearly three hundred years since the Tuberose first flowered in Europe, having been sent from the West Indies, by Father Minuti, to one of the celebrated gardens near Toulon, about the year 1594. It is to day the same pure, modest, unassuming and deliciously fragrant flower it was then. It is one of those gems that no one would change if they could, or could if they would. It may be considered perfectly beautiful from the fact of its being the first sought after on all occasions, whether of joy or mourning. It is, too, one of the few flowers that can be had at all seasons of the year. The only difficulty being the selection of bulbs, which should in all cases be left to the experienced grower or responsible dealer, as not one-half the bulbs sold will produce flowers under any circumstances; not that it is difficult to grow good bulbs, but it is to properly cure and keep them ready for planting. Dry bulbs can be obtained at all times which are the ones for forcing or planting out. It is of but little use to take up bulbs that have grown in the garden during the summer for flowering in pots in the "Window." To be successful use five inch pots, fill with a mixture of loam and well rotted manure in equal parts, press the bulb in about one-half its length and place it in a hot bed, or plunge the pot on a bench of the green house where they can have a gentle bottom heat, which is a necessity for flowering. They very soon begin to grow and should be kept warm and watered freely. Soon as they throw up the flower stalk remove to the conservatory, when they will soon flower and remain in bloom for several weeks. Good bulbs should average twenty flowers to a spike. After flowering throw away, as the bulb only flowers once. Stock is kept up by off-sets. Those who do not have the convenience of a green house or hot beds for starting the bulbs must do the next best. We have frequently started them on the mantel in the kitchen, by taking a box narrow and long enough to hold three or four pots, which are put in the box filled with ashes or tan which should be kept wet to better retain the heat. They will start very well in this way using wood ashes for mulch. A Bulb which we once had flowered in the pot and gave us forty-five large and perfect flowers. For an ordinary Window Garden, one or two pots at a time is quite sufficient. The

Fig. 37.—Glasses used as Bouquet Holders.

most convenient way and about as cheap a one as any, is to buy bulbs with flower stalks started from a florist. This is meant to apply to the large number that love flowers but do not like to work for them.

Achimenes.

These tuberous rooted plants, generally classed with bulbs, are charming for growing in pots, pans and hanging baskets, either in assorted or individual colors. The flowers combine great individual beauty with richness and brilliancy. Much importance should be attached to the Achimenes from the ease in which they can be induced to flower in the winter. The best soil for growing them is a light rich loam. The tubers should be put singly in three inch pots and placed in as warm a situation as the conservatory affords. Where bottom heat can be given them they will do much better. A moist atmosphere, with the thermometer from 70 to 80 degrees at mid-day, are requisites for specimen plants. After flowering, gradually withhold water, turn the pots on their sides, in a dry place where they can remain until wanted the following season. When at rest they should remain in the pots. If long exposed to the air the roots become worthless. By starting at intervals of three to four weeks a succession of bloom may be kept up the whole season.

Lily of the Valley.

Who does not know and admire this, the loveliest child of the floral family? Why it is not found in every garden, conservatory, "window," or greenhouse, it is difficult to imagine, for there is scarcely a plant more easily cultivated than this. It is easily forced into bloom, and may be kept in succession from Christmas until May. For winter or spring flowering, take from the border, clumps as large as will fill pot, box, or any device in which they are wanted to bloom, using a rich strong loam. After potting, plunge out of doors, where they will be sure to freeze hard. Any time after, they may be brought into the greenhouse or conservatory, where they should be given bottom heat, and kept at the highest possible temperature; 100° with a moist atmosphere, will very soon bring them into flower; a less heat will answer, but they will not come into flower as quickly. Light is by no means necessary, as they do quite as well on the floor, under the bench, or the pipes, as anywhere else. When once in flower place in any desirable situation. To maintain a succession a reserve should be kept in a cold frame or pot, and brought in as required. For small pots it is best to select only the strong crowns; place four to six in a pot three inches in diameter, and treat as above stated. After flowering, separate and plant in a strong rich soil, where they should remain undisturbed for two years, when they will be strong enough for forcing again.

Illustrations.

The Jardinets illustrated in Figs. 24 to 27—are constructed of pottery ware, filled with sand in the interior, with here and there an opening for the spike of flowers to grow from the bulb. Figs. 28, 30 and 31—are costly porcelain, intended as elegant mantel piece ornaments. The remaining illustrations are very SIMPLE, and need no special explanation.

CHAPTER XIV.

FERNERIES, WARDIAN CASES, AND FERN DECORATIONS.

The fern case offers to us the very simplest of all means of household plant pleasures. Many who cannot afford a green house, or conservatory, or go to the expense of fitting up a plant cabinet, will find an abundant solace in this simple and inexpensive method of growing indoor plants.

The use of these small glass cases for plants, are numerous. They occupy very

Fig. 38.—Fern, (Platyloma cordata.

little room, are usually ornamented enough to be placed on any table or parlor stand. When once filled, they need little or no attention for many weeks; require no unusual care as to watering; can be readily removed from one room to another; are not as quickly affected by changes of temperature as plants in the open air of our sitting rooms.

But a more favorable feature in their use is seen when we say that they afford the only successful means for obviating the effect of the dry heated air of our dwellings. They are reached by no dust, are free from the noxious exhalations

Fig. 39.—Interior of Fernery.

of coal fires or gas lights ; and when a breath of cold air accidentally enters the room they are not chilled nor frosted if the thermometer in the room should chance

to go below 35°.   Their styles are so various and prices so reasonable, that any.
one can be suited at prices of from $3 to $25.

To any one living amid the anxieties of a troublesome parlor garden, which
they cannot manage, there are but one or two satisfactory ways left for enjoyment.   Either get a fern case, or be satisfied with a simple hanging basket.

The Wardian Case.

The history of the Wardian or fern case, dates back to 1829, when a gentleman
by the name of Ward, of London, first noticed, accidentally, the growth of vegeta-

Fig. 40.—A Parlor Fernery.

tion under a close glass.   He had laid down the chrysalis of an insect with some
mould within a glass bottle, and covered it over.   A short time afterward, as he
describes it, "a speck or two of vegetation appeared on the surface of the mould
and, to his surprise, turned out to be a fern and a grass.   His interest was
awakened ; he placed the bottle in a favorable situation, and found that the
plants continued to grow and maintain a healthy appearance."

This was the first idea of the Wardian case.   In 1842, Mr. Ward published
his discovery relating to the "growth of plants in closely glazed cases," in a volume which contained the result of his experiments in raising plants, and also the
way he made his discovery.   In 1851, the Wardian case made its first successful appearance in public, at the "*Worlds Fair*," and from that time to this it
has become more gradually known and better appreciated.   Very few have yet

any knowledge of it, but it is one of the few things which in time will be as popular as flowers themselves are, and every window will be decorated with their presence.

It has been an invaluable means of introducing to the floral world, and successfully growing many most delicate plants from the tropics which otherwise would scarcely ever have been seen out of their native haunts. By its use the Botanist has been enabled to transport plants to and from great distances through extremes of climate ; and yet so unfailing has been the working of it that cases judiciously planted have been known to maintain their freshness and vigor for nine years, and no air or water was ever supplied in that time.

It is quite curious to watch its operation, and to many it is evidently as mucn of an enigma as a pleasure.

Apparently, moisture is constantly being condensed and deposited on the glass sides of the case. This supplies the plants within, who give it out again, and yet none escapes ; thus affording the spectacle of a little world by itself.

This moisture is very desirable for the growth of ferns, and in no other form can they be so successfully and evenly maintained as here ; nor can any other variety of plants furnish so interesting a study.

The Lycopodiums are very suitable and grow very satisfactorily. They drop their pendant roots, and, under the influence of the moisture, spread rapidly along the surface of the earth in the case, and filling up the bare spots, make a velvety covering of light feathery green, thus inducing shade and moisture.

Fig. 41.—A Fern Vase.

Countless seedlings of ferns and lycopodiums will spring up, of the different varieties, and their unfolding fronds and subsequent development will be exceedingly interesting to you. You will be agreeably astonished and surprised when some fern, supposed by you to be dead, suddenly raises its head above the surface and shoots rapidly upward to let you see its vitality is not to be questioned.

As a pleasure, then, the Wardian case deserves a cordial reception ; but it will be far more welcome to that class of our plant lovers who have often felt the disappointment in their pot plants, many of the best of which, notwithstanding the closest care, will show the yellow leaves and drop off, or the buds develop but an imperfect blossom ; the fern case will prove to be their refuge in distress, a never failing source of interest and amusement.

Principles of the Fern Case.

Let us understand the principles of fern cases and the operation and life of plants within. Those of you who have observed plants under bell glasses or

Fig 42.

shades, have noticed that the moisture often collects so quickly inside as to actually obstruct or prevent the plant from being seen, and have wondered where this moisture came from.

The answer to this question is simple : " *From the earth, the plants, by exhalation,* i. e. *vegetable perspiration.*" But you ask again : " *Why does it collect so largely ?*" and we reply : "Simply because we confine it, and prevent its escape and evaporation by making our case airtight. If the case were ventilated, its temperature would be moderated to correspond with the atmosphere of the sitting room. And this is the very thing we do not want. Our case then should be made air tight, for the purpose of not only confining this moisture, but of keep-

Fig. 43. A Large Fern Case.

ing a constant and abundant supply of it, for the plants must have a congenial atmosphere of their own and cannot live without the proper moisture.

You cannot expect your ferns or plants to grow nicely in this moist atmosphere if you open the case every few days: It has the same effect as change of climate, or open air exposure to a sick person accustomed only to the air of the house. The confinement of ferns in these close cases has the tendency to make them delicate, and the sudden opening of the case, with the introduction of the hot, dry, dusty air from the rooms, is against all reason.

Fig. 44.—A Fern Window and Aquarium.

It is sufficient to say, therefore, that when once planted and closed, the fern case needs no ventilation. Let it live by itself.

Drainage.

This point comes up for discussion, and the only answer we give is to ask another question : " Do plants need drainage when the water is being constantly evaporated a n d thrown off in the open space above the plants ?" In other words, the plants are draining themselves constantly. Here is one great advantage of the fern case over the pot plant, the latter requires constant watering, the former none at all, for no water escapes. Then a fern case may be handled with impunity by one in whose hands we would not trust a row of pot plants, and so is beyond the reach of the careless or forgetful.

Management.

Whether your case is of wood, glass, or metal, you will require a pan in which to hold the plants. Zinc pans answer every purpose, combining economy and durability. Tin should not be used as it will soon rust and wear out.

No pan should be less than four inches deep, unless the plants are very dwarf specimens, and then an inch less in depth will do, though there might be some risk of crowding the roots too much. Then, again, too great a depth is objectionable. The best rule to observe is as follows : Ferns, whose fronds are not over eight inches in length, should be planted in a pan four inches in depth. Larger ferns may require a pan five to six inches in depth, but four inches will generally be found sufficient for all purposes.

Those who try the shallow and deep pans will soon find how much more freely their plants grow when plenty of space is allowed for their roots. A side opening to the glass case is to be preferred in all cases, whether by hinged doors or sliding panes. This avoids reaching in at the top of the fern case, which, besides being extremely awkward, often results in the breaking of the fronds or the leaves.

The *height of the case* is an important point. Under glass, a plant or fern, will often develop a greater length of frond, than under any different circumstances. Make your cases high, so that all fronds may have room to develop and expand to full size ; and the height should not be less than twice the diameter. In cramped quarters, and cases chosen perhaps too small, filled with too robust plants, their growth is often summarily checked by reaching the top of the glass ; there the fronds with no chance to get higher, lie flattened out against the surface of the glass collecting an undue amount of moisture, which soon causes it to mould or damp off. It becomes unsightly, and the beauty of many rare and fine looking specimens is endangered.

The forms and construction of fern cases will differ with the tastes of each individual. We do not recommend attempts at "home made" cases, on the

Fig. 45.—Ferns in a Window Garden.

side of mere economy, for there are now cases already prepared for use, at so cheap prices, and obtainable at proper places, that it is a waste of time to make one yourself. Very desirable cases are now imported, constructed of bases of pottery, with dishes all complete, and the glass shade ready to fit upon the top—only wanting the soil and the plants from the florist. Very good cases are also made of wood bases, and the cost for either will not exceed $3 for circular cases 12 inches in diameter, to $6 or $10 for 18 inches to 2 ft. in diameter.

The larger your case, the better, provided it is not too bulky. It should be in a form easily handled, light in weight ; and if square, or in any other form than round, should have a small door to reach the plants without lifting the glass top. *The soil for fern cases*, should be carefully attended to; no common garden earth will answer; get it from the most reliable florist if possible,—and even some of these may not know exactly the needs of the plant. For ferns, choose leaf mould one part, silver sand one part, dry friable peat two parts. Avoid that peat which comes from wet unhealthy situations. Wherever you see ferns growing near the edge of woods or running streams, you can be safe in taking some of the same soil, if you cannot get a good compost anywhere else. English florists, who have access to special materials, make up a particular compost of the fol-

Fig. 46.—Heated Fern Case.

lowing materials which is described as perfect. Mix equal parts of silver sand, good loam, powdered charcoal, refuse of cocoanut fibre. If you wish, you may cover the bottom of the pan with a layer of powdered charcoal, or bricks or gravel broken to the size of hazel nuts, to a depth of one inch, if pan is four inches deep; or one and one-half inches if 6 inches deep. Do not take the advice of those who recommend filling the pan half full with small charcoal; such a proportion is unnecessary. When the soil has been placed in the pan press firmly that all the plants may be set solidly.

Location for fern cases. They will do well *anywhere*, and that is just what the

Fig. 47.—Fern Case.

amateur wants. They may be shifted from one window to another at pleasure, with little fear of dangerous consequences. If placed in the south window keep them back a little from the heat of the midday sun. A half shady position is much better than a sunny one. A northern out look will suit them admirably if not too cold,—and an eastern or western one is at all times suitable.

It would be best to have tables provided especially for the fern case to rest upon. This should be strong and yet easily moved by castors, (use the brass ones, not the rubber or wooden ones.)

Fig. 48.—Fern Pillar.

If the cases are quite small, say within 9 inches diameter, they may be suspended, and some of these hanging ferneries are quite ornamental.

The secret of good management is told in a few words, viz., *water well after planting*, then shut up your case, and leave it to itself.

A successful fern case grower, writes us that " the most success ful winter I ever had with ferns, was one in which I only watered the case once after planting, and only opened it a few times in the seven months from November 1st to June 1st—and then to remove dead fronds."

If you water sufficiently at time of planting, (and you need not water any more than ordinarily for pot plants,) you will have no occasion to water again. The closed case prevents all evaporation.

Some fronds of course will die or turn brown. These must of course be removed. Insects may invade your little plant home, and these must be removed, but there will not be many and they are easily disposed of.

Some of our florists recommend ventilation for the case, feeling that the plants will be much the better for the pure air and the sunlight. This may be done only when the temperature of the outer and inner air is about the same, and only for a short time. It should not be done frequently, but may be tried at long intervals of one or two months.

Avoid too much moisture. If there should be too much inside the case, open it daily until a little has evaporated into the outer air, and then close again. It will not need watering or opening again for a month or more.

Plants for The Fern Case.

In arranging your plants place the strongest growers in the centre, and the smaller at the sides.

Besides standard plants in the fernery, there are often introduced little hanging plants suspended from the top of the glass frame. Plants for this purpose are simply taken out of their pots, their balls of earth are surrounded with moss, tied with copper wire, a loop running from which is fastened into a hook in the top, and then it becomes a miniature hanging basket. In England small pots of gutta percha are manufactured for this express purpose.

You will perhaps be advised by some florists not to choose for your fern case any of our native plants, because it is difficult to transplant them from their native soil, just at close of summer when they have done growing, and compel them to continue life continuously thereafter, in opposition to their nature, which demands rest during the winter season. Nevertheless it is done, and many a pretty fern case is indebted to some plant treasure of this character stolen from Sylva's bowery retreats, to grace the setting room; they still thrive, despite the prognostications of wise

Fig. 49.—Parlor Fern Stand covered with Glass.

heads as to failure. The *Lygodium Palmatum*, or Climbing Fern, is very suitable, and can be usually found in shady or moist spots in any of our Eastern States. It has a slender running root and stalk, from which proceed twining flexible stems, with very smooth palmate leaves or frondlets; these running stems or stalks are often three feet long, and the whole plant resembles in growth a delicate little Ivy. Besides its suitableness for the Fern Case, it is especially desirable for Rock Work in a conservatory.

The *Partridge Vine*, (Mitchella,) is also invaluable, for its brilliant scarlet berries enliven the sober green of the ferns or form an excellent contrast with the mosses. Take up large vines of it, with as many berries as you can procure;

if they are green when found, they will turn red very shortly; for covering soil and otherwise, naked or exposed, it is excellent.

The *Trailing Arbutus* (Epigœa repens) usually forms its buds in October or November, and blooms with full flower by January. These flowers are highly prized for their delicious fragrance, and it may be considered one of the choicest for our selection.

Fig. 50.

The *Maidens' Hair Fern* (Asplenium) is the first favorite for the Fern Case, the loveliest of our native ferns. It may be found on some sheltered hill side, or away in some deep, moist w o o d s, known by its black, hair like stems, and curiously shaped fronds. Gather some of the very smallest specimens, and let them grow; take them up roots and all. When you gather up the roots take up also soil enough to fill your zinc tray or box. It will stand transplanting better if its proper soil is carried with it. It will not be amiss to take home an abundance for other purposes, to fill in the pots for Fuchsias Roses and Carnations, which grow in your windows. Among other plants which you can transplant from the woods, are

The *Gaultheria procumbens,* or Wintergreen.

Chimaphilla, or Pipsinima, various species.

Pryola, or False Wintergreen, various species.

Sarracenia purpurea, or Side Saddle flower; their cups must be kept full of water.

Cypripedium, or Lady Slipper, or *Maccaron Flower.*

Speranthes, or Lady Tresses, various species.

Dionaea, Muscipula, or Venus' Fly Trap.

The *American Lycopodiums,* or Club Mosses, are all very desirable. Many of them are used freely for decorations at Christmas. The best varieties are *Denticulatum, Wildenovii, Umbrosa, Dendroideum, lucidulum.*

The daintily cut foliage of the (Captis trifoliata) or Gold Thread, will form a pretty feature, and the Linewood, or.*Hepatica,* with its blue eyes, will be no less lovely. The Wild Lily of the Valley (*Convallaria*) will open its tiny white bells long before they open in the meadow or at the brookside.

If you look for other mosses, larger than the *Lycopodium*, you can take the *Polystichum*, or Hair Cup moss; *Patraphis*, or four toothed moss; *Splachnum*, or Umbrella moss. You will need plenty of these green mosses or white lichens or the Sealing Wax moss, to pack about the roots of your plants, and help keep up a cool, wild, woody home-like retreat. The following are the most generally preferred Ferns :

Polypodium, various species.

Struthiopteris, Ostrich Fern.

Fig. 51.—Group of Fern Shells.

Pteris, or Brocken.

Adiantum, or Maiden Hair.

Cheilanthes, or Lip Fern.

Woodwardia.

Camptorum, or Walking Fern

Asplenium, or Spleenwood.

Dicksonia.

Crystopteris, or Bladder Fern.

Woodsia.

Polystichum, or Shield Fern.

Onoclea, or Sensitive.

Davallia Canariensis, or Hairs Foot Fern.

If your fern case is large enough you may add one or two large plants, such as the *Dracaena term alis,* or *Nobilis;* the *Dieffenbachia variegata,* is very showy. The *Pandanus* or *Ananassa* may be admitted, and if you have plenty of room, there is no objection to the Crotons with their handsomely variegated foliage, the

Cissus Discolor, with blood red leaves and half trailing habit, the variegated leaved *Begonias,* also the *Gesnerias, Caladium, Colocasias, Marantas, Cacti, Saxifragas, Sedum.*

Avoid complication or crowding. If your case is of but moderate size, say two feet in diameter, use only one or two large upright plants; but if smaller than this stick only to the ferns and mosses.

Among other additional plants are :

The (*Goodyera pubescens*) Rattlesnake Plaintain ; leaves variegated, dark green, with white veins.

The (*Erythronium*) Dogs' Tooth Violet, whose leaves are green mottled with brown.

For trailing purposes perhaps nothing is better than the *Lysimachia,* or Moneywort, and the Coliseum Ivy. *Orchids* may be added, if there is plenty of room,

Fig. 52.—Ornamental Fern Case and Stand.

and nothing will give more satisfaction.

Do not expose those ferns with variegated foliage to severe sunlight, as they will suffer injury. Neither should delicate ferns be watered on the leaves. Some whose leaves appear but mere powder or dust, such as the Golden or Silver Fern, will lose their beauty if thus treated, and perhaps may be killed outright.

Exotic, or Green House Ferns.

Should you have ill success with your native plants and be undecided what to do we think it best for you to fall back upon something more suitable, and begin in a more simple manner, by going to the nearest green house, where ferns are grown, and procure some small seedlings. These come up in great quantities in the pots, also on the earth of the pan on which the pots rest, and in fact everywhere that the spores chance to sow themselves. You can in this way frequently get a half dozen varieties of ferns. Among them probably one or two *Adiantums*, a *Doodia*, and several varieties of *Pteris*. These are the ferns most likely to produce seedlings, when the spores are scattered over a moist surface.

After these have been transferred to the fern case, their daily growth will afford you a very pleasant and interesting study; the gradual change and growth of the frond from the first appearance to the full development will amply repay you for your patience in waiting.

This is the true way to enjoy plant cases; begin with the rudiments and learn step by step the nature of the plants.

For moderate sized cases we must select ferns of size and habit suitable for them.

The best of those found in green houses are :

Adiantum Capillus Veneris, A assimile, A acristatum, Doodia Aspera, D. Caudata, Pteris geraniefolia, P. Cretica, Albo lineata, P. hetero-phylla, P. serrulata, Blechnum gracile, Asplen-ium auritum, and *A. bulbiferum.* There are many others, but a simple list like this is suf-ficient.

For tall ferns choose *Polypodium Aureum, P. appendiculatum, Pteris argyrea, Asplenium Brasiliense, Adiantum Macrophyllum, Anemia hylitidis.*

In planting your ferns do not crowd them together, but give room for the full development of the fronds; their growth is rapid and many soon double their original size when first pur-chased. Alternate the different varieties if pos-sible, and do not get two or three plants of the same kind together. A fine delicate fern always

Fig. 53.—Parlor Fern Stand.

looks more graceful and pretty beside a variety with a full broad frond. So a light green or variegated plant will show to better advantage beside one with a dark green frond. In choosing your soil, make say of three parts rich, black peaty mould, one part coarse sand and gravel siftings mixed, and one part broken charcoal, see that the pieces of charcoal are broken to the size of cranberries, and well mixed with the earth; the whole should only be broken up, not sifted.

After you have put the plants in the case, water with a small watering pot with a fine nose. Saturate the earth pretty thoroughly, but not to make it muddy. There are many other varieties of the *Lygodiums* not mentioned above. *Lygodium, Apodum, densum, caesium, arboreum, lipidophyllum,* their roots will extend over the earth, covering all the bare spots with a fresh green carpet of delicate growth.

Should we be able to procure a plant of the greenhouse species of climbing fern, *Lygodium flexuosum,* or *L. japonicum,* another beautiful object will be added.

Among the climbing ferns, are some of the most graceful ferns in the whole family of *Filices.* There is one plant, however, not a fern, which does exceedingly well in a fern case, and is remarkably interesting. We refer to *Ficus Stipulata.* This plant, a vine, is a free grower, and climbs up the sides of our case by its roots, which, aided by the moisture on the glass, spread and adhere to it.

Fig. 54.—Plant Case.

It is a hard wooded plant, roots quickly from cuttings, and grows so freely as to fill a moderate sized case very rapidly.

After you have become accustomed to growing ferns in the case, you will perhaps crave a little variety. This can be easily had. Suppose you look a little into the curiosities of growth and reproduction.

If you look on the under side of the fern fronds, you will find something resembling a brown powder, adhering to them thickly in regularly distributed masses of varied shapes, depending upon the species.

Examining with the magnifier or microscope, you find them to be seeds or spores.

Shake these spores, which appear like the veriest dust, over the surface of the earth in an ordinary fern case, after it has been well smoothened. The earth should be watered very thoroughly previous to scattering the spores.

In about a month or six weeks, looking carefully across the surface of the earth, you see the slightest specks of green; again examining with the microscope you find them living organisms of vegetation ; and when at a later date they become of good size, it is with no little satisfaction to be able to say, that they were the seedlings sown by your own hand. If in your travels in the woods, you carry an herbarium with you, you can gather the fronds of every variety you meet, which contains fertile spores.

Spores from such an herbarium should be planted as soon as convenient to insure germination. Spores have been known to germinate as long as eighteen months after being gathered, while under favorable circumstances germination in spores has taken place, when sown eight or ten years after they were collected. From your spores you will get a quantity of seedlings, many of them of strange forms, and some to differ from the parent plant.

Fig. 55.—Arborette.

We may find frequently several fronds on the same plant differing very materially. Thus your love and knowledge of plant life increases, and you willl cherish your fern case with more than customary pleasure, for it opens up a new world to you.

One thing only remember *i. e.*, keep out of your fern case all the common bedding plants, such as Geraniums, Petunias, Verbenas, Roses, Fuschias, &c., for they cannot well stand the confined moist air.

Designs for Fern Decorations.

A home made plant case can be constructed as follows : Get your carpenter or cabinet maker to construct a shallow box, of fine wood, say black walnut, about two feet wide, and three or three and one-half feet long. The bottom board should be about an inch and a half thick, and project about an inch beyond the sides. The sides should be of inch stuff, and the depth six or seven inches. See that the corners are well dovetailed together, and on the inside of the tops cut a groove, into which to set the glass.

Fig. 56.—Ferns in Arborette.

The size of your glass should be about two feet square for the ends, and two feet by thirty-six inches for the sides and top; but if this is too large and expensive a case, you can construct one of but half these dimensions, viz., twelve inches square for the ends and twelve by eighteen inches for the sides and top. Many like to have their cases made for them with pitched roof, like design No.

40, and with wooden frames same as for windows.   All that it needs is to fit the glasses into the frames and seal the sides up tightly with putty.

The frame, as it sets into the lower wooden box, should also be fastened well with putty, to make it tight; and on the outside you may fasten a very pretty

little moulding, which will cover the top of the wood, and set snugly up to the glass. You will of course take care to have a little door cut in the back glass, say about six inches by eight or ten, opening or sliding, whenever necessary to introduce water, or remove insects and dead leaves.

In Fig. 42, the upper pane may be made movable. Next you will need a tray to go inside the wooden frame work. This should be of nearly the same size as the box, but smaller so as to fit inside. This tray should be constructed of zinc, and may be made with a double bottom of an inch in height, a small hole being cut in the upper one, for the purpose of carrying off any surplus water. The filling and

Fig. 57.—Arborette.

planting have already been described. Place some broken charcoal, or fine brick or gravel, in the bottom of the upper pan, and then your compost over this. If your wood is well moulded, and sides ornamented, the case will be a very handsome ornament. Cases such as we describe, are now made and sold at prices of from $20 to $30, by all our large floral warehouses.

Should you wish to construct a little rockery in the fernery, select pieces of stone, sharp pointed, or with rough jagged sides. You will often find them in some moist spot in the woods, already half covered with moss; then build them up one above the other until you have made the form of an arch. Start the stones from the very bottom of the tray, mix the soil well with them wherever possible, into all the interstices, and if it is necessary to get cement to make them firm, do so. Then set set your ferns in all the rugged interstices of the stones, wherever you have placed the earth, and they will soon cover it with their leaves, and their roots will reach into all the crevices.

Fig. 58.—Arborette.

Design No. 40, is about the size we have described, constructed in a more than a usually ornamental style. It is very suitable for all kinds of ferns, and *Lycopodium, Small Orchids,* small species of the *Dracaena, Croton pictum, Cr variegatum, Aphelandra Leopoldi, Gymmostachys, Vershaffeltii, Eranthemum, ifineum, Passiflora trifasciata, Alocassia, Caladium,* and *Fittonia argentea.*

Fig. 41 shows one of the simplest of all fern decorations in the form of a neat vase; the bowl is filled with the proper soil, and its surface is covered with moss. In the centre is a nicely shaped plant of the *Maiden Hair Fern*, whose appearance gives a delightfully cool and refreshing feeling in the room. A very pretty effect could be produced by inserting little tubes of glass or tin (such as are used for holding cut flowers,) in the soil here and there among the moss, then filling with water and inserting at intervals clipped blossoms of some of your winter blooming flowers, Geranium, Roses, Fuchsias, &c., or perhaps a clipped blossom from your climbing vines. Arranged any way it is in fact a beautiful object for the drawing room or conservatory.

In Fig. 39, is shown a most charming fernery, the property of Mrs. Shirley Hibberd, at Stoke Newington, London, England. This conservatory was located where sunshine was excluded on account of neighboring buildings and large trees, and a fern house was constructed. Rockeries were built up on two sides of the house, and in the crevices were planted ferns and lycopodiums. The floor was covered with neat tiles, and with the naturally graceful character of the plant the conservatory was peculiarly ornamented. The rockeries were made almost entirely of big blocks of peat, and on the top near the glass were planted a few Sedums, Sempervivums, and

Fig. 59.

other succulent plants. Mr. Hibberd, in his description of the fernery, in his volume "Rustic Adornments for Homes of Taste," states that for the past twelve years about a hundred and fifty species and varieties have thrived here, making summer all the year round in their perennial greenness.

The finest selections of ferns, as recommended by him for such a house, are the *Adiantums, Asplenium, Adiantum, Nigrum, Athyrium, f. f., A. f. f. Crispa, Gymnogramma leptophylla, Doodias, Scolopendriums, Woodwardia radicans, Equisetum, Sylvaticum,* and *Selaginellas.*

Water was given daily during the warm weather; in spring and autumn, twice a week was sufficient, and in winter once in two or three weeks. The plants must, however, never be left to get dry.

Fig. 60.

Miss Maling, an English lady writer on indoor plants, has invented a case (Fig. 42) which contains room for a hot water apparatus in the zinc pan. Her principle is to supply a cool or a heated end in the fern case, according to the necessities of the plants. "Hardy or greenhouse plants last long in flower at one end in the cool temperature; stove plants and forced flowers come on beautifully in the heated part. If all your plants in the case are hardy, then use no heat. If our ferns or flowers, though not wanting heat specially, should damp off; we give heat just for a time to change the air entirely. At ten minutes notice the heat can be raised to any degree up to 90°. The cases are of two sizes, the larger ones being about four feet long, by two wide, and two high, while the boxes on which the glassed frames rest are eight inches deep. The boxes are lined with zinc, and fitted with hot water apparatus. No lamp or any heater is required, hot water only being used, which is poured in through a concealed opening from without, and when cold is let off by another opening.

This water maintains the temperature at a height sufficient for most plants for twenty-four hours without refilling; but when greater heat is required it can be raised to any degree from 65° to 90°, by adding more hot water after the first twelve hours. The upper glass sash is movable, and by a button or hook is lifted at any time ventilation is needed or you wish to examine the plants. This principle of heating the case is principally for the sake of bringing into flower and keeping in good health many tender stove plants, as well as other delicate plants which cannot stand either a cool or a dry atmosphere."

Fig. 61.

The general outline and construction of Miss Maling's plant case is very similar to the "home made case" we have previously described. Heating will be unnecessary if amatures will only choose but the ordinary native or greenhouse ferns, and keep the case well closed away from cold air.

But it seems to us if the case is to be heated at all, it should be divided into two apartments, one end for plants needing the warm temperature, the other for the cool temperature, or else put no plants in the case unless they are all to be treated alike.

Whenever, in the mind of a beginner, there appears to be a doubt as to what to choose, take the *Lycopodium denticulatum,* and other varieties of *L. caesium, apodum, heloctica,* or *variabilis* will always appear to advantage ; also the *Pteris cretica albo lineata,* or *Cyrtomium falcatum,* do remarkably well, being very strong growers."

Fig. 62.

These Fern Pillars are also made of Terra Cotta, in England, with openings in appropriate places for setting in the bricks. The columns are also constructed as to permit a glass screen to shut completely over them and rest upon the base, thus giving the same effect as a Wardian Case. Fig. 49 shows another design on a table, with a glass top also. Fig. 50 shows one of the largest styles of fern bricks, as it rests fitted into a fire screen.

Fig. 51 is much more elaborate, and shows what may be done either in the side of a wall or a conservatory, or to occupy a large fire place. These are made in the form of square pieces of pottery, which may be nailed flat against the wall. In the lower portion of the front appears a projection of a shell, and within it is a small cavity for holding the plants. Being of various sizes, any style of arrangement can be ingeniously formed, and at slight expense.

These designs are as yet unknown in the United States, but can be quickly imported to order by any one; or our pottery manufacturers could soon supply any demand by making any pattern and casting therefrom.

They are elegant in appearance and effect, and the general testimony is to the effect that the ferns thrive very well in them.

Fig. 63.—Fern Stand.   Fig. 64.—Fern Stand.

Figs. 52 and 53 introduce several pretty Parlor Ferneries, of easy manufacture, the former in the shape of a rectangle, about 2 feet long by one and a quarter foot wide, and two feet in height. The other with six sides, curving to the top, from which suspends a little wire hanging basket. These designs are soon constructed by any cabinet maker.

A pleasant story is told of a gardener near London, England, who, instead of following the invariable fashion of devoting the high stone walls surrounding his enclosed garden, to wall fruit, determined to cover it with ferns.

"The wall was 14 feet in height and 400 feet in length. It was then very old, and having been originally built of a dark red brick, much in use in that day in the district, it had a venerable and picturesque appearance. From the ground line to the summit it was all the summer long dotted over with ferny tufts of herbage, some sparkling with the hue of emerald, others shading off to rich shades of brown and orange; and the delicate tracery of those with finely divided fronds, wonderfully set off like vegetable lace against the dark background of the weather-worn brick.

Nail holes had been made here and there, where in former times were fastened the branches of peach, apricot, cherry, and plum trees to ripen their crops; but they had long ago been given up. The idea occurred to him to convert it into a perpendicular fernery. He first of all thrust into some of the large holes in the wall, tufts of common *Polypody*, making their creeping roots comfortable with turfy peat, and securing them from falling out by means of a copper wire passed across the hole and held to the bricks by small staples. As these were found to flourish and give the wall somewhat the aspect of a ruin, he began to make holes to plant others; and by degrees the wall was covered with Hearts Tongue, *Asplenium adiantum*, the Wall rue fern, the Mountain Polypody, the *Alpine cystopteris*, and dozens of others that bear drought patiently, and naturally inhabit rocks and waysides. In the shady chinks next the butteries, he managed to coax the *Maiden hair* to make luxuriant fillets of herbage, and at the

Fig. 65.

foot of the wall there were tufts of *lastrea, osmunda royal*, and other ferns which the wall itself refused to nourish. The majority of these held their verdure far into the winter; the Hearts Tongue and common Polypodium were usually quite green the whole year round; and during the winter their rich dottings of golden spores sparkled in the most cheerful manner against the dark back ground of sheets of ivy and red brick. Of course the wall itself was crowned with *Snapdragons, Wallflowers*, and other gay tenants of ruined towers, or pines, that make riot of man's work, and glorify the decay of art with the triumph of nature."

Figs. 55, 56, 57, 58, introduce several "*Rustic Terra Cotta Arborettes.*" These are made of Terra Cotta, or pottery ware, cast in a rugged form resembling the projecting limbs of an oak tree just clipped, and with cavities opening downward for the reception of earth and holding plants. Some of them have a solid interior, and each basin is by itself. These are undesirable, having no opportunity for drainage; but where the interior is entirely hollow and can

Fig. 66.

be entirely filled with earth, no rustic ornament is more suitable for ferns or other plants to live in. They may decorate the hall, parlor, conservatory, or out door lawn. Their size is from one to three feet high.

The strongest growing ferns may be placed in here, taking care to put a few crocks of broken brick or charcoal in the bottom of each basin for drainage.

They may be used also for spring flowering Bulbs, and filled with hyacinths, crocuses, scillas, snowdrops, narcissus ; and then when these are over, the contents may be emptied and refilled again with summer flowering plants ; but it is usually best to devote them to such classes of plants as will flower the year round without any change.

Figs. 59 to 66 show the different styles of mounting Fern cases with the customary cylindrical glass shades.

In Fig. 43, we see one of the larger styles of Miss Maling's designs, intended to set upon a table. This is most charmingly filled ; and perhaps we cannot do better than let Shirley Hibberd himself, who filled it, tell us what is in it :

Fig. 67.—Fern or Flower Case.

" It fell to my lot to construct the mimic archway (a rockery,) and fill it with pockets for the reception of small ferns. For that purpose I took two square seed pans, and placed them bottom upwards, on the zinc bottom of the case, as abutments, which, of course when the case was filled with soil, were hidden from view. From the flat foundation of clay thus provided, I began to build, using small pieces of coke dipped in a batter of cement, and spending a few hours every day for four days in succession upon the work ere it was completed. In the pockets were inserted specimens of *Cystopteris regia, Camptosaurus rhizophyllus, Asplenium flabellifolium, Scolopendrium, vulgare var. ramosum, polyschides,* and *vulgare ramo marginatum, Adiantum hispidulum,* and a few *Selaginellas.* The latter soon grew so as to smother the whole fabric, forming a rich bell of various tints of blue and green, with the fern pushing through them. On the right hand side of the arch was planted *Nephrolepis exaltata,* one of the most suberb of Wardian Case ferns, and remarkably distinct, with its graceful arching polypodium-like fronds.

Fig. 68.—Case for preserving flowers fresh.

On the left hand *Nephrolepis pectinata,* which is of the same habit of growth, and a very beautiful and interesting fern ; nevertheless, less beautiful than the other, as it is also less vigorous. A small plant of *Platycerium grande* was then planted in the shell of a cocoanut, and suspended by copper wire to the crown of the arch, and this spring its new growth was so vigorous that it had to be removed to the greenhouse, where it is now flourishing. Two more notable ferns were introduced, namely : *Pteris flabellata, var. crispa,* a very erect and characteristic fern of large growth, quite cheap and common, and one of the best for glass cases, of at least two feet in height within. The other was our fine old hardy friend, *Cyrtomium falcatum,* which is worth a place anywhere among ferns, and fortunately it will grow anywhere, and is always noble.

The rest of the plants consisted of various small, yet choice subjects. *Pteris scaberula,* very beautiful in the lace-like divisions, and light green hue of its fronds. It is really a gem, and always grows well in peat, cocoanut, or any soil of a light spongy texture.

Doodia lunulata and *caudata,* are of small growth, and serve well with *Lomaria lanceolata* and *L. spicant,* to fill up green tufts between ferns—of very distinct and striking appearance. In the centre of the case, but on the side opposite to the view here given, and hence hidden by the *Platycerium*—a plant of *Phlebodium sporodocarpum*—made a fine effect. It is one of the most distinct and beautiful and easily managed of all Wardian Case ferns, but must have always a nice peaty mixture.

Fig. 69.—Ladies' Plant Case.

The remaining ferns are *Polypodium phegopteris* and *rugulosum, Campyloneurum phyllitidis, Adiantum formosum, pedatum* and *tenellum.*

An important point in all fern cases is to have them so constructed as to be easily turned about and moved around, so that the plants may all share equally in the sunlight. If the case is too large, many plants will receive an undue proportion of the sunlight, while others will be totally deprived.

The Germans, who have a greater fondness and taste for *Window Gardening* than any other nation, have some very tasteful fancies in the way of Ferneries and Rockeries in the windows.

Fig. 44 will illustrate one of them projecting outward from the side of the house. The arch frame above is also on the outside. Looking at the rockery within rising up out of the aquarium, we find the following plants which do well in the constant evaporation of the water :

Adiantum tenerum, cuneatum, formosum ; Davallia, pixidata ; Gymnogramma Peruviana ; Lomaria spicant ; onychicum japonicum ; Pteris serrulata ; Selaginella calsia ; Selaginella, umbrosa, Africana serpens, and *Wildenovii,* with *Acorus gramineus folius fol var ; Sibthorpia Europœa ; Panicum variegatum ; Torrenia Asiatica ; Ficus stipularis ; Tradescantia Zebrina ; Hoya bella,* and *Æschynanthus zebrinus.*

We mention the plants particularly, as perhaps some one may be disposed to copy the designs literally. We know of no form of Window Gardening so exquisite as this. A climbing vine may be twined around the outside of the window casement. The water in the aquarium must be contained in a vessel with glass sides, so that all portions may be discernible to the eye.

Fig. 45 is another of the designs for Window Gardens, similar to those described in our second chapter. Now it is peculiarly suitable to hardy ferns, and such native plants as the Partridge vine, Mosses, Lycopodiums, etc.

Fig. 46 is known as the Pickard Plant Case; but we do not discover any special feature different from those constructed by Miss Maling. It contains the same metal box for the soil; but instead of having the glass sides and top stationary, all are movable, and easily put up or taken down. The glass sides all come in sheets, which fit each into a light frame of their own; yet any one of these may be removed from the other without disturbing the rest. The front can be taken out in an instant by lifting, or fixed back again in its place by a couple of hooks and eyes; in short each side has a frame of its own, and when all are shut up together they are held firmly by hooks and eyes at top and ends. The interior of this case is filled with Calodiums, Begonias, and other plants of colored foliage, as well as ferns. It is intended specially for a case of soft wooded plants, such as are usually grown in the pots of the greenhouse.

A very pretty fern case is that of Fig. 47, also in the possession of Shirley Hibberd. The base is a stone vase, with hollow interior; the foot is a frame of wood; inside the vase is a zinc pan, wherein the ferns are placed, and the frame of glass fits over the pan; a couple of doors furnish access to the interior

Fig. 70.—Wardian Case.

Fig. 71.—Wardian Case.

and open or are closed by a little button fastener. The size is as follows : Height of vase and glass, 5 feet 9 inches ; width of vase, 2 feet ; height of glass frame, 3 feet.   In the top of the glass frame Mr. Hibberd suspended four half cocoanut shells, in which he planted some ferns ; holes are cut in the bottom for drainage ; and copper wire only used for hanging them.   The contents are thus described by Mr. Hibberd in his Floral World : " This case contains at the present time two pretty climbing plants ; one is the common Ivy of the British woods, *Hedera helix ;* the other is *Lygodium scandens,* an elegant climbing fern.   The palm-like fern in the centre is *Nephrolepis exaltata*—the finest fern in the world for a centre piece ; both because of its character and also that it may be cut without spoiling it, if it happens to grow too tall.   With it are examples of *Pteris cretica albo-lineata,* an elegant variegated fern ; *Niphobolus lingua*—a hardy tongue-like fern ; *Onychium Japonicum,* most delicately divided ; *Pteris crenata, Lastrea glabella, Doodia caudata, Asplenium viride,* and some bits of *Selaginellas, Anemone nemorosa,* and a few *Mosses.*

The Ivy gained a footing quite by accident.   This, with other of our cases, is frequently exhibited.   On one occasion, in preparing some cases for a festive meeting, we introduced into this a number of little twigs of common Ivy among the ferns.   The case was left undisturbed afterwards, and then on removing the Ivy one of them was found to have rooted.   It was allowed to remain and it soon formed a rich shell on one side of the glass, without robbing a single fern of a ray of light.   There it remains to this day ; it is now some nine years old as an inhabitant of this case, and is as vigorous as ever.   A few lengths of fine copper wire serve to train the Ivy and the *lygodium,* which add very much indeed to the beauty of this little garden.   This case stands in the window, and has only the warmth of an ordinary room in winter.

For a fern case to stand in the sunshine all the time, and with a room of high temperature, choose the following tender ferns : In the centre place a fine plant of the *Cheilanthes farinosa ;* then add here and there *Anemidictyon, phyllitidis, Olfersia cervina, Diplazium radicans, Asplenium fragrans, Lomaria attenuata, Pteris calomelanos, Fadyenia prolifera,* and a few tufts of the *Selaginella caesium* and *S. laevigata.*"

Among fern decorations nothing is so striking, and yet so novel, as the fire brick.   For filling a vacant fire place and making the screen appear ornamental, nothing is of better fitness.   They are the invention of a physician, Dr. G. Churchill Watson, of Chester, England, and so constructed as to fit into the sides of walls of conservatories, ferneries and greenhouses, affording a convenient method of rendering a blank wall useful as well as ornamental.   They are made of porous material, usually pottery, and round or oval shaped, with a concave centre, in which may be placed wet ferns, mosses or Lycopodiums.   They are of different sizes, from 3½ inches in diameter to 14 inches, and adapted to the place where they are most needed. The largest can be used to fit into the niche of an unused fire place, and the smaller ones can be used to fit the niches of a fern column or pillar.   A fern pillar is one of the curiosities our parlor gardeners do not often behold; and yet a glance at illustration No. 48, will show how pleasing such a decoration might be, and how simply it could be made. This design is constructed of wood, in the form of a hexagonal pillar, with vase at the top.

At various places in each side are little niches or openings, into which are introduced the fern shells; these are filled with earth, usually holding a pint to a quart, and the fern grows gracefully outward. This pillar holds 19 vessels, and affords a rare opportunity of cultivating quite a variety. If the centre of the pillar is hollow it must be filled up by hand with some earthy material, and either moss or cocoanut fibre or dust may be pressed firmly. The soil for the bricks should be peat two parts; loam or woods mould one part, silver sand one part.

An English lady, filling such a case, once adopted this selection of plants. As mentioned in the Gardener's Magazine, "In the vase at the top were some plants of the *Asplenium flabellifolium*, one of the most elegant of all the small trailing ferns. To help out the effect of this, a tuft of the pretty rush *Isolepis gracilis* is introduced. This falls over in most graceful glass-like outlines, and as it loves moisture it is quite at home under a bell glass. In the shells at the sides of the column are specimens of *Adiantum eapillus veneris, A. hispidulums,* and *A. cuneatum,* the last of which may grow too large; if so, it should be removed. One of the most suitable of all ferns is *Woodsia Ilvensis,* which grows marvelously, and seems to be at home in the porous ware of the vessel. Other good ferns are *Asplenium fontanum, A. rutamraria, Doodia lunulata, Doodia caudata, Woodsia obtusa, Cystopteris fragile Dickeana, Camptozaurus, rhizophyllus,* (one of the rarest of the exotic Hearts Tongue ferns,) *Scolopendrium vulgare, v. proliferum vamo marginatum,* and *v. polyschides, Lastrea filix-mas v. Schofieldii, Adiantum Setulosum, Hymenophyllum Wilsoni, Athyrium f. f. diffissum.*

These are the cheapest of all designs for the window. Fig. 59 and 60 being obtainable at almost any glass store, at prices of $2.00 to $5.00 complete. Figs. 61 and 62, are in a basket vase. Figs. 63 and 64 are with pottery ware or lava boxes, resting upon stands. Fig. 65, is made of rustic wood and has a wooden bowl, upon which the glass cylinder rests. Fig. 66 is an iron stand, with a plain earthen bowl beneath the fernery, the outside of which is decorated with a network of wire.

Among the various designs of Wardian Cases, for the drawing-room or saloon, there are often met a few of much simpler material, which can be used for other purposes. Figs. 67 and 68 are so constructed that they can be used at one time for growing ferns within, or they can be used merely for holding cut flowers in moist sand or water. In Fig. 68, the top is movable, fitting into a brass groove, and must be lifted entirely off the table when the plants are to be placed inside or need any attention. All the ornamental work around the edges of the stand, and the frame work for holding the glass plates, is made of brass; the stand itself is of wood. The size of the interior is about 18 inches in diameter, by 12 inches high.

Fig. 67 is much more symmetrical in shape, and easily made. The frame of this, too, is made mostly of polished brass, and the glass sets down upon a groove made in the top of the stand, which is of wood. The interior is hollow, with a zinc basin for holding plants.

Fig. 69 is a *Lady's Plant Case,* a kind of Wardian case in miniature; and though not affording very spacious accommodations inside, still there is a good deal of novelty in its construction, sufficient to render it a very interesting object for either the drawing room or library.

A bell glass, or shade, fits closely at its base into a groove running all around the edge of a stand constructed usually of wood.

The plants inside are in small pots not over four inches in diameter, although the proportions of the case may be enlarged from 18 inches in diameter up to 3 feet, and afford greater room. Any manufacturer of glass shades could make such a shade in a special mould, and any cabinet maker could fashion a tasteful table or stand beneath.

Figs. 71, 72 are sketches of two very pretty Wardian Cases, exhibited at one of the Horticultural Society Exhibitions, and was much admired. They admit of considerably greater outline than the previous designs of Ferneries, and are more ornamental. Fig. 70 is 7 feet high, 4 feet 2 inches wide, and 2 feet 6 inches in breadth.

Fig. 71 is 4 feet high, 3 feet broad, and 1 foot 11 inches wide. These are constructed mostly with bright metalic frame work; the best quality of sheet glass is used; castors are fitted to the base, and at the back there is a little door to allow the entrance of the hand for watering the plants or removing dead leaves.

Such designs as these, made to cover an entire collection of plants, should be generally adopted, and their manufacture encouraged. They do away altogether with the daily task of watering, they are absolutely free from dust, and the plants have a perpetual moisture inside, which affords not only the most desirable and uniform temperature, but conduces to health of habit, and freedom from insects. Our Window Gardeners must learn by practical experience that there is but one practical solution to the difficulties of Window Gardening, "*The plants must live in an atmosphere to themselves, shut out alike from the air of the room, and from the outer air.*"

In apartments lighted with gas, the use of these glass covers or shades is again made obvious, for no gas fumes will ever touch them.

An opinion is general among amateurs, that these Wardian Cases must be perfectly air tight. This is not quite true; although they are fitted pretty close, yet they are not absolutely air tight. Indeed it is sometimes quite desirable that the case should be lifted a little to permit a free circulation of the air betwixt the interior and the exterior, especially if there is a surplus of moisture inside, and condenses so constantly upon the glass that the plant cannot be seen.

A fact may often have been observed by flower lovers, that when two flowers are plucked, the one stuck with its stem into a bottle or vase of water, and the other thrown down into a wide basin of water, so the petals as well as stem are in the water, it will be found that the latter will keep fresh and sweet the longest. The explanation is only in the greater humidity. In the former case, the air of the room being too dry, evaporates the water from the surface of the petals faster than the stem can supply, while in the latter the flower is completely surrounded with all it needs.

Observing this principle then in your cut flowers or bouquets, if you will take care to place them in pans of water, or sand and water, and then cover with bell glasses, they will have a humid atmosphere entirely to themselves, retain their freshness for double the length of time, as they would if exposed to the dry air of the sitting-room.

The Wardian Case then, in principle, is not only the most practical in operation, but beneficial in results.

List of Ferns.

For a Wardian Case kept in a room with a high temperature, use :

Adiantum *cuneatum, tenerum, *formosum, trapeziforme, Veitchii, rubellum, concinnum, Farleyense.

Anemia *hirta, flexuosa, villosa.

*Asplenium viviparum.

Blechnum *brasiliense, corrovadense.

Cheilanthes Alabamensis, Borsigiana, hirta, microphylla, pulveracea, spectabilis.

Davallia *decora, *Mooreana, *polyantha.

Didymochlaena lunulata.

Doryopteris nobilis, *pedata.

Gymnogramma *tartarea, *chrysophylla, Laurheana, Peruviana.

Hemionites *palmata.

Microlepia Davellia, hirsuta-argusla.

Nephrolepis *exaltata, *pectinata.

Notorhlaena chrysophylla, *nivea, tenera.

Polypodium aureum, omyxifolium.

Pteris *haslata, tricolor.

Selaginella.

Selaginella caesia arborea, *Africana, atrovirens, cauleriens, *conferta, Lyallii, *umbrosa (erythropus), Kasleniana, *serpens, *imbricaulis, Wallichii, Warcswewitzii.

The above Ferns and Selaginellas are also suitable for general decorations in a well heated room. Such marked * are useful for the window without glass covering.

2. For a Wardian Case in a moderately heated room :

Acrostichum *alcicorne (Platicerum.)

Adiantum affine, *capillus, Veneris, assimile, *colpodes, *formosum, *rubellnm, reniforme.

Asplenium *palmatnm, Fabianum.

Blechnum *australe, Cyathea medullaris, australis.

Cytomium *falcatum.

Davallia *canariensis, *pixidata.

Dicksonia *antarctica.

Lygodium scandens, palmatum.

Asplenium nidus, avis.

Aspidium *molle, *violascens, *Kaulfussie.

Nephrolepis *exaltata, *tuberosa.

Notorhlaena trichomanoides.

Oleandra *neriifolia.

Onychium *japonicum.

Pteris *arguta, argyraea, *cretica alba, *serrulata *hastata, longifolia.

Doodia aspera, caudata, *rupestris.
Doryopteris *palmata.
Drynaria coronans.
Lastraea glabella.
Lomaria *gibba.

Woodwardia radicans
Selaginella apoda, *caesia, *denticula-
ta, stolonifera, formosa, involvens,
Sohottii, *Martensii albo var, *Wil-
denowii.

The above named Ferns and Lycopodias are also suitable for general decorations in a moderately heated room.   Those marked * are useful for the window.

3. For a cold room, open hall, veranda, rockwork, or for cool shaded places
near the building:

Adiantum pedatum.
Allosurus crispum.
Aspidium goldianum.
Asplenium septentrionale, fontanum,
Trichomanes, Ruta-muraria, viride.
Anthyrium felix foemina, gracile, mul-
ticeps.
Blechnum boreale, occidentale.
Ceterach officinarum.
Cystopteris montane.
Lastraea Oreopteris, dilatata, filix-mas,
rigida.

Onoclea sensibilis.
Osmunda regalis, cinnamomea.
Polypodium vulgare.
Polystichium angulare, Lonchitis,
Scolopendrium officinarum and varie-
ties.
Struthiopteris germanica.
Pteris aquilina.
Woodsia hyperborea, ilvensis.
Lycopodium clavatum, alpinum, selago,
dendroideum.

The above named Ferns and Lycopodia are also suitable for window decoration during the summer season, but require some shade.

CHAPTER XV.

THE CAMELLIA.

The Camellia, when cultivated in window gardens, requires great care on account of the tendency of its flower-buds to drop off.

Too much or too little water, and great variations of temperature when the buds are swelling, cause this trouble ; yet with care it can be flowered in profusion without any artificial heat. A northern or northeastern exposure is the most desirable, and a temperature from 40° to 50°, better humid than without, the most advisable.

When the plant has flowered, if it is a young, small sized plant, it should be shifted into a pot one size larger ; but if an old, large plant, it need not be repotted oftener than once in two years. The soil should be composed of equal parts of black peat and rich loam, but if the peat is not within reach, sandy loam, enriched with one-third leaf mould, will make the plant flower well.

After potting, the plant can be placed in the window of a room where a fire is kept, but it does not require much sunshine. (In its native woods it grows in moist, shady places.) While new leaves and buds are forming, water should be given every day, and the leaves and branches frequently sponged or showered, as the dust will adhere to the leaves. The plant requires light, but does not need the direct rays of the sun.

In the spring, when it has ceased growing, it can be placed out of doors in a shady situation, yet not under the dripping of trees or shrubs, and where it will be exposed only to the morning's sun. Early in September it must be brought in doors, for it would lose all its flower-buds should the frost touch it. If the plant is in good health, it will now be filled with buds. One hour's drought, or a soaking wet soil, will bring down the buds and destroy all hopes of flowers. The air should be too cold for a person to sit comfortably in the room, until the flower-buds open ; then the plant can be brought into the parlor. When the mercury marks 40° or 45°, a couple of hours of fresh air will be useful to the Camellia, but do not place it in the fullest sunshine.

When the buds swell for flowering, a little more water is needed ; give it in plentiful doses, turning away all that runs out into the saucers. Apply the water directly to the soil, for the flowsrs are injured by sprinkling ; never shower the foliage when the sun shines upon it, lest the leaves should be blistered or spotted. After the plants have flowered, and fully repaid you for all your attention, observe the same routine of culture again.

In the Southern States and in California Camellias grow into large shrubs or trees, and need no protection in the winter. They are propagated from seeds, cuttings, grafting, and marching.

The seeds are a long time in vegetating; sometimes two years will elapse before the first leaf is developed, and then the blossom may not repay the care it has demanded ; but a graft from a handsome variety will make a fine plant.

The cutting should be taken from the base of a leaf, or at a joint, as soon as the wood is ripened, and placed in damp sand under glass. When it shows signs of growth, transplant it to a small pot filled with rich, dark soil. If you desire large flowers, allow only one bud to remain on each terminal shoot. The best time to graft the Camillia is from the middle of August to the middle of September. The chief care is in making a perfect junction of the parts, and carefully tying the graft in place. The graft having nothing to support it, must not only be firmly secured to the branch, but moisture and shade must be given it so as to promote its growth, and the roots must not be soddened with water.

Inarching, or grafting by approach, is generally done in July. A thin portion of the stock is sliced off, and a corresponding portion of the variety to be inarched. The slice should be made so deep that it will take off a slit of the stock, with bark attached, for about two inches; the graft is cut to fit exactly, and the parts fastened closely together and wound about with zephyr wool; moss can then be tied over it to keep it damp, and this must be moistened as it dries until they have grown together.

Camellias are most extensively grown in Philadelphia, New York, and Boston, by the florists, and are highly prized for house and table decorations, wedding ornaments, and funeral wreaths, crosses, and anchors.

The Double White, Fimbriata, Candidissima, Mont Blanc, and Alba Plena are all very desirable for window culture, and if their pure, spotless white flowers are protected from the sun they will retain their exquisite beauty for a fortnight. Among the colored varieties are :

Imbricata, crimson and white.
Landrethii, the richest rose color.
Dutchess of Orleans, striped pink and white.
Juliana, a rosy blush color.
Benneyii, crimson, striped with white.
Conspersa, striped carmine.
Prince Albert, pink, striped with rosy carmine.
Reine des Fleurs, of the richest crimson.
Sacco Nora, exquisite pink, blotched with rose.
Jubilee, rosy pink, striped with cherry color.
Storyi, a waxen rose color.

History, &c.—A sketch of the history of this flower calls up some very interesting facts. The Camellia Japonica was introduced into Europe by Father Kamel, a Moravian missionary who traveled in Asia, and saw the beautiful tree growing in China ; and the plant was Latinized into *Camellus* in honor of him.

Although brought from China, it is a native of Japan, whence its name *Japonica*, and belongs to the germs of the Tea Plant, the *Bohea* and *Virivis*, which supply the well-known black and green teas of commerce.

The first plants were brought to England in 1739, but they died from being treated as stove plants; yet the idea of them was given, and it only required time and perseverance to make them what they now are—the ornament of every greenhouse, conservatory, and window garden.

The commencement of the general culture of the Camellia began in 1792, when the single red variety was again imported from China. The double white and the variegated red were the next kinds introduced, and they were followed by the Waratah, or Anemone flowered, and the fringed white, the pale black, and the striped and variegated. The single white was not introduced until 1818. Mr. Fortune, who has traveled extensively in both China and Japan, and added many valuable plants to our collections, met with specimens of Camellias growing wild in the woods of Poo-to-san, some of which were tall trees, being from 25 to 30 feet high. Their glossy, evergreen foliage, and magnificent blossoms—red, white, buff, yellow, crimson, variegated, and blotched—render them one of the most beautiful features in an Oriental landscape. The trees are so plentiful in Japan and China that the seeds are used in cookery and medicine, and from one species an oil for anointing the hair is extracted.

Camellia Maliflora, or the apple-flavored Camellia, has beautiful little flowers resembling the apple blossoms in color and form, but are double. This species is more tender than the common kind. It was not introduced into England until 1816.

Camellia Sasanqua is still more tender, and has a small, single flower, like that of the green tea plant. It is more densely allied to that species, and its leaves are used for tea. The hybrids which have been produced from the Camellia Japonica are very numerous, and every year some new varieties are added to the catalogues.

CHAPTER XVI.

THE ROSE.

The romance of the Rose, and its exquisite loveliness, will never permit it to be left out of the window garden, notwithstanding the occasional trouble and difficulties of its culture.

THE ROSE IN ROMANCE.

Sappho says of it in one of her poetic strains: "If Zeus had willed to set a King over flowers, the Rose would have claimed that distinction. It is the ornament of the earth, the glory of the plants, the eye of the flowers, and the blush of the meadow.

Luther, in his admiration of it, says: "If a man could make a single Rose we should give him an Empire"—and he chose the Rose for the emblem on his seal.

In Germany there are various superstitions concerning the Rose, many of which are very singular, and the relation of the flower to blood is widely credited.

Thus one hears in France and Italy as well as Germany the saying that a drop of one's blood buried under a rosebush will bring rosy cheeks. There is a legend that the thorn crown of Christ was made from rose briar, and that the drops of blood which issued from His head fell to the ground and blossomed in Roses.

Mrs. Howe alludes to it in these lines:

"Men saw the thorns on Jesus' brow,
But angels saw the Roses."

In Ancient Greece there was an Academy whose statutes were couched in these words: "The Academicians think much, write little, and talk less."

A famous Professor desired to become a member, and when a vacancy occurred hastened to obtain it, but arrived too late—a candidate had been chosen. The Academy desired to number Dr. Zeb upon its rolls, but it had just granted to power what belonged to merit.

The President, not desiring to give a refusal in words, desired a cup of water to be brought, which he filled with water so that even one drop more would cause it to overflow. The doctor understood the emblem, but he saw at his feet a rose-leaf, which he placed upon the top of the water without displacing a drop

His ingenuity procured him the desired admission, and he was received by acclamation as a member of the Silent Academy.

The phrase "*sub-rosa*," implying secrecy, is said to have originated during the wars of York and Lancaster, when the red and white Roses played so prominent a part; but in ancient days it was the custom to suspend a Rose over the heads of the guests at banquets and feasts, to signify that the conservative was not to be repeated.

In mythology the Rose was dedicated to Harpocrates, the God of Silence.

When the Roman pontiff desired to confer a particular distinction upon a crowned head, he presented a consecrated Golden Rose. Both Henry VI and Henry VIII, of England, were honored in this manner.

Calture.

The list of varieties of Roses is very extended, reaching over 600 or 1,000. As many as 600 have been known to bloom in a single garden in this country, and in some nurseries 100,000 have been under propagation at one time.

The various sub-families of the Rose are numerous, yet for window gardening we need only to use the ever-blooming or monthly species, *Tea, China,* and *Bourbon.* Of these the Tea and China are the best adapted to winter flowering. They delight in a very rich soil, composed of decomposed sods and manure; cow manure is the best of all others for Roses, but it must be so decayed that it will crumble easily in the hand. They will grow in almost any soil, yet no plant requires a richer compost or better repays the cultivator for preparing it.

If the compost is heavy add enough sand to make it a little friable, but it prefers a rather stiff soil. When it is in rapid growth it requires a good supply of water, but not enough to make the soil too damp. When in a dormant state it needs but very little.

Roses that are transplanted from the garden require a time of rest, and it is much better after potting them to put them in a dark cellar where they can remain until February; then bring them up, prune away the old wood, and give them all the sunshine you can, for they require plenty of it to bloom in perfection. Amateurs fail in not pruning sufficiently; all the finest flowers are produced upon new shoots; so be sure to cut back the long, scraggy branches within three or four eyes of the main stem. There is no plant which requires such close pruning. Very few flowers are found upon the old wood, but are produced on the new, fresh shoots, and the branches sent up from the roots.

Roses are propagated by seeds, cuttings, layers, budding, and grafting. The process of growing them from seed is too slow for amateurs to care to attempt it, as the plants will not bloom for six or seven years.

Cuttings are the easiest means of cultivation, and fine bushes can be raised from them. The manner of growing them is described in Part I, the chapter on Propagation, and little can be added to it. They will strike much more certainly under glass and with bottom heat, but in May and June they can be grown in sand with but little attention.

Layers are made by " tongueing " a branch, and bending it carefully down to the soil, pressing the cut firmly into the ground, and twisting it a little, so that the end of the tongue may have a downward tendency in the ground. May, June, and July are the best months for layering, and by November they can be cut off from the parent plants within two inches of the tongue, and potted in small pots for the winter.

The Chinese mode of layering differs a little from ours. They select in July a strong shoot of the same year's growth, tongue it as described, cutting it just below a bud or joint, and put in a little pebble to keep the slit open. Then bind a ball of green moss around the tongue; keep the moss constantly moist, and roots will speedily shoot into it, and by six or seven weeks the layer will be ready to cut off; it should then be planted in rich soil, without disturbing the moss, and it can be sent, as a present to a friend, to any part of the country.

There is a diversity of opinion regarding the best time for pruning Roses, but M. Paul, the celebrated English Rose-grower, says :

" A Rose in vigorous condition, healthy and full of sap, requires less pruning than when it is of moderate or weak growth. The same degree of pruning, applied to each condition would produce opposite results. Close pruning would be the means of improving the health and flowering of a weak plant, while it would induce a strong one to form wood shoots rather than buds."

But it is a good rule to thin out the weak, unhealthy shoots, and even some of the stronger ones, as soon as the plant has done flowering. This allows it to make fresh roots, and then will follow new shoots and fresh buds.

When the plants are out of flower remove the soil to the depth of an inch, if you can do so without injuring the roots, and fill up with the richest soil you can procure. This treatment will cause a fresh, vigorous growth, and insure many buds to come. The decayed flowers should be at once removed, and the stems cut back.

Nothing but patient hand-picking and weekly showerings will keep away the green fly. In the Chapter of Part I, which treats upon " Insects," antidotes are given for all insects.

No plant thrives better under applications of liquid manure, but care must be taken not to give it so strong as to make all the leaves fall. A decoction of soot is also good for it. Dissolve a tablespoonful of it in two quarts of warm water, and apply to the roots once a week, and the growth of your plants will surprise you.

The Tea and China Roses are large shrubs in their native climes, and bloom profusely ; but our northern seasons do not allow them to grow so rapidly, yet they fill our hearts with much pleasure. The buds of these varieties are much handsomer than the expanded flowers, which are open in the centre, and frequently show the stamens, while the Hybrid Perpetuals are very double.

For winter flowering the following list embraces some of the best varieties :

TEA.

Aurora, rich yellow, shaded to rose.

Adam, deep rose, very sweet; shaded to salmon color; very large and full.

Bon Silene, a blending of purple and carmine.

Devoniensis, blush white; magnolia fragrance.

Clara Sylvain, snowy white; very extra.

Isabella Sprunt, a bright canary yellow.

La Pactole, light buff; the most abundant bloomer of any known.

Madame Maurin, purest white.

Pauline Lobante, light cream color.

Marechal Niel, the best yellow Tea Rose in cultivation; its perfume is unequaled, and its buds are perfection.

BENGAL, OR CHINA.

Agrippina, the deepest crimson, with an occasional stripe of white in the centre.

Bourbon Queen, rich blush; very fine.

Count de Rohan, purplish red.

Louis Philippe, rich, rosy crimson.

Madame Morel, cream color; centre pink.

Napoleon, blush; very large.

Virginale, rose and crimson

Vesuvius, deepest crimson.

Madame Rohan, pure white.

BOURBON.

Bouquet de Flore, deepest carmine; very fragrant.

Crimson Globe, purplish crimson.

Edward Desfosses, brightest rose.

Glory of Algiers, bright crimson.

Henri Plantier, deep pink; perfect form.

Hermosa, rosy pink flowers; a profuse bloomer, and general favorite.

Leveson Gower, salmon rose; very double and fine.

Phœnix, deepest rose, with the fragrance of the old fashioned Damask.

Psyche, light rose; very double.

Splendens, richest of crimson.

Souvenir de la Malmaison, flesh color; splendid.

Sombrienil, blush white; strong grower; very fine.

Vicomte de Cassy, cherry red; extra

Vulcan, dark shade of carmine.

NOISETTE.

Aimee Vibert, one of the best white roses under cultivation.

Chromatella, deepest yellow; very delicate.

Gloire de Dijon, blush white; buff centre.

Lamarque, white; yellowish centre; very fine.

Minette, light crimson; very double, and large clusters of flowers.

Ophirie, salmon, shaded to orange color.

Susanna, yellowish white ; very fine.

Souvenir d' Anselem, deep carmine.

Sir Walter Scott, dark purple.

Solfaterre, deep straw color ; extra fine.

Washington, pure white; semi-double ; full clusters.

Triumphant, double rose ; very large.

Wells' Pink, carmine rose ; full clusters.

Zobeide, crimson, and purple shaded.

For City Gardens,

Choose those varieties that are strongest growers and freest bloomers.

Of crimson varieties, the best recommended are *Agrippina, Gen. Washington,* and *Giant of Battles.*

 Of Pink—*Formosa and Eugenie.*

  Yellow—*Sabrona, Mme. Falcot.*

  White—*Mme. Maurin, Sombriel.*

  Carmine—*La Phenix, C. Bobeistsky.*

  Straw color—*La Pactola, Isabella Sprunt.*

  Blush—*Pauline, Fleur de Cymes.*

Climbing Roses are our favorite plant for adorning piazzas, balconies, pillars, and the outer decorations of the window. The usual varieties are Baltimore Belle, Prairie Queen, Fulgens, and Gem of the Prairies.

A fact worth noticing in the window culture of plants, is that the delicate varieties of China and Tea need a light soil. Mr. Parkman recommends a mixture of loam, manure, leaf mould, and sand, in the proportion of two bushels of loam to one bushel of manure, one of leaf mould, and one-half a bushel of sand; but for the more robust growers the proportions of loam and manure should be greater.

One of the favorite methods for producing flowers in early winter, is to take the autumnal flowering varieties, clip off their blossoms as soon as they appear until they are ready to transfer to the window, and then permit them to bloom at freedom.

Of the different classes of Roses, the China are the most easily managed, yet are less fragrant than the *Tea,* and not equal in beauty, still fully as abundant in bloom, which constitutes their chief merit.

Of Tea Scented Roses, none are more delicate than the Devoniensis, with its large double form and light yellow, its only fault being shyness of bloom.

The Glorie de Dijon, however, is most suitable for training over the supports, columns, or rafters of greenhouses and conservatories ; a very robust grower.

The *Bourbon* varieties are of great value for window use or forcing purposes, being both free bloomers, and having fine forms and brilliant colors. The strongest of them need to be well pruned back, especially the ends of the largest shoots, which, when cut off, will develop fine side branches. They have rich, luxuriant foliage, and flowers are produced in large clusters, very fragrant and lasting. The finest variety of this class, and unsurpassed among all Roses, is the *Souvenir de La Malmaison,* a very large flower, of full and beautiful form, light flesh or fawn color; needs to be well drained.

The *Noisette* Roses are distinctive specially for their blooming in clusters, partaking the nature of true climbers, and usually quite vigorous. The Aimie Vibert is the prettiest of the group; flowers purest white, borne in large clusters. The *Lamarque* is a universal favorite among greenhouse owners; flowers pale lemon yellow, very large, double, and beautiful; growth very vigorous.

CHAPTER XVII.

The Fuchsia.   The Myrtle.

These graceful flowers have a curious history. They are natives of South America, and were first brought to England nearly a hundred years ago. Mr. Lee, a well-known English florist, introduced them to the public in 1774. A customer purchasing plants of him said: "I saw, in a window at Wapping, a prettier flower than all your greenhouses can produce. The flowers hung like tassels from the drooping branches; their color was of the richest crimson, and in the centre were folded leaves of the brightest Tyrian purple dye."

Mr. Lee enquired the exact locality where this rare novelty was to be seen, and hastened to behold it. At a glance he knew its worth. Entering the house he told its mistress that he would pay any price that she chose to ask for her plant. No, she could not sell it; it had been brought by her sailor boy from over the sea, and for his sake she cherished it.

Mr. Lee must have it; so he emptied his pockets of their contents of gold, silver, and copper, amounting in all to over eight guineas. Placing them on her table, he said:

"All this money is yours, and the plant mine. I'll give you one of the first cuttings I raise; and when your boy returns the plant will be quite as handsome as this one."

Money always has a potent force, and the woman reluctantly consented, and Mr. Lee hastened away with his treasure. He cut it into joints, these he forced in hot beds, and the smallest branch took root. Every effort was employed to increase his stock, and in two months he had three hundred plants growing finely.

As soon as the first plant bloomed the pot was exhibited in his show window. A lady of rank was the first visitor; she was delighted with the loveliness and grace of the flower, and must have the plant, for which she gladly paid one guinea. That night the Duchess entertained friends, and her rare plant was much admired. The following day Mr. Lee had many visitors, but only two plants were in bloom.

Others were engaged, however, and before the summer closed he had made three hundred guineas from the Fuchsia. Since that time one cannot estimate the amount of money that has been expended upon these plants, nor the time and patience that has been given to their culture; but the results are seen in the hundreds of varieties now offered for sale, and they increase yearly in size and beauty of coloring, and popular favor. The variety from which they originated is now rarely seen; its flowers are small and its foliage very different from those we now cultivate. Although so insignificant, when compared to its gorgeous sisters, yet its fragile flowers press beautifully, and they are great acquisitions in a bouquet or wreath of pressed flowers.

Culture.

Fuchsias do not require a high temperature; a very warm, dry atmosphere is not favorable to their growth, but they need light and air—not so much the direct rays of the sun as roses and geraniums—but if kept in too dark a situation they will loose their leaves and drop their buds.

Good rich soil is needed for luxuriant growth, and well rotted turf mixed with peat, is quite to their taste; the dark soil from the forests, composed in a great degree of leaf mould, with a little sand added to it, will make them grow luxuriously. A *Seratifolia* and a *Speciosa* have grown three feet high in one winter in such a soil, and they were covered with a wealth of buds and flowers. Their growth was magnificent! The above named are winter flowering varieties, and will bloom in window gardens from nine to ten months in the year.

The Fuchsia is a gross feeder, and requires a good deal of room for its roots when it is growing rapidly. It can be planted in small pots, and as the branches increase, watch the roots and do not let the plants become root bound.

Two years old plants will bloom profusely—often having hundreds of flowers upon them—but they must have liquid manure once a week to be grown in perfection.

When raised from cuttings, they strike quickly in damp sand, and should be transplanted into rich soil, in three inch pots. In two weeks tie the main branch to a small stick and train the plant into a symmetrical shape. When the branches are two or three inches long pinch out their tips, and two or three branches will start from each one.

A really beautiful plant of handsome shape is obtained only by care. The accompanying illustration, Fig. 72, is a specimen out of thirty others grown from a small cutting in twelve months. The cutting selected should be strong, healthy and woody, with no less than three or four joints; each leaf should be pulled off, and then set the cutting two or three inches in the soil, and about one inch out. The proper temperature is 55° to 65°; atmosphere moderately moist; use rainwater of same temperature as the atmosphere.

Many persons prefer to have young plants every year or two, and let the old ones die away. But the old plants can be judiciously managed, and make very pretty plants for years to come. Set them in the cellar until late in January; let them lose every leaf; then take up, and cut back severely. If you want a pyramidal shape cut back all the branches, and some of the top also.

If you like an umbrella shaped plant, choose the drooping kinds, and cut off the lower branches close to the main stem, within two or three feet of the pot; then cut the branches next higher up, to within a few inches of the stem, and cut the top off entirely. Turn out of the pots and trim some of the straggling roots, and put it in a twelve to fourteen inch pot; prepare soil of rotted turf and hot bed manure, or well decomposed cow manure, with a small handful of sand.

When potted, water with warm water, and thoroughly sprinkle once a week.

Fig. 72.—A well grown Specimen Plant of the Fuchsia. (From a Photograph.)

Always encourage the main stem to grow straight, and tie it to a stake; then form your plant as you please. Often you will have to cut back so as to make a skeleton from which the branches can start as you choose to have them.

Fuchsias are greatly troubled with the red spider, and for antidotes consult chapter on Insects, Part I.

When the plants are in the cellar they will not need any water, but when growing rapidly and flowering, they desire a good supply, yet not too much; don't keep them soaking or let them become dry; either condition will make them drop their buds.

In training plants due heed should be paid to their natural habits. A plant like the Pride of England—which always grows like a shrub—cannot be forced into the umbrella or spreading form; while those like the Souvenir de Chiswick, naturally inclined to the tree-shape, cannot be forced into a shrub. They must follow out their own peculiar habits to thrive well. In California they bloom every month in the year, and grow as tall as the honeysuckles of the Atlantic coast. The Double Fuchsias are most beautiful, and when studded all over with their gorgeous wealth of pendant floral gems, are unsurpassed by any other flower. They are not inclined to bloom in the winter, but if all their buds are pinched off, and they are kept in the shade, and little water given until October or November, they will bloom in January and February.

The varieties are very numerous, and yearly the florists produce new ones. They are raised from seeds by most careful hy-

Fig. 73.—A Fuchsia trained in Umbrella form.

bridization, and they will bloom in two years. The seeds require careful treatment, bottom heat, and a gardener's care to germinate well; but a young child can raise a cutting, so easy is its culture. There are no plants which more fully repay the attention you may give them; and they are so graceful and attractive that they strike even the dullest eye with admiration.

The Fuchsia was named in honor of Leonard Fuchs, a German botanist of repute.

The most desirable varieties besides those already named, are:

Single Fuchsias.

Arabella, white sepals, with rich rose corolla; the best early variety.

Brilliant, purple globular-shaped corolla, scarlet sepals.

Charming, large violet, saucer shaped corolla, with scarlet sepals.

Conquest, bright scarlet sepals, corolla, rich dark purple; very free bloomer.

Conspicua, snowy white corolla, with bright-scarlet sepals; very beautiful.

Empress, long, white corolla, with rich crimson sepals; extra fine.

First of the Day, scarlet sepals, with well expanded lavender corolla.

Father Ignatius, brilliant carmine sepals, with rich indigo blue corolla.

Evening Star, blush sepals, with pinkish scarlet corolla.

Lustre, vivid crimson corolla, sepals waxy white; free bloomer.

Minstrel, pink sepals, with rosy lavender corolla.

Marginata, white sepals with pink corolla, edged with deep rose-color.

Freund J. Durr, richest scarlet sepals, with purple corolla, the stamens changing to petals.

Prince Imperial, corolla dark purple, sepals bright scarlet; the earliest of the dark varieties.

Rose of Castile, sepals blush white, purplish corolla, changing to crimson.

Rhoderic Dhu, very large lavender blue corolla, sepals salmon-tinted scarlet.

Starlight, pure waxy white sepals, clear bright lake pink corolla.

War Eagle, sepals rich crimson, corrolla very largely expanded, of a dark purple striped with rose.

Double Fuchsias—Select List.

Elm City, rich crimson sepals, with dark purple corolla, fully double,

Emperor of the Fuchsias, white corolla large and fine, sepals crimson.

Giant, immense double purple corolla, with bright rose sepals.

Gloire des Blanc, snowy white corolla, crimson sepals.

Madame Crouse, white corolla, very long, scarlet sepals.

Marksman, sepals bright carmine, corolla very large, of a rich dark violet; extra fine.

Norfolk Giant, deep purple corolla, with scarlet sepals.

Queen of Whites, pure white corolla, very double, with crimson sepals.

Surpasse V. de Puebla, scarlet sepals, with white corolla veined with scarlet; extra fine.

Symbol, crimson sepals much reflexed, creamy white double corolla, very beautiful.

For a select list choose *Lustre, Rhoderic Dhu, Elm City, Marksman*. These four are the best of the entire collection.

The Myrtle.

The use of the Myrtle for decorations reminds us of the esteem with which it was held by the ancient Greeks, who dedicated it to Venus, the goddess of beauty. Its leaves were used to improve the flavor of wine, and to increase its invigorating properties, while its berries were taken as a medicine. Garlands of it were woven to adorn the brows of their chief magistrates, and it was always used to crown the dead. The early Christians continued this custom, but it was prohibited on account of its use by the idolaters; yet the Myrtle has always been retained as a religious decoration, and, in Germany, composes the bridal wreath. The Italians have a great passion for this plant, preferring its odors to that of the most precious essences, and their baths are often perfumed with water distilled from its leaves, as it is considered a promoter of beauty.

In Australia the Myrtle grows to a great size, having a large stem or trunk, and sometimes it is one hundred feet in height.

The Myrtle we cultivate is that spoken of in the Bible, and the Jews still regard it with veneration, and always use it to adorn the Feast of the Tabernacles —literally obeying the command of Nehemiah to " Fetch olive, pine and myrtle."

Culture.

There is a broad leaved variety, a narrow leaved, the box myrtle, and the Chinese. The last named produces purple flowers, the others bear pure double white flowers, and are always most lovely shrubs for window gardens.

It does not flourish in a close hot temperature, but will bear a cool, shady window, with a northerly exposure. It needs fresh air and frequent washings, to grow luxuriantly. It does not form roots rapidly, like the Rose and Fuchsia, so will not require repotting often; and yet do not let it become root-bound, for that will check its blooming. It is propagated by cuttings, which will soon strike under glass, and with a little bottom heat, but not so quickly without them. This plant was formerly to be seen in all window gardens. Why it is not more common now we do not understand, unless it be that the Ivy is more popular.

The cuttings should be made with four or five buds or joints, and covered an inch under the sand. When it begins to show fresh leaves, pot it in good, rich sandy loam, in a three or four inch pot, and keep it shaded for nearly a week. The best soil is two parts loam, and one part rotten dung. It blooms early in June.

The Periwinkle or Vinca, is sometimes called Running Myrtle, because of its evergreen leaves, which resemble those of the broad leaved myrtle.

It grows luxuriously in the open garden; is perfectly hardy, and can be transplanted into a large sea-shell or any hanging vase filled with good loam; water it weekly with some stimulant, and it will flourish beautifully; and early in February place every one with its lovely lavender chalices opening to the sun. It delights in moisture, so must never be allowed to become dry.

The *M. communis* is the usual sort chosen for window use, having many varieties with leaves both large and small, variegated flowers, single or double. But the Chinese species, *M. tomentosa*, has also claims for popularity, on account of its vari-colored blooms from purple to white, and other shades between; often many colored flowers on the same plant.

CHAPTER XVIII.

The Heliotrope.

The celebrated JUSSIEU, while botanizing in the Cordilleras, suddenly inhaled the most delicious odors. He looked eagerly about to discover their origin, expecting to find some brilliantly colored flower, but only perceived some large bushes bearing clusters of flowers of a pale lavender hue. On coming nearer he observed that the flowers turned towards the sun. Struck with this peculiarity, he gave the plant the name of Heliotrope, which is derived from the Greek words signifying "sun," and "I turn." Delighted with the charming acquisition, the learned botanist collected a quantity of seeds and sent them to the *Jardin du Roi*, at Paris, where it was first cultivated in Europe, in 1757.

It soon became a treasured household flower, and is found in every window garden and bouquet. Three species have since been introduced from the south of Europe and Asia.

The Heliotrope has been called emblematical of flattery. The Orientals say, that its perfumes elevate their souls toward heaven.

It is prized more for its fragrance than the beauty of its flowers; though *Voltaireanum* has deep purple flowers that are very handsome, and many of the later varieties are rich in coloring as well as in perfume.

The cottagers of England used to call it " cherry pie," from a fancied resemblance of the fragrance of the flower to the odor of nicely cooked cherries. The variety introduced by *Jussieu* was called *Heliotropium Peruvianum,* and is still cultivated; and it was many years before much change of color was effected in the flower, and now its shades are either lighter or of a rich purple. It will bloom the whole season; is never without flowers in California, where it grows in immense bushes, and blooms most luxuriantly.

It is a favorite with every one, as its odors are not so strong as those of many other flowers, and pervade the atmosphere to a small extent. The older the plant, the more profuse are its flowers, but it must be kept in a healthy condition to bloom in perfection.

Cuttings grown in open borders become very rank and succulent, but if kept over the next season, this disappears and a woody stem succeeds it.

They can be grown as standards and make fine showy plants. Prune off all the lower branches, and let a single leading stem remain, with a head of several feet in diameter. *Peruvianum* is well adapted to train in this manner, for when the plant is three or four years old its branches assume a drooping habit.

These plants require close pruning to flower profusely. If you desire to keep the plant for winter flowering, do not turn it out of the pot, but keep it in a sunny location, and in August trim off a great many of its branches, then the young growth will push forth, and by January it will be covered with blossoms.

It will flower in a warm atmosphere, from 68° to 70°, but it can bear a heat of 50° and do well. The green fly never touches it, but the red spider will sometimes ruin it; yet frequent spongings will keep it away. It likes a good, rich soil, with a moderate admixture of sand.

Cuttings root very easily, either in sand or vials of water, and if struck in March will make fine plants by another winter.

They must have the sun; they cannot grow in a shady location. The varieties vary considerably in habit, some being of rampant, robust growth, while others are dwarf and compact.

The freest bloomers are:

Boule de Niege, blush white.
Alexina, deep bluish purple.
Corymbosa, dwarf, light lavender.
Gem, dark bluish purple.
Jane Mesmer, rich dark purple.
Triumphe de Guascoi, robust growth, pale lilac.
Madame Parker, very dark purple.
Madame Rendatler, very bushy, light lavender.
Jersey Belle, dwarf and compact, lavender.
Voltaireanum, bluish purple.

The Lantana.

This plant was given the ancient name of the *Viburnum,* because its foliage resembled it. It was brought from the West Indies in 1692. The flowers are a little like those of the verbena, but change in color from yellow to a deep orange and red, or from yellow to a rich rose-color. The florists have experimented with it, and produced many new varieties, among them a pure white flower, which is much admired. It grows very robust in a rich but sandy loam, and needs plenty of sun and water when in flower. It is propagated either by seeds or cuttings. The latter can be started in April or May, either in water or sand, and will make large plants by another spring.

This plant can bear the knife well, and can be trained into a graceful shape. It needs repotting every spring, and then is the time to prune it, and shorten in the branches. Towards autumn give less water to harden the wood. If large plants are desired to be kept through the winter for bedding out another summer, place them in a cool cellar, frost proof, however, and let them remain until March without any water, unless the soil become dust dry; but in a damp and perfectly dark cellar this rarely occurs.

The handsomest varieties for window gardens are:

Lantana Alba grandiflora, large flowered white.
Crocea superba, brilliant orange turning to scarlet.

Comtesse Mory, blush turning to rose.
Fillonii, yellow, changing to purple.
Fulgens mutalilis, scarlet and yellow.
Garibaldi, lilac.
Imperatrice Eugenie, blush and white
Snowball, purest of white.
Surpasse, lilac, with yellow.
Zanthena, scarlet buff and lemon-color.

The Hoya, or Wax Plant.

This plant will thrive splendidly in a close, hot room. It does not require much moisture, but loves heat. It is a fine plant to droop over pictures or train about windows. The pot can be placed on a high shelf near a window, and the branches trained so that they will have the warm air at the top of the room.

The Hoya requires a soil of peat, loam and a little sand, and if liquid manure is given every fortnight it will not need repotting oftener than four or five years, as it does not root vigorously.

The flower stalks bloom anew year after year, so they should not be cut off when the petals drop.

The best way of propagating this plant is by layers, though cuttings can sometimes be started with much bottom heat.

The leaves are of a deep, waxy green, and the flowers are cream-colored, with dark chocolate stamens, and possess a peculiar fragrance, often likened to the odor of fresh baked bread. They bloom in full clusters, and secrete a honey-like juice.

The Hoya is not commonly cultivated, yet it merits attention.

CHAPTER XIX.

The Geranium.

The improvement in the Geranium by English and American florists, both in the size of the individual flower, or their clusters, or their foliage, are really wonderful when compared with the flowers of fifteen years ago.

Frequently the single flower is now as large as a silver quarter of a dollar, and the trusses will often measure over six inches in diameter, while colors are seen from the purest white to most delicate rose, brilliant scarlet, richest crimson, loveliest salmon-color, and striped pink and white.

The foliage is also much improved; it is margined with gold or silver, zoned with chocolate, white, black, crimson, and gold, and in a few choice varieties, like *Lady Cullum* and *Madame Pollock;* nearly all these colors may be seen in one separate leaf.

Their habits are also changed from the straggling growth of former times, to dwarf, compact shrubs, which are in perfect shape.

The florist's skill has taken still another step, and produced the Double Flowered Geranium, whose individual flowers are double as a Chrysanthemum, and do not drop their petals as the single varieties, but each flower withers on its stem; and by cutting it off the other flowers fill its place, and the beauty of the cluster is preserved for a long season. These varieties run through the same series of colors as single species, although a pure snowy white has not yet been produced, but a peach blossom variety shows that the white will soon appear.

The flower clusters are often enormous—sixty flowers having been produced on one truss—and they are exceedingly beautiful for bouquets, baskets, and vases.

With the other improvements have come a Lilliputian variety with smaller foliage, and a compact, dwarf growth, very vigorous in habit, while the flowers equal in beauty those of the taller varieties.

The Ivy-leaved species have yielded to the effects of hybridizing with the zonale class, and the results are great improvements in the foliage, variegating the leaves with yellow, pink and white, while the flowers have increased in size and color, and approach nearer to those of the Zonales.

The sweet-scented Geraniums have also increased in number, and a variegated leaved Rose Geranium has been introduced whose foliage is very attractive.

These different varieties are propagated by seeds and cuttings chiefly. The seeds require sandy soil and warmth to vegetate, but will sometimes spring up of themselves in the open ground.

Cuttings are easily struck, as recommended in Part I.

The plants require plenty of sun, air, water; a rich loamy soil, with weekly waterings of liquid manure, and a season of rest. A good compost is made of one-half two years old manure, and one-half good fresh loam.

For winter blooming, the plants should be repotted early in September; shake all the earth away from the roots, prune back the tops closely, and cut in the branches with due regard to the shape of the plants. Press the fresh earth closely around the soil, and keep the plants shaded for a week or so, then give more sun and water, and by December they will be stocky, thrifty plants, with buds well set, which will keep in bloom for many months.

They do not require a warm temperature, and should be kept cool at night, and ought not to be crowded as they want a free circulation of air through the branches and leaves; but draughts of air will injure them. When the buds begin to show they need to be stimulated with liquid manure.

In summer, when the weather is close and hot, it is well to keep saucers under the pots, and give water twice a day, as the foliage will wilt and become injured if the roots get dry, and they do not need the noonday sun; are better if shaded from it.

It is difficult to give lists of the very best when all are so good, but a few choice varieties are herewith appended:

ZONALE GERANIUMS.

Azucena, salmon-color shaded to white, large flower.

Cheerful, bright cherry-color.

Christine, richest rosy pink, nosegay variety.

Distinction, brilliant carmine, bordered with white.

Gloire de Corbenay, bright salmon pink, tipped with white.

Knight of the Garter, deepest orange scarlet, marked with pink, nosegay variety.

Cybister, the most dazzling scarlet nosegay.

Madame Chandon, bright rose-color, extra large flower.

Madame Paul Hibon, white ground, bordered and veined with blood-red; extra.

Madame Chate, salmon-color, marked with white, and bordered with rose-color.

Ne plus Ultra, pure rose, spotted with white.

Snowball, purest white, dwarf habit.

Vicomtesse de Flavigny, bright rose, marked with white; extra flower.

Madame Dupanloup, blush white, nosegay.

TRICOLOR GERANIUMS.

Lady Cullum, margined with gold, mingled with crimson, and bronze; scarlet flowers.

Mrs. Pollock, zone of red, belted with crimson and gold-color; scarlet flowers.

Sir Robert Napier, broad, black zone indented with brilliant scarlet, and margined with gold flowers, peach-color, with rose centre.

Sophie Dumaresque, chocolate zone, margined with golden yellow; scarlet flower.

Beauty of Oulton, broad, bronze zone, on a yellow green leaf; flowers cerise scarlet.

Beauty of Calderdale, broad zone of a reddish bronze, margined with yellow; scarlet flowers.

Italia Unita, broad, white margin; flowers scarlet.

Sunset, ground color, golden yellow, veined with crimson, black and green.

Mountain of Snow, pure white margined leaves, scarlet flowers.

LILLIPUTIAN ZONALE.

Baby Boy, scarlet, white eye.
Beauty of Sureenes, rich shade of pink.
Bridesmaid, rosy salmon-color.
Cybester, orange crimson.
Little Dear, delicate rose, with white spots.
Little Gem, brilliant vermilion, white centre.
Pretty Jemima, brilliant scarlet, white eye.

DOUBLE FLOWERING.

Conseiller Ragon, rich orange red, very fine.
Capt La Hermite, rich scarlet.
Andrew Henderson, brightest cherry scarlet.
Jeanne de St. Maur, bright dazzling vermilion.
Le Vesuve, very double scarlet flowers, habit dwarf and compact.
Ferre Promise, a bright satiny red, dwarf, bushy growth.
Emile Lemoine, crimson scarlet flowers, very double.
Marie Lemoine, rosy pink, very fine dwarf.
William Pfitzer, orange scarlet-color.
Victor Lemoine, brightest scarlet, dwarf and bushy.
Triomphe de Lorraine, rosy carmine, striped with white.

SWEET SCENTED.

Under this head are comprised the several varieties of Rose-scented
Rose Capitatum.
Capitatum Major, large leaf, rose.
Denticulatum, cut leaf, rose.
Odoratissimum, apple-scented.
Doratissimum-erectum, nutmeg-scented.
Shrubland Pet, variegated foliage.

Lady Plymouth, variegated foliage, rose scented.
Dr. Livingston, lemon-scented.
Quercifolium, eximum, oak-leaved.

Ivy-Leaved Geraniums.

Aurea variegata, golden margined.
Lateripes, the common variety, white flowers.
L'Elegante, brilliant green foliage, with broad bands of creamy white, pure white flowers ; extra handsome.
Duke of Edinburgh, (Hollywreath,) variegated with gold and silver margins; pink flowers.

The Pelargonium.

Pelargoniums are also among the most beautiful plants we have for house culture. Fifteen years ago, or more, great attention was paid to their cultivation, and veined, spotted and white flowers, which rivaled the Pansy in size and beauty of coloring, were yearly the pride and boast of the florist. Of late years the Zonale and Double Flowered Geraniums have been more attended to, but they can never equal the flowers of the Pelargonium.

They are natives of the Cape of Good Hope, and trace their name to the resemblance of the Capsules to the Stork's bill ; hence from *pelargos,* the Latin for Stork, comes the title. Nothing can surpass the richness of coloring of these flowers.

Mr. Henderson places it as his first choice. " If I were confined to grow but a single genus of plants for conservatory decoration, the Pelargonium would be chosen." Their hues are in every shade of scarlet, crimson, cherry, pink, purple to lilac and white, while they are blotched, marbled and spotted with velvety black, maroon, and all its shades.

Their growth is very vigorous, and they require repotting both spring and fall to bloom in full perfection.

They are most charming flowers for all kinds of grouping, and their colors blend and mingle in great beauty.

They are easy of culture, but require a rich soil to flourish well. Cuttings rooted in the spring make large plants by autumn. The old roots can be wintered in pots or boxes in the cellar, and brought forward to light and heat in March, and should not be allowed to wilt for want of water.

New varieties are raised from seeds sown as soon as ripe, or in March or April. When the fourth or fifth leaves are well developed transplant into three inch pots.

Some of the newest varieties are :

Belle of the Ball, rose-color, veined, and blotched with crimson.
Butterfly, deepest crimson with black spots and veins.
Captivation, purest white, blotched with deep crimson.
Emperor, lower petals nearly white, upper ones dark maroon.

Eugene Duval, light purple with dark blotches.
General Taylor, carmine with crimson spots.
Grand Duchess Stephanie, brilliant carmine with very dark blotches.
Invincible, crimson, veined with white.
L'Avenir, rosy scarlet, striped with white.
Monarch, maroon, crimson and rose.
Madame Leroy, violet purple, with bluish lilac centre.
Sunrise, delicate scarlet and crimson, with dark blotches.
Unique Miellez, cherry scarlet.

CHAPTER XX.

THE OLEANDER; BOUVARDIA; MAHERNIA ODORATA.

The Oleander is a native of the Holy Land, and Keble alludes to it as follows:

"In the flowery land of Palestine it is always found wherever rivers or water courses invite its thirsty roots.

The banks of the Jordan are clothed with this beautiful plant, aptly styled "a gem among flowers; and it blooms at the overflow of that river, its roots being then partly immersed in water; yet it will endure the extreme heat and baked soil of an Eastern summer when the brooks and rivers are shrunk into the narrowest streams."

A rich turfy loam must be provided for it to grow in, and from the end of September until March or April, it should receive no more water than will prevent the soil from being crumbly; and during the rest of the year it should have a most bountiful supply, and the tub or pot should be immersed in a saucer or a half tub filled with water.

It is very easily propagated by cuttings during the spring or summer months. They should be taken from the young shoots and cut off close under the fourth joint, cutting off the three lower leaves, but without injuring the bark of the stem.

The most simple way of rooting them is in vials of rainwater, hung in the windows of a warm room. The cuttings should not be deeper in the water than half way up to the second joint. In a short time tiny white roots will make their appearance, and when these are about half an inch long, take it carefully out and pot in light sandy soil; keep moist and shaded from the sun until the bright color of the leaves show that the roots are growing.

Water and warmth will produce roots rapidly, but cannot sustain growth. So when cuttings are rooted in water, they should be transplanted as soon as the rootlets are from half an inch to an inch in length.

Dwarf Oleanders that will flower the succeeding spring, when not over a foot high, can be produced as follows:

Early in September or October, according to your climate, cut three to four joints from a topmost branch, leaving a joint at the end, strip off the leaves, take a six inch pot filled with turfy loam, and a little moss at the bottom of the pot, press it firmly in, and make holes around the edge of the pot about an inch and a half apart, pour into each hole half an inch of sand, and plant the cuttings firmly in it. Cover the top of the pot an inch deep with sand, saturate the whole with water, and see that each cutting is fixed and immovable without a strong pull. Upon the close contact of cutting and soil depends half of your success. Keep in a temperature not over 50° during the winter, and among the cuttings will be found several which have the heads of future bloom in the upper leaves, and the perfect flowers will expand by April or May.

Of course the cuttings must not be allowed to become dry. Most plants collect during the summer a greater store of nutriment than is required for their support during the winter; so if cuttings of Oleander, Hydrangeas, Cacti, etc., are taken late in the season, they possess quite a store of nutriment, and will grow better, and flower more profusely.

The only trouble is that these late cuttings require more care to keep them alive during the winter than if they had been made in the spring, but where there is no difficulty, there is no honor.

Bouvardia.

These winter blooming plants are invaluable in every conservatory or indoor garden. They are of a shrubby character, of the easiest culture and becoming exceedingly popular. They have the merit of being free bloomers, flowering in clusters of varied colors from pink to crimson, scarlet and white, and their flowers are considered excellent for bouquets. As plants for the decoration of the lawn, also, it is doubtful if they have any superior. In outdoor culture they will bloom from August down until cold weather, and if lifted within doors before frost, they will continue blooming down until March.

They are popular with every florist on account of their profusion of bloom, and the number and excellence of varieties seems to increase yearly. Still they are little known in any of our country homes or family flower gardens. They are essentially lovers of the hot house during the winter, needing a temperature at night of 55° to flower well.

They are propagated chiefly from pieces of the roots, as cuttings do not grow easily; yet it is best for all amateurs at first to procure their plants already started, and then by degrees learn the art of reproduction.

The plants require training, and the tops should be nipped off frequently in the summer to give them a bushy shape. They are also tender, and a slight chill only will prove injurious. Give them a good supply of water when in full flower, less in summer.

The usual method of culture is to let them grow during the summer in the common garden border ; then in the fall lift them, pack very closely in sand filled boxes, and store in the cellar to keep through the winter. If desired to bloom during the winter, cut back one-half the wood, water sparingly, place in the cellar for six weeks, then bring to the heat and light, give a copious watering, and in a few days you will have a fine bloom.

The soil for potting should be loam, leaf mould, peat, and a little sprinkling of silver sand ; pot firmly. If you wish immediate bloom, let the plants stand out doors in the fall, two weeks before you bring them to the conservatory, and then you will soon be repaid by numerous clusters of bright, sweet-scented flowers.

Our list of varieties, by constant improvement, has become quite excellent, but originally there were only two principal varieties, *B. Leiantha* and *Hogarth Angustifolie* has flowers of a very rich orange scarlet, a dwarf growth and neat foliage. It blooms constantly during the summer.

Hogarth, bright scarlet, long tube, and splendid raceme, a very vigorous grower, and fine habit.

Elegans, a sport from the Hogarth, light scarlet carmine, with the novelty and merit of flower trusses, of immense size, sometimes measuring 4 to 5 inches in diameter. Comes true from root cuttings.

Leianthe, bright dazzling scarlet; an old, well known, and desirable variety.

Jasminoides, a most valuable acquisition, discovered in a private collection of plants in London, England, origin unknown, but supposed to have been produced from seeds sent from South America. Its merits consist chiefly in its ease of propagation. By cutting, its growth is rapid, yielding an abundance of flowers of waxy whiteness, said to resemble the jasmine in appearance and fragrance.

For bouquets and baskets of cut flowers florists esteem it invaluable.

Vreelandii, a sport from Hogarth, pure white, a compact and vigorous grower, profuse bloomer, bearing tresses of largest size, readily propagated from root or top cuttings; considered by many to rank at the head of the white varieties.

Jasminoides compaeta, dwarf habit, white flower, yields a very agreeable fragrance, and quite a profuse bloomer. Both this and the Jasminoides are very valuable for vases and drawing room boquets.

Mahernia.

A delicate little plant, always pleasing with its freedom of bloom. It is more properly called Hermannia, named in honor of Hermann, a Dutch Botanist, yet among florists its popular name of Mahernia is still retained. Nothing can be more lovely than a pot of it in full bloom, thickly hung with its lemon-colored bell-shaped flowers, which possess the most delicious odor, resembling that of the Lily of the Valley.

It is easily raised by cutting started in damp sand, and when they have struck, transplanted to pots filled with a peaty loam.

It likes moisture, but not too much of it, and an application of liquid manure should be made once a week or so. The *Odorata* is the variety usually grown, although there are other kinds, Hector and Diana, orange and pink. If too luxuriant, pinch in unsparingly.

CHAPTER XXI.

THE VERBENA, PETUNIA, PYRETHRUM.

Bedding plants like these are not to be recommended generally for window culture, still window gardeners will have them, and we can only give directions for their culture.

Very great improvements have been made in the last few years in the Verbena, both in the size of the individual flowers and the form of its clusters; also in the great variety of its brilliant colors of crimson, scarlet, lilac, bluish purple, and all their intermediate shades, with eyes of white, deep crimson, rose, purple, and yellow, and still others are striped and spotted.

They are great lovers of the sun, will not thrive without it, yet will not grow in the hot, dry atmosphere of many sitting rooms, but require a cool room during the winter months, and a goodly share of fresh air when the frost is not in it.

When grown as a house plant they must be placed close to the glass, and the mercury should not be over 50° during the day and less than 45° at night, until March. They do not like moisture in the winter, but should be kept a little dry; when you do water, give a good supply, and pour away all that falls into the saucer.

Shower the foliage weekly, to keep it clear of the green fly which injures it greatly. The Verbena Mite, which produces the "black rust" upon these plants, is also very destructive to them, but plentiful showerings and washings will keep it way.

These plants are particular as to soil, blooming plentifully in sandy or clayey loam, if it is enriched with well decayed manure, or liquid stimulants.

The young shoots root very rapidly, and they are to be selected to make plants for window gardens. The reason why many fail to keep them through the winter is, that they attempt to keep the old plants, or layers from them, instead of striking cuttings in September or October from entire new growth.

The sulphate of ammonia is an excellent fertilizer for Verbenas, giving the foliage a dark green, healthy appearance, and it is easily prepared and applied. Dissolve one ounce of the ammonia in four gallons of warm water; it can be given once a week. Keep the soil well stirred up in the pots; this is very essential to the healthy growth of all pot plants, for their roots must have air to flourish well.

The cuttings should be pinched back to keep the plants stocky and robust.

In raising them from seeds, the soil should be very sandy, and kept uniformly moist; the seeds should also be soaked before sowing. When the second row of leaves is well developed transplant the seedlings into shallow boxes.

As a plant for a vase, either outdoors or indoors, the Verbena has few equals, its bright cheerful colors and steady bloom being well calculated to please the fancy of any one.

Many Verbenas are grown in the house during the summer season, although more pretty in the open garden border. Yet we suppose every one has their fancy and like to keep something pretty constantly on their window sill. They need only plenty of light and air ; not too much watering, and careful pinching.

A good soil for potting Verbenas is sand 1 part, loam 2 parts, and leaf mould or decayed manure 2 parts. Keep it well drained. If you have a conservatory place them upon a top shelf until ready to bring to the window for show. Dampness causes mildew, and then comes the green fly, the destruction of which is secured only by fumigation with tobacco.

If they grow too straggling, train them, and a convenient trellis or frame work may be made for them by using some of the wire or wooden frames used in floral stores, set sloping outward from the edge of the pots.

The list of varieties is indeed formidable, and every florist has not only his fancies, but seedlings of his own year after year, so that new varieties are abundant enough not to attract any remarkable attention. Our bright summer sunshiny days are very suitable for the development of seeds ; hence our American florists are able in many cases to produce handsome varieties surpassing those of Europe.

Special List.

Annie, one of the very best, white, striped with crimson ; blooms constantly, and vigorous grower, truss large.

Black Bedder, very dark maroon, rich.

Conspicua, ruby scarlet, with white eye.

Colossus, crimson, violet eye, very large.

Ceres, light blush, crimson eye.

Decorator, light cherry scarlet, yellow eye.

Diadem, large white, violet bordered.

Enoch Arden, blush, crimson and maroon.

*Formosa, large pink, white eye.

*Gazelle, deep blue, clear white eye.

Harlequin, pure white, striped and splashed with rosy carmine.

Ivanhoe, rich bluish purple, white eye.

King of Blacks, deep maroon.

Lafayette, scarlet crimson, with white centre.

Fire Gleam, light scarlet, dwarf habit.

Pink Beauty, bright pink, with white eye.

Purple Standard, rich dark purple, white centre.

Silver Star, dark maroon, with large white centre.

Ultramarine, the best blue raised, very fragrant.

White Beauty, purest white.

Warrior, crimson maroon, violet eye.

Beacon, fine dark scarlet.

Those marked with a star are considered best novelties for this year. Lists change so frequently, and new ones are formed so quickly, that many a variety becomes old and forgotten in a few seasons. The public in this respect are dependent solely upon the annual announcements of the florists. We could wish good varieties might be a little more permanent and less shifting.

The Verbena derives its name from the Celtic for *Verrain,* a common wild flower. It bears its flowers in long spikes, while the Verbena is a cluster flowered variety. The *Verrain* was called holy herb; it grew plentifully on the Capitoline Hill at Rome, and was much used in religious festivals, and also employed as a symbol in making treaties of peace.

The Druids, of Great Britain, held it in high esteem, and used it in foretelling future events, and in casting lots; but for these purposes the plant must be gathered "when the daystar rose at such a time as neither the sun nor the moon should be above the earth to see it," and also that before they take up the herb they bestow upon the ground where it greweth honey with the comb, in token of satisfaction and amends for the violence done in depriving her of so holy an herb."

The Verrain is said to grow in the vicinity of villages and towns, and never in the wilds, which has gained for it the name of "Simpler's Joy."

The Verbena is found growing wild in Kansas, and there is a species called Verbena Montane, which grows in our western territories, but its flowers are small compared to those we cultivate.

The Petunia.

Here we meet some very charming favorites. The common single Petunias will grow in any soil, being usually quite hardy. The large double varieties are very fragrant and frail, and though easily raised for cuttings produce few if any seeds.

Start cuttings in April or May, and plant them in damp sand, keeping it moist all the time. When rooted pot in rich garden loam and press the soil carefully around the roots; keep in the shade until the roots begin to grow, then give it all the sunshine you can. Pinch off the flower buds during the summer, to allow the plant to become bushy, and do not give too much water to make the sprouts spindle out. There are no handsomer house plants than the improved Double and Single Petunias, and their culture is very simple. Some varieties will train easily, and require a frame for support. The Double varieties are blotched and striped like Pelargoniums, or Picotee Pinks, and are exceedingly beautiful and attractive. Among the finest are:

DOUBLE.

John Lyons, very large size, violet.

Vick's New Fringed, a new strain with fringed or frilled edges, various colors, long tube.

Queen of White, pure white, too good for bedding out.

B. K. Bliss, white blotched with violets.

Dame Blanche, pure white.

Dexter, crimson and white, marbled.

Edward Beck, very large blush pink.

Gov. Geary, white blotched with crimson.

Mrs. Colt, pure white, striped and spotted with violet.

Magnet, habit compact, growth very vigorous, flower white blotched, with purplish crimson. Measures often five inches in diameter. The best of all the doubles.

THE SINGLE VARIETIES.

Admiration, white, blotched with lilac.

Ceres, pure white, purple throat.

Enchantress, white carmine edges.

Gen. Grant, white, marked with fine crimson bars.

Louisa, crimson, beautifully striped with white.

Maculata, white blotched with lilac.

Triumph, white edged with rose, purple centre.

The Pyrethrum.

This is a species of Chamomile which also bears the name of Fever Few, and is of the same order as the Daisy and Chrysanthemum. Its delicate green foliage and pure white double flowers, make it a very beautiful plant for house culture, and it is desirable for dressing the hair, and many other purposes of ornament. It is very hardy, will bear a severe frost without injury, and will live out in the coldest climates if protected by sods.

It is propagated by cuttings and divisions of the roots. The cuttings strike with great ease if the piece is kept in water a week; the roots will form very quickly. They will grow in any soil, and prefer a shady location, where they will bloom in great perfection. Do this in March or April.

The Pyrethrum is also called Mountain Daisy, because it is a native of high places like the Caucasus and the Ural Mountains.

An enthusiastic gardener describes the best of the named varieties as extremely beautiful; "many of them are like Pompone Chrysanthemums; others like Anemone Chrysanthemums; others like Marigolds. Their colors range from purest white to the deepest crimson and purple, the shades of crimson being particularly brilliant."

CHAPTER XXII.

The Mignonette. How to Form a Tree. Cineraria. Wall Flower. Stockgilly.

The Mignonette, or *Reseda odorata,* is very desirable for winter bloom because its perfume is so delicious. Linnæus compares its odors to those of Ambrosia, and it is sweeter and more penetrating at the rising and setting of the sun than at noonday.

Its floral language is, " Your qualities surpass your charms," for its flowers are very insignificant when compared to the brilliant colorings of many others.

For blooming in the house, the seeds should be sown in August, in the pots where they will bloom ; and when started, pull up all but three or four good strong roots, keep in a shady place, and pinch off the top shoots to keep the plants from straggling; give liquid manure once a week, and by November you will have a pot full of branches ; then let the buds form at their pleasure, and before December is out, the flowers will be in great profusion.

For soil in the pots, use 3 parts loam, 1 part dung, and 1 part leaf mould. When water is applied, do so in the morning, so that the foliage may be dry before night.

To have Mignonettes the year round, begin sowing as early as February, then again in April, in September and October. Thin out the plants as fast as they grow up, to but five in the pot ; shade from the sun, in the heat of the day, as otherwise the foliage might have a yellow and unsightly appearance.

For training, five small stakes may be stuck into the pot at equal distances from each other, and tie the plant thereto.

In thinning, keep the largest in one pot and the smallest in others so as to give a succession of bloom. If it is desired to cause any to bloom late, pinch off the tops of a few as soon as they begin to flower ; they will break out again and bloom three weeks or a month later than others of the same sowing.

In boxes they are very pretty. It is best to grow them in pots first until just ready to bloom, and then transfer them to the box, where they can branch out and flower for a long time.

The Mignonette is a native of Egypt and Barbary. In France and England it is much cultivated in boxes made to fit into windows and balconies.

To Form a Tree.

This is an interesting operation, and one particularly agreeable to window gardeners, from the careful superintendence it requires, as well as the singularity, beauty and fragrance of the plant, and it shows so conclusively what results can be obtained from close pruning and attention.

Some persons think that the Tree Mignonette is a distinct variety from the common kind grown in gardens; but it is not so; upon the process of formation alone does the difference rest. Sow the seeds as directed above. The soil should be rather rich, but friable, not heavy. When the plants come up, thin out the weakest, so as to leave only one strong growing plant directly in the centre of the pot.

Push a stiff piece of wire down by the side of the plant, and when it is two inches high commence tying it loosely with a worsted thread to the wire, and keep it well supported. Every side branch that appears from the main stem must be pinched off; but the leaves must be allowed to remain on the stem as their functions are needed for the health and support of the plant. In four or five months turn out the ball of earth to see if it requires a larger size; but do not give it unless the roots are curled around the edges of the ball.

Fig. 74.—Tree Mignonette.

When the plant is a foot or more in height, according to the fancy of the cultivator, the side shoots can be permitted to grow, but they must have their heads pinched off occasionally, to force them to form a bushy top of ten or twelve inches in diameter. This will be accomplished in from nine to twelve months, and then one plant will be sufficient to perfume a large room. Every year it should be repotted, and it will bear an abundance of fragrant flowers for many seasons.

The *Reseda Odorata*, or Sweet Mignonette, is our most popular variety, unless we except

The *Parsons New White Mignonette*, which is white also, but much more vigorous. The flowers are larger, but some do not consider the color any different or superior. In other respects it is, however, an improvement.

The Cineraria.

This plant is usually grown in pots or boxes, and it flowers abundantly during the greater part of the winter and early spring. The variety of its colors, the beauty of the leaves of some of the plants, and the spicy fragrance of others, makes it suitable for the smallest collection of plants.

It requires a friable loam, and does not need the sun during the warmest part of the day in the summer.

There are three methods of increasing this pretty plant : by *seed,* which ripen abundantly in this country, and from which the various beautiful hybrid varieties recently introduced have been obtained; by *cuttings,* and by *divisions* of the roots. Seed sown in sandy soil in May, will make fine blossoming plants in January.

Cuttings strike readily in damp sand or water. The dwarf varieties are quite an improvement upon the older sorts.

The Wall Flower.

The Wall Flower is an old fashioned flower, not much cultivated in these days of novelties. Yet many flowers, much less worthy of admiration, are seen, and the double varieties are particularly attractive, on account of their sweetness and peculiar colorings. We read in old literature of " The yellow Wall Flower stained with iron brown," and again

> " The rude stone fence with fragrant Wall flowers gay,
>   To me more pleasure yield
>   Than all the pomp imperial domes survey."

Tradition associates with this plant one of her wildest fantasies :

In ancient days a noble castle stood amid woods and wilds near the Trent, and a fair damsel had long been detained a prisoner within its walls, because she had given her young love to the heir of a hostile clan ; and although the youth was of equal birth, and renowned for feats of arms and strength, the deadly hatred of those fierce days forbade all thoughts of their marriage.

Many stratagems did the youth devise to obtain possession of his love, but they had all failed. At length a serving woman came to his aid, and it was arranged that with a silken ladder she should descend the fearful height and meet her lover, and the poetry thus describes her fate :

> "Up then she got upon a wall,
> Attempted down to slide withal;
> But the silken twist untied,
> So she fell, and bruised, she died.
> Love in pity to the deed,
> And her loving luckless speed,
> Turn'd her to this plant, we call
> Now, the Flower of the Wall."

Hence, the Wall Flower has become an emblem of fidelity.

The ancient English dames took much pleasure in cultivating this plant, and in wearing its blossoms, so that the title of " Dames' Violet " was applied to it.

The blossom is cruciform, having in its natural state only four petals ; but cultivation has changed the stamens into petals, as is often the case. It will not bloom until the second year from the seed, but if potted in September will bloom by March or April. Unless the soil is very rich the double flowers will become single.

Cuttings must be raised in sandy loam, and then transplanted into rich soil, or they will degenerate from the parent plant. With but little care Wall Flowers will live for many years and blossom profusely.

Stocks.

These are biennials, and blossom in the early spring of the second year from seeds sown in April.

The later varieties are very beautiful, and make most showy and fragrant plants for house culture.

The varieties most suitable for winter flowering are the German Brompton, or Cocardeau; the flowers are very bushy; the latter have a single stem and flower and formed in the shape of a pyramid.

These stocks are in the richest of colors, varying from scarlet, crimson, pink, purple, lilac, to white and cream-color.

The roots can be lifted from garden borders into pots or boxes, and kept in the cellar until March, when they can be brought forward to the sunlight, and will soon be covered with their brilliant, fragrant flowers.

If the seed has been sown in spring in the garden, the plants can grow until autumn, and then be transferred to pots for indoor culture, and flowering during the winter.

If sown in July and August, and grown in pots, they will bloom the following spring and summer.

The culture of Stocks for the window garden is destined to make them one of the most popular fancies of the amateur. Their bloom makes a most desirable display.

CHAPTER XXIII.

THE CARNATION.

The Monthly Carnations are the species most in request for window gardens, as they bloom several times a year, though scarcely every month, excepting in California. There the soil and climate is peculiarly adapted to their needs, is exactly formed for their culture, and the flowers bloom in the greatest profusion, of the largest size, and in the most perfect colorings.

Many of the best species are brought from Italy and Germany, and the imported seeds come from Erfurt, and some parts of Thuringia, where the culture of the Carnation is a *specialite.*

There are three kinds of Carnations—*Flakes, Bizarres* and *Picotees.*

The *Flakes* have only one color disposed in broad stripes on a pure white or yellow ground, and it extends through each petal from its margin to the base.

The *Picotees,* from the French *picoti,* was formerly spotted with purple, scarlet or crimson spots on a yellow or white ground, but the florists have changed its character, and it is no longer a spotted Carnation, but one with all the color confined to a border around each petal.

The *Bizarres* have two or more colors running from the margin to the base of the petal, in irregular stripes of purple, scarlet, cherry, pink or lilac, on a white or yellow ground.

Each of these classes have passed through transformations, and there seems hardly any limit to the rare shadings, veinings and marblings which the flower has assumed. A good, rich compost is indispensable to the production of fine flowers; there is scarcely any plant to which a congenial soil is of so much importance. It does not like a wet soil, but one that is rich in leaf mould and perfectly decomposed cow or horse manure. Many years ago the weavers in various counties of England and Scotland were celebrated for their Carnations, and there were various receipts for composts which were jealously kept from the public. One of these receipts ran thus: "One half one year old horse manure, one-sixth good garden soil, one-sixth leaf mould, and one-sixth coarse sand. Mix together, and let it be exposed to the frosts all winter, turning it as often as possible."

Carnations are propagated by seeds, layers and cuttings.

The seeds should be sown in April or May, in sandy soil, under glass, and transplanted when two inches high.

Layering is best done in July or August. Take a fresh, young shoot, strong and vigorous, which should be four or five joints in length; strip off all the leaves nearest the root, leaving only those on the two or three upper joints. Stir up the soil about an inch, and fill up the pot with light, rich soil, then take the shoot in the finger and thumb of the left hand, and bend it upwards, inserting a sharp knife below the third joint from the top; cut upwards through the centre of that joint to about half or three-quarters an inch above it; then cut off the tongue directly under the joint, taking care not to cut it, as it will not make roots so well; the future roots will spring from this joint; any injury will prevent their formation. The incised shoot must then be gently pressed into the soil, taking great care not to break or crack it at the joint.

As there is considerable danger of breaking the shoots on account of their brittleness, it is well to place the plants in the hot sun, and withhold water; this will cause them to wilt, and become more limber; and as soon as the layer is well fastened into the ground by a thick hairpin, leave the point of the shoot well exposed. The plant must be well watered and set in the shade.

Not more than a quarter of an inch of soil should be covered over the joint; and none of the leaves should be covered, because they will decay and communicate it to the shoot, which will " damp off," as the gardeners term it.

If the plants are kept moist and shaded from the noonday sun, they will be rooted in three or four weeks. Then they can be cut off from the parent plant, with about half an inch of the stem which connects them to it, and planted in rich soil.

Carnations are more hardy than many greenhouse plants, and require much air, and a cool atmosphere until the flower buds begin to form. The flower-pod or calyx, when nearly its full size, is apt to burst, letting out the petals at one side, which presents a loose, ragged appearance, and spoils the circular symmetry of the flower.

This must be prevented by tying the calyx around with a bit of green wool or thread. Some make a ring from a piece of cardboard, and slip it over the bud, so it will keep the petals in regular form when the calyx bursts. Propagation by cuttings is more difficult than by layer, as they do not strike well without artificial heat. If soaked in water for twenty-four hours, they will root more quickly. A celebrated Carnation grower states that the chance of obtaining a handsome Carnation from seed is as one to a hundred.

Manure water will often force flowers upon barren plants.

LIST OF VARIETIES OF CARNATIONS FOR PARLOR OR GREENHOUSE CULTURE.

Remontant or Monthly Carnations.

Astoria, white ground, with yellow, red and scarlet colors.
Bozzaris, blush mottled purple, clove scented.
Brightness, large bright scarlet, very double, clove fragrance.
Canary, yellow ground, slightly tinged rose.
Darkness, very dark crimson.
Defiance, deep crimson, large and fine.

Fortunii, crimson.

Flatbush, snowy white, deeply fringed, very strong in habit, and profuse bloomer.

Little Beauty, carmine edge, yellow ground.

Solfeino, dark violet purple, fragrant.

Unique, pure white, fine form.

Peerlesss, pure white, shaded with blush, large size flower, compact, brushy habit, and immense bloomer.

Gen. Grant, pure white, blooming in clusters.

De Fontana, Orange, shaded purple.

Ma Glorie, red and yellow, very showy and attractive.

Best Winter Flowering Carnations.

President De Graw, pure white, shaded with blush, very large, deeply fringed.

La Purite, rosy pink, profuse bloomer, one of the best for winter flowering.

Variegated La Purite, carmine, striped with black.

Vaillante, richest scarlet, deeply fringed, very fragrant, dwarf in habit, and blooms profusely.

Edwardsii, pure white, large and perfect flower.

Donaldi's Pride, white, tipped with deep rose.

CHAPTER XXIV.

ALPINE PLANTS.

Among the great number of plants, which are acceptable for Window Gardening, we find the Alpine plant is one of the least cultivated for this purpose. On account of the interesting shape of most of these plants and the tiny space required for them by their pygmy appearance, they ought to take the main part of the so said Lilliput Gardening. How is it, that even our nurserymen lack a good deal of the true Alpine plants in their collection of plants, and are in some ways to blame for the want of them amongst our decorated windows? The answer is easily found. It is the fault of the present fashion. Gardeners supply their customers rather with Coleus, Verbenas, Pelargoniums, Heliotropes and other bedding plants, than with the exquisite fine Alpine plants, which, of course, cannot be propagated in so short a time as common bedding plants. The public is mostly satisfied with the latter plants, believing that the culture of Alpine plants is one of great difficulty.

Most of all who have seen these beautiful, modest plants, with their vividness of color, displayed in endless variety in perfect loveliness on the fringes of the glaciers, near steep crevices or ghastly slopes, or in elevated plains and pastures, in Switzerland, Tyrol and Savoy, have learned to love and cherish the sweet flowers, and would like to grow them in their own home. Formerly, when cultivation of Alpine plants was accomplished only in botanical gardens, many difficulties arose; but now, after much patience, experience and experiments, made with all kinds of these plants, the general error, that the true Alpine plants only grow on high mountains in a cool temperature, has thus been dispelled. It is a fact, that many Alpine plants which are found plentifully on elevated plains or near glaciers, do often grow and flower in valleys or lowland regions. Such are, for instance : *Gentiana bavarica* and *verna, Dryas octopetala, Mœhringia muscosa, Silene acaulis, Soldanella alpina,* and several various kinds of *Saxifraga.* Some again, found near slopes or crevices, grow well in pots. Such are : *Gnaphalium leontopodium, (Leontopodium Alpinum),* various kinds of *Primulas, Primula Cortusoides* and *Acaulis, Aster Alpinus, Ramondia Pyrenaica,* all Alpine. *Sedum* and *Sempervivum, Saxifraga umbrosa, Pyramidalis.* Others, which are met within sight of or among fields of snow, or in places beyond our reach, are very difficult to cultivate, and therefore not fit for window decoration. We mention especially several kinds of *Saxifragen;* some *Androsacen, Draba frigida Silene glacialis, Dianthus glacialis, Rannunculus glacialis,* and others. Of Alpine plants, can be used those for Window Gardening, which bear well a hot summer. Of course, we need shady places for most of them. On the high mountains of the Alps, where in summer the temperature is much lowered at night, the plants like full light to spread forth the brilliancy of their colors. To protect now, by cultivating Alpine plants of durability, the same against high temperature during our long and hot summer, we recommend the following arrangement and treatment:

Fig. 75.—Alpine Window Garden.

Have a flat box made about eight inches high, and wide enough as to be easily placed into the window casing. Cover the box, which is best made of zinc, at the bottom with sand about an inch in depth, then arrange the pots in it according to their size. Give to plants of a tall growth the centre, and surround them by the smaller ones. Then fill up the spaces between each pot with a compost of coarse sand, small stones or broken bricks, and some charcoal; water this mixture well and cover it lightly with moss. By such management the plants in pots will have a cool moist stand, which is just required for Alpine plants.

The soil for planting Alpine plants has to consist of a compost of leaf mould, rich loams, some peat, sharp sand and a few pieces of broken bricks; for in-

Fig. 76.—Alpine Plants in Window.

stance, for *Saxifragen, Sedum* and *Sempervium.* Another compost has one-half of good rich loams, mixed up with one-half of leaf mould, a little sharp sand and charcoal. He, who has much peat on hand, mix it up with coarse sand and good old manure. Be careful in watering the plants; do not give too much or too little water, but a sufficient moisture, protect the plants against the hot midday sun, keep the leaves clean, do not allow any worms to hurt the plants, keep off the dust from the leaves with a sponge or syringe, and in accepting these prescriptions you will enjoy an excellent growth and good health of your Alpine plants.

The following list contains only such Alpine plants which are adapted for Window Gardening and will stand a hot summer. These plants can be brought through the winter season in an unheated room or cellar, leaving them in the same boxes and keeping them moderately moist. These fine boxes may stand also in the yard or garden, but must be lightly covered, when frosts begin, with dry leaves or a little mat, made of straw, which is placed six inches above the box. The plants will have, by following this rule, protection and cleanliness, and will pass the winter season well enough to show when brought out again in March, the first lovely spring blossoms.

List

Of Alpine Plants for Window Gardening. Only such species, which are easily cultivated and to be had in American nurseries, or raised by seeds as other herbaceous plants:

1. *Achillea tomentosa,* with yellow flowers in spring, and downy leaves, of a dwarfish growth.

2. *Adonis vernalis,* with large yellow flowers in spring, on the stalks, about ten inches high, useful for the centre of a group.

3. *Alyssum saxatile compactum,* with fine yellow flowers in spring, of a dwarf habit and nice appearance.

4. *Anemone nemorosa,* with pair rosy flowers.

5. *Anemone angelosa (Hepatica),* with beautiful blue flowers, which appear very early in spring.

6. *Anemone hepatica (Hepatica triloba),* with red, blue and white flowers, and varieties with double flowers, and of a dwarf habit.

7. *Anemone ranunculoides,* the golden yellow wood *Anemone,* height, five or six inches.

8. *Antennaria tomentosa,* a very dwarfish silvery leaved plant; a native of the Rocky Mountains.

9. *Arabis albida fol. variegata,* a native of the mountains of Greece, and of a dwarf habit; flowers are white and blue, leaves beautifully variegated.

10. *Armeria vulgaris,* a very pretty little plant, with soft lilac or white flowers springing from dense cushions of grasslike leaves.

11. *Aster alpinus,* the blue daisy of the Alps, of dwarf habit and large pale blue flowers with a deep yellow eye.

12. *Bellis perennis, fl. pl.,* with white and red flowers.

13. *Calandrina umbellata,* a native of Chili, of a dwarf habit, with crimson flowers like the *Portulacca.*

14. *Campanula garganica,* a fine dwarf Harebell, with kidney shaped downy leaves and bluish purple flowers.

15. *Campanula pulla* (*pusilla*), with dark blue or white flowers; plants of a diminutive habit, a very fine little plant.

16. *Campanula Raineri*, a very dwarf species with large dark blue flowers; a native of the Italian Mountains.

17. *Cerastium tomentosum*, a very fine little creeping plant with silver white leaves and star like white flowers, and of easy propagation and cultivation.

18. *Dianthus chinensis nana fl. pl.*, the dwarf China pink in various colors.

19. *Dryas octopetala*, a native of European and American mountains, with creeping stems and large creamy white flowers.

20. *Erinus alpinus*, a very neat and distinct little plant of the Alpine, Tyrolean and Pyrenæn mountains, with violet purple flowers, in short pubescent racemes ; of a very dwarfish habit.

21. *Gentiana acaulis* (*Gentiana verna*), species of a dwarf habit and very large beautiful blue flowers.

22. *Gypsophyla saxifraga*, plant of dwarf, mosslike habit, with fine white flowers.

23. *Helianthemum vulgare*, the little sunrose with single and double flowers of white, yellow and red colors ; it is easy to propagate by seed.

24. *Holeia japonica, fol. var.*, a fine plant, with beautiful variegated leaves, and with spikes of very fine white flowers.

25. *Iberis sempervirens*, a very fine little plant, with dark green leaves and fine large white flowers.

26. *Leontopodium alpinum* (*Gnaphalium Leontopodium*), the "Edleweiss," translated "Nobly white," of the Tyrolian or Switzer Alps; a very pretty plant with downy leaves and beautiful white leaflets around the pale yellowish flower.

27. *Lotus corniculatus*, an interesting plant with yellow flowers, and of a creeping habit.

28. *Lychnis Haageana*, has large flowers of a splendid scarlet or crimson, and stems from eight to ten inches high.

29. *Myosotis alpestris*, the Alpine Forget-Me-Not, with beautiful blue flowers; propagated from seed.

30. *Myosotis Azorica*, a native of the Azorean Islands, of dwarf habit, with beautiful dark flowers.

31. *Myosotis palustris*, the common Forget-Me-Not with pale blue flowers.

32. *Nirembergia rivularis*, a very beautiful little plant with the habit of a Daisy and with large cuplike flowers of a creamy white tint.

33. *Œnothera pumila*, a very dwarf species from the Rocky Mountains, with small yellow flowers.

34. *Ænothera taraxacifolia*, a native of Chili, and profuse flowering; flowers are very large white with a rosy tint.

35. *Omphalodes verna*, the large creeping Forget-Me-Not with beautiful blue flowers.

36. *Phlox setacea* (*Phlox subulata*), the moss pink with beautiful pink, or

seldom with white flowers; plant of a creeping habit, but of profusion of spring flowers.

37. *Phlox reptans* (*Phlox repens verna*), another creeping American species, with very fine flowers of a pink or mauve color.

38. *Plumbago Larpentæ*, a very dwarf, shrubby-like plant, with slender wiry branches, covered with light green leaves, and in September with close trusses of fine blue flowers at the ends of the stems.

39. *Primula cortusoides.* This species is most fit for Window Gardening in regard of its easy culture; it is a native of Siberia, and bears early in spring fine pink flowers.

40. *Primula acaulis fl. pl.*, of very dwarfish habit, and double flowers of white pale lilac, red, yellow and purple double colors; shape like small roses.

41. *Pysidansthera barbulata*, a very interesting American plant, growing in the pine barrens of New Jersey and Carolina, of a moss-like habit, with beautiful white flowers, which are in not opened buds of a fine rosy tint; a very pretty species; requires sandy peat soil.

42. *Ramondia pyrenaica*, also a very distinct and interesting form; very dwarf in habit; leaves stand in rosettes and close on the ground; the large flowers on stems of five or six inches in length, are of a purple violet, with orange yellow centre; native of the Pyrenees.

43. *Sanguinaria canadensis*, the Blood Root, an interesting American plant of dwarf habit, and with white flowers early in spring.

44. *Saxifraga Arizoon*, a native of high European and American mountains, with leaves standing like silvery rosettes; a very showy little plant.

45. *Saxifraga cotyledon*, habit like silvery rosettes, with elegant pyramids of white flowers.

46. *Saxifraga hypnoides*, the mossy sasifraga forms, mossy tufts of the deepest green, with small white flowers.

47. *Saxifraga umbrosa*, a very interesting species, with broad dark green leaves and red spotted white flowers.

48. *Saxifraga sarmentosa* and *Saxifraga Sieboldii fol. variegata*, both species very well known, are suitable for Alpine groups.

49. *Sedum acre* and *hexangulare*, the common stonecrop with yellow flowers.

50. *Sedum daisyphyllum*, one of the most interesting Alpine plants of a glaucous color, with creamy white flowers.

51. *Sedum Sieboldii fol. var.*, an elegant well known plant, with light pink flowers in summer and fall.

52. *Sedum carneum variegatum ;* species with fine variegated leaves.

53. *Sempervivum arachnoideum*, the cobweb houseleek from the Alps and Pyrenees, with fleshy leaves in tiny rosettes, covered at the top with a white down-like spider web.

54. *Sempervivum montanum;* the leaves are very regularly arranged in fine light green rosettes.

55. *Sempervivum californicum,* a larger species; leaves are of a dark green color, with reddish margin and dark points.

56. *Silene alpestris,* a very fine plant of dwarf habit and pure white flowers.

57. *Silene maritima fl. pl.* The leaves of this species are of a glancous color, and the flowers are like small snowballs.

58. *Soldanella alpina,* a lovely little plant of an interesting appearance, with leathery, shining, roundish leaves and beautiful blue bell-shaped, fringed flowers.

59. *Tymus zerpillifolium fol. var.,* the variegated Thyme.

60. *Viola cornusa,* the Pyrenean Violets with very large blue and white flowers which appear numerously during the summer season.

Finally, we observe, that in a collection like the preceding one, many plants could be added, which would match well with the Habitus of Alpine plants but which would anyhow require another treatment; for instance, a warmer place for the winter season, while others are in a resting state during the summer.

Such are : *Cyclamen Coum, persicum, repandum, vernum, europaeum, hederaefolium ; Echeveria secunda, glaucovirens, gibbiflora; Linaria cymbalaria; Spigelia Marylandica ; Scilla Sybirica, amoena, praecox; Leucojum vernum ;* various kinds of *Crocus* and *Snowdrops; Iris pumila; Sibthorpia Europœa; Portulacca flore pleno;* dwarf kinds of *Mesembrianthemum, Saponaria ocymoides; Sanvitalia procumbens flore pleno; Nycta vine capensis; Sedum coeruleum; Grammanthes Gentianoides, Ionopsidium acaule,* and various kinds of *Nemophila.*

CHAPTER XXV.

Miscellaneous Plants.

The Azalea.

This has of late years become a popular window plant, and most justly, too, for with their profuse masses of flowers they make every window or balcony a bower of bloom.

The plants should have a light dry soil, of leaf mould and loam. The best for this purpose is a mixture two parts loam, rich vegetable matter; two parts rotten peat from the swamp, and one part sand, and be sparingly watered—yet the roots must never become dry. They need a temperature of 65° by day, and at night coolness of 40° to 45°, for rest.

While dormant they need shade and but little water, but when the flower buds are swelling, they desire more. It is a shrub that needs little pruning, only enough to keep in good form.

The usual months for blooming are April and May, but a succession of bloom can be kept up from February to May, by storing in the cellar the previous winter, in a cool place, dormant plants of the chosen varieties, then bringing them one by one to the window, where they are hastened into bloom. When done blooming, take them away, and fill their places with new ones.

Ordinarily, after Azaleas have done blooming, it is best to set the plants in the shade out of doors until September. If desired to propagate new plants, take cuttings in May, in moist sand under glass; but since so good plants are purchased at so cheap prices at the florists, propagation for window purpose only is not worth the trouble.

Most of the varieties brought to the window will bloom for three weeks; yet some will last six weeks; by bringing up new plants successively, the blooming season, may be extended several months. The following is a select list of those most suitable for window purposes. Those with a star are the most desirable of the collection:

Amaena, very early.
Amarantina, rosy purple.
Belle Gantoire, rose and striped with white.
**Charles Quint,* rose.
Criterion, light salmon, edged with white, upper petals spotted with crimson.
Delicata, rose.
Exquisita, violet pink, edged with white.

Indica alba, white.

* *Fielden,* white ; very early.

* *Minerva,* scarlet ; profuse.

Modele de Marque, splendid form ; rose.

Grande Dutchesse de Bode.

Iveryana, white, striped with rose.

Perfection, rose ; good form.

Vittata crisiflora.

Vittata, variegated.

* *Punctata,* splendid, variegated.

* *Punctata omnicolor,* early bloomer.

* *Narcissiflora plena,* six weeks in bloom.

President, scarlet.

The Daphne.

Of all woody plants that are suitable for parlor culture, the Daphne, especially *Daphne odorata,* deserves the first mention, for it flourishes under the most adverse circumstances ; patiently putting forth group after group of its dark glossy evergreen leaves, each group through the winter months wearing right royally its cluster of pearly blossoms, whose delicate throats constantly distil a most delicious fragrance.

In foliage this shrub greatly resembles the laurel, and hence bears the name of that beautiful maiden who being beloved by Apollo, but not favoring his suit, besought the gods for aid in escaping him, and in answer to her prayers was changed into a laurel-tree.

Though the Daphne is capable of enduring heat and dryness, it grows most luxuriantly in a cool, moist atmosphere ; and it should be frequently syringed with tepid water, its leaves kept clean with water by washing them often with a soft sponge. Give it a soil of garden earth mixed loosely with a little vegetable mould or stable refuse and a small quantity of sand. In May prune it closely to make it grow tall and symmetrical ; at the same time repot it, and then keep the plant in the shade with slight watering till September ; then give it sunshine and water freely. In early October take it to the parlor. Of the prunings make new plants by immersing the stems in a bottle of water and keeping the bottle in the sunlight till it is filled with white fibrous roots ; these roots are very tender, and when they are placed in soil care must be taken not to injure them. The young plant must be kept under a bell-glass or an inverted tumbler for a fortnight, with a scanty sprinkling of tepid water every morning. It should have the sun three hours, at least, each day ; but make the air of the room moist and let it not rise above 58° by day or 45° by night, if you would promote its rapid and healthy growth. It blooms almost constantly from December to the last of March.

The Abutilon.

A beautiful parlor tree is the Abutilon, with its maple-like foliage, and its bell flowers of gold and crimson. It needs a light sandy loam, for if the soil is too rich it will grow too tall to form a handsome shaped tree. Ordinary garden soil loosened with sand will answer. If the air of the room it occupies is too close and hot, it will not bloom, so give it air frequently, shielding it from draughts as you would a geranium, and water it well.

It grows easily from cuttings; prune in spring, and root the best of these prunings in wet sand to get new plants.

Abutilon striatum is hardly ever out of flower; its bells are of a golden yellow, veined with brown, and they are very graceful and lovely.

Abutilon venosa has larger flowers, with deep red veins, and is very handsome.

A *Marmaratum* is a charming hybrid, blossoming all the year, and producing white flowers, marbled and veined with rose.

A *Mesapotanicum* is a species which differs in the shape of both flowers and leaves. The calyx being scarlet, with golden yellow petals, the flowers beautifully marked; they hang in regular rows down the flexible branches, and are very valuable for cut flowers.

A *Thompsonii* is another distinct variety with variegated leaves, its leaves being mosaiced with yellow.

A *Santana* is a new plant with flower bells of a much larger size, and of dark brownish crimsom, veined with orange color; it is the darkest sort cultivated.

A *Album* is pure white, and very much admired.

The Orange.

Small orange trees are very desirable window plants, on account of their exquisitely fragrant flowers, and beautiful evergreen foliage which contrasts finely with other plants. The prettiest for house culture are the dwarf varieties, and the dwarf Mandarin or China orange bears excellent fruit. The dwarf *Otaheite* is a more common kind, but not as suitable ; for neither its flowers nor fruit equal those of the Mandarin.

Early in the eighteenth century, orange trees were quite the fashion for house culture, and although the fashion has passed away, there are few plants that still combine so much perfection in foliage, fruit and flower.

Oranges are usually raised from seed, and in a year or two, grafted from a fine variety. Seeds sprout readily in any light loam, but the orange blooms the finest in good rich soil, and requires liquid manure once in a fortnight or even oftener. The foliage is handsomer, if the pot stands a little away from the full noonday sun.

The Lemon.

The Lemon belongs to the same genus as the Orange *viz.:* the *Citrus,* to which also belong limes, shaddocks and citrons; all the species are characterized by fragrant flowers, glossy evergreen leaves, and delicious fruits.

The golden apples of the Hesperides are supposed to belong to this family.

Fine trees are raised from seeds, and when the shoots are two years old they can be budded from fruitful trees.   The blossoms of the Lemon are smaller than those of the Orange, and they are not as purely white, the under side of the petals being tinged with purple.

Oranges are over a year in ripening, and often remain for two years on the tree. Lemons ripen irregularly, and fall off when ripe.   Every six or seven years both orange and lemon trees should be pruned closely.   Shorten in the shoots several inches, and they will throw out an abundance of fresh green leaves.

If they flourish well, they will not need repotting oftener than once in five or six years.   Then the mouldy roots, and smallest fibres should be cut back, and the ball of earth well shaken off.   Pot in soil of light loam, leaf manure, and two years' old cow manure, equal parts, with a good sprinkling of charcoal dust. Keep in the shade for two or three weeks, and water less frequently than when in flower.   It loves the light, but not the hot sun until the fruit is ripening.

The Sweet Verbena.

The Sweet Verbena or *Aloysa Citriodora,* is much cultivated for its lemon-scented foliage.   Any soil will suit it, but in rich loam it makes a more vigorous growth.

It is of a deciduous habit, will lose its leaves, and its admirers grieve when they fall, but like the elm and the maple, it buds out afresh in March or April, and from the old wood, cuttings will strike as easily as currant cuttings.

When its leaves have fallen, it can stand in any dark, cool place where the frost will not touch it, and where the roots can be kept rather dry.

It makes an ornamental standard plant, if trained to a single stem to a height of three feet, and then allowed to branch out in a graceful form.

The young shoots will strike root in May or June, if planted under glass, and well shaded for awhile.   The flowers are borne in large spikes and are very minute, white, but not much esteemed, as the foliage is the most desired part of the plant.   Its generally neat appearance always gains much admiration. Trim old plants and repot them in the spring.   Root the trimmings in wet sand, under a glass; then give those young plants a soil of garden earth, vegetable mould and gravel in equal proportions.   Set the pots in a garden-bed, plunged to their rims, till September; then stir the soil often with an old table-fork, water sparingly, giving liquid manure once a week; take them to the parlor in October, let them have the sun six hours every day, keep the atmosphere moist, and not above 65° by day or 45° by night, and they will flourish wonderfully.

Eupatoriums and Stevias.

By reason of the contrast of their delicate blossoms and graceful foliage, with those of the Geranium, the *Eupatorium* and *Stevias* deserves high rank, as popular favorites.   The eupatorium gets its name from Eupater, king of Pontus, who first used the plant in medicine.   We have many species growing in their native beauty in the lovely mountain passes and valleys of the North, as well as in the sunny meadows farther South; and the florist has transplanted them and carefully watched and tended their growth till the foliage has attained unwonted smoothness and beauty, and the hues of the tassel-shaped flowers have become clearer and brighter. Their large clusters of snow-white, or lilac blossoms, have a fine effect among geraniums, and they have always been much sought after as a winter blooming flower. The white varieties are most cultivated, being used for funeral crosses, and crowns, also for wedding bouquets.

They prefer a sandy, peaty loam, with a good supply of water. In the spring, after blooming, shake out the old soil and repot in good loam and sand mixed in equal proportions. Make new plants of the cuttings. Start them in damp sand under glass. Water them much and frequently. Set them in the garden till September, then accustom them gradually to the indoor atmosphere. They will bloom from November till February. When in flower they do not need much sunshine, as it dims the whiteness of the flowers.

Eupatorium ageratoides, E. Mexicanum and *E. Elegans* are the varieties most usually cultivated in conservatories and window gardens. They are of a beautiful feathery whiteness, and most desirable for purposes of decoration. In saving the seeds, cut the flowers while in full bloom, as they ripen quickly, and fly away, but they germinate easily.

The *Stevias*, of similar foliage, but a yet more delicate and feathery flower, of a creamy white, cultivate in the same way. Pinch out all buds that appear on these plants during the summer. No plants can be so effectively grouped as geraniums with heliotropes, eupatoriums, and stevias, if proper attention is paid to an agreeable contrast of their blossoms,—the purple or lilac being always flanked with white—never with red or crimson or rose,—and the white mingled among scarlets, crimsons, reds, and salmons—the white predominating.

The Chinese Primrose.

The *Primula Chinensis* is the gem of the collection of window plants. None surpass it in beauty; and for continuous bloom, certainly none can be found more desirable. It is one of the best of all plants for the decoration of the drawing room or dining table, and always at home in the conservatory or greenhouse. For nine months out of the twelve they may be made to yield flowers, though most profusely from November to May, and with their colors of red, white, crimson, purple, and pink, they form objects of curious ornament.

They are objects of easy care, requiring attention only in watering; the soil should not be allowed to get dry, and yet the roots are so tenacious of life, they will cling closely till the last moment around any particle of moisture in the earth. Keep the soil moderately moist, but not over saturated; if evaporation or drainage is slow, and the circulation through the pot impeded, the plants will turn sickly and die off. We do not advise manure water; plain warm water is the best. The best varieties for window gardens are the *Double White Primroses* and *rubra plena*, a double red variety, indescribably charming. The single fringed varieties are very fine, but the above are now the most popular. One great advantage which the Primrose possesses over most winter flowering plants is that it is rarely ever infested with green fly or other troublesome pests. Primroses are propagated mainly by *cuttings and seeds.* Cuttings taken from the side shoots in April will make vigorous plants by autumn. From June to October they should be kept from the hot sun, in a shady location, with but little water. The soil should be largely composed of leaf mould.

The single varieties are largely grown from seed which should be sown in April or May, under a square of glass; when four or five leaves are developed, plant in small thumb pots, and shade for two or three days. During the summer keep the pots in a shady location, but in the winter the nearer they are to the glass the better and brighter will they flower.

If any unusually fine flowers reward your care, they can be increased by cuttings. The Primrose is a perennial; the seed is usually sold in mixed colors, but they can be recognized nearly as soon as the leaves appear, by the color of the stems. No plant flowers more profusely, and sometimes five hundred florets are gathered from one plant.

The Pansy.

The Pansy never blooms so well as when the plant is small and well rooted, for as it increases in size the blossoms become smaller, and, although abundant, inferior. They can be cut back after spring flowering, and all the buds kept off until December, then they will bloom for the whole winter. If planted in boxes in a conservatory or window, they make a fine show; indeed, there are few plants more desirable for window gardening.

They are most easily raised from seed, and it is well to purchase the most expensive varieties, so as to be certain of the finest flowers.

Cuttings strike quickly, and are more sure of fine flowers, as they always reproduce the parent plant. They should be cut about three inches long, and taken from the points of the shoots, and cut off directly under the joint. Strip off the lower leaves, and insert them in saucers of wet sand, pressing it closely around the joint. Keep tumblers over them, and in six weeks they will be well rooted and ready to transplant into small pots filled with the richest compost.

Pansies are gross feeders, delighting in the richest soil you can prepare; in rotten tanbark, leaf manure, and cow manure, equal parts, they will bloom magnificently.

No plant is better adapted to house culture, as they can bear changes of atmosphere, and a good deal of water, while their bright faces are very attractive in the gloomy wintry days.

They can be increased by dividing the roots, and keeping them in the shade for a week or ten days. If the amateur desires to save seed from her plants, she should select the largest, brightest flowers, and cut off all other buds and blossoms. As the seed pod matures it can be tied up in gauze to prevent the seed from scattering, and when fully ripe, can be planted directly in sandy loam When the seedlings flower those should be rejected that are not very handsome.

The best location for Pansies is a northwest window, for they delight in shade, and desire to shun "the gairish eye of day," and hide their lovely blossoms from his scorching rays.

The Sweet Violet.

These require a rich compost to enable them to bloom luxuriantly, and a cool temperature, say 40° to 45°; all the fading leaves must be cut off, and if the plant is desired to bloom profusely, the runners should also be cut off as soon as they appear. Water must not settle at the roots.

They are propagated by divisions of the roots, or usually by cuttings taken in June, and raised in wet sand under glass.

The dark blue English variety, or the double blue *Neapolitan*, are most generally cultivated as parlor plants.

The Czar or Russian Violet has been much admired; leaves are large and the flowers are borne on very long footstalks, five to six inches in length. The flower is single, but large, and fine; color of a light blue; blooms all winter from September to May, and fills the air with its delicious fragrance.

King of the Violets. Flowers very double, like a miniature rosette, very fragrant, color of a deep indigo blue, with occasional stripes of white; flowers borne in profusion.

Double Blue Neapolitan, the best standard sort we have. A bouquet composed of a statuesque camellia, embedded in blue violets, with a fringe of cliver or gypsophila, is the perfection of floral arrangement, combining beauty, fragrance and grace.

The Daisy.

Its botanical name, *Bellis*, signifies beautiful, pretty. Cultivation has given to it many petals, and also brighter hues.

It is frequently used in this country as an edging for beds and borders, but it is a pretty plant for house culture, with its tufts of lovely green leaves crowned with numerous bright pink blossoms.

It flourishes best in a rich soil, and is propagated by offsets, or division of the roots. For winter flowering, the pot should be kept in the shade, with little water during the hot weather—only enough to keep it from drying up—till the first of October. Then it will need all the sunshine to make it bloom well, and liquid manure will greatly increase its blossoms.

The Daisy will bear transplanting, even when in flower, if the soil is kept about the roots. Every spring fresh earth should be given, and the roots should be divided. The Belgium Daisy is best adapted to house culture.

The Calla. (Richardia.)

The *Calla Æthiopica* is a very attractive plant, its large, broad, glossy, green leaves, and its white, thickly textured, scroll-like blossom making it peculiarly graceful. There is no better plant for the centre of a group of flowers.

It blooms equally well in greenhouse, conservatory or window garden; may be allowed to be rather dry in the summer after flowering, but care should be taken not to injure or break off the leaves. When budding it requires much water, and its saucers should be supplied night and morning. It is propagated by suckers and divisions of its roots. It desires a clayey loam with a third of leaf mould. It is very tender, feeling a slight chill.

Its flowers are in great request at Easter to adorn the churches, when white lilies are sought as emblems of the risen Redeemer, and the florists grow them in large quantities for this purpose.

The best method of growing Callas is in a hollow stand lined with zinc; eight or ten flowering bulbs can be planted in a stand three or four feet long, and eighteen inches wide. It should be eight inches deep, and the surface of the pots should be covered with moss, and moss filled in between the pots. Its appearance is exceedingly ornamental in a bay window, and it is very easily taken care of, the chief essential being plenty of water, and a weekly sponging of the large leaves; and the stand should be occasionally turned, as the large leaves turn towards the light.

Such a stand of Callas can be set out of doors in a shady place during the summer and brought in before fear of frosts. Soon they will make vigorous growth, and will flower abundantly from December to May. No flower better endures furnace heat and gas, and so it is particularly adapted to window culture.

Dielytra Spectabilis.

For window flowering and conservatory, this plant is very valuable. Take up the tuberous roots in October, in a six or seven inch pot, and set in a sheltered place for a month or so, giving a little water daily, and keeping it warm. When the shoots appear, bring to the light, and give it as sunny a situation as possible, but the atmosphere need not be warm. It will do well in a chamber window where the temperature is about 60°. As it grows and produces more flowers, increase the supply of water.

It will grow best in light sandy loam, but enjoys a weekly measure of liquid manure. When done flowering, set in a shady place, but give water in small quantities as long as the leaves are green; when they fade, give only enough to prevent its dying from thirst, and in the following autumn proceed as above, giving a fresh supply of soil to make its blossoms more plentiful.

It multiplies from the root, and must be given enough pot room, or its roots divided yearly.

The Calceolaria.

The Calceolaria,—its name comes from the Latin for shoe—the blossom resembles an ancient Roman slipper,—is singularly beautiful with its heavy clusters of golden, crimson, maroon, or rose-colored flowers—sometimes plainly tinted, at others curiously mottled and flecked. It needs a sandy soil—garden earth and common sand in equal proportions; should be kept rather warm, in an atmosphere of 60° to 65° by day, and 50° at night; and be sparingly watered. Give liquid manure once a week after the flower-buds start. Pot old plants in May, in the same manner as eupatoriums, and keep them in a warm but shady place, out of doors, till September, with only water enough to prevent them from drooping. Before potting cut them in closely, and make new plants of those cuttings by rooting them in moist sand under a glass, in the sunshine; or plant the seed in a sunny and sheltered spot. In August pot them and tie carefully to a light trellis till they are two feet high, then trim off the most slender branches—in fact cut them in pretty close and let them stand alone. This is a delicate plant, but may be strengthened and hardened by this close trimming and a careful management of its supplies of heat and moisture. It needs a good deal of air—does best when wide breathing space is allowed.

The Lantana.

The Lantana requires similar soil and treatment to the Calceolaria—except that it is of a stouter, a more woody nature, and needs no support. Its compact head of flowers of different and changing hues—white, crimson, scarlet, orange, and yellow, sometimes all in the same spike, is always an object of great interest, though its peculiar perfume is not universally agreeable.

The Pyrethrum.

A very desirable window plant is the Pyrethrum, sometimes called Mountain Daisy; it is found in great profusion in the mountainous regions of Asia. This will grow in ordinary soil with very little care, and its delicate light green foliage, crowned with dense clusters of snow-white blossoms, contrasts finely with the deeper colorings of Calceolarias and Lantanas. Old plants should be cut to their roots, and both roots and cuttings be set in a garden-bed in May or June, and treated as common out-of-door plants. Pinch out all flower-buds till they are taken to the house. In September pot them with the same soil in which they have been growing. Keep them in the shade, with occasional watering, for a fortnight, then bring them within doors. The Pyrethrum does best in a moderate temperature with scanty watering.

The Chrysanthemums.

The Chrysanthemum (it gets its name from the Greek words for gold and flower—many species bear yellow flowers), though commonly classed with out-of-door plants, should be made to lend its beauty to every parlor through the months of October, November and December. After flowering, Chrysanthemums must be set in a dark, cool place—a cellar, or any damp dark place where they will not freeze—till May. Then give them the same treatment as Pyrethrums, with which they are often classed; but they require free watering. Soapsuds will make them grow stout and strong through the summer. After they are potted give liquid manure twice a week till the buds begin to unfold, then withhold it entirely.

A very desirable feature of the Chrysanthemum as a winter blooming plant, is that the blossoms are finely formed, of brilliant colors, keep well, and are produced in great abundance. The dwarf or Pompone varieties are now the most used in consequence of their beauty of form, with diminutive habit of growth. Any florists' catalogue will give a good list of varieties.

The *Ch. Laciniatum* has a novel and elegant appearance. The flowers are double, nearly three inches in diameter, delicately fringed, and of the purest white. It is especially a plant for winter flowers. By pinching off the flower buds as they show, it can be had in flower from December to March.

The Salvia.

Another splendid flowering plant, which has been supposed, until recently, to expend all its energies during the autumnal months, and to require the open air for the perfection of its beauty, is the Salvia. *Salvia angustifolia*, with its elegant foliage and long spikes of clear blue flowers, is particularly fine ; so is *S. patens*, bearing blossoms of a still more "heavenly hue;" yet none are so attractive, nor so hardy, as *S. splendens*, with its plumes of dazzling scarlet. Any of the Salvias are easily raised from cuttings; trim all the foliage from these slips and set them in damp sand to root. Start them in May.) When rooted set them in the garden, but keep them shaded from the sun with a paper screen till the new leaves are well developed. Water freely. In September pot those you wish for the house, and pinch out the buds. If then left to themselves they will store up strength for the winter. But before the frosts come, be sure to take them within doors, and give the fertilizer once a week till in bloom. Cut them to the root in May, and set the root in the garden. It is best to start new plants every year for the house. Salvias need a light loamy soil, and a temperature of 60° by day, and 45° by night.

The Mimulus.

The *Mimulus*—its seeds resemble the face of a monkey, and hence its name, which comes from the Latin—is a very thirsty plant, does best in a mixture of leaf mould and garden earth, with just enough sand to keep the soil from being heavy, and frequently needs watering twice a day ; but it thrives in the atmosphere of any family room, and with its gorgeous blossoms of gold spotted with maroon and crimson, is a great addition to any collection. Propagate it from cuttings rooted in water. The young plants should be kept in the shade all summer out of doors.

Pinks.

Pinks—*Dianthus Chinensis*, the China Pink, and *Dianthus caryophillus*, the Carnation—are well known parlor plants. The China Pink, though not fragrant, is so beautiful and so easy to manage, no collection should be considered complete without it. Plant seed in June in good garden soil ; pinch out all flower buds till September ; then take them, with a ball of earth about their roots, to pots of the same soil. Keep them in the shade a fortnight. Water sparingly till more flower buds appear, then give moisture generously—weak liquid manure twice a week, also. It will bear great heat, 65° to 70°; but 60° suits it best. In that temperature in an open, airy situation, it will put forth its deep crimson, velvet, very double, flowers in great profusion all winter.

Achyranthes.

The best varieties of Achyranthes are now freely used for window decoration, and have become quite common as standard plants for the centre of hanging or standing floral baskets. They need only a moderate temperature of 50° to 75,° and are easily taken care off. Their rich crimson tints have made the people crazy to use them wherever it is conceivable to do so.

Achyranthes Lindeni has foliage of the deepest red, each leaf having a conspicuous mid-rib of a lighter shade ; when the sun shines fully upon it it is of a perfect claret color, habit dwarf, leaves narrow, lanceolae, and considered the most ornamental of the class of fine foliaged plants.

A. Aureus Reticulatus, is of the same habit of growth as the *A. Verschaffeltii*, but its leaves are of a rich apple green, marked with a net work of yellow, while the stems are a ruby crimson, affording a fine contrast with the leaves.

A. Verschaffeltii, Var Gilsonii. This variety has leaves of a still brighter tint, a full carmine, with the stems of a deep shade of pink, rendering the plant decidedly ornamental, and giving a very rich appearance. This variety is now generally used in place of the old Verschaffeltii.

Coleus.

We do not recommend too free a use of this for the window or room culture. It needs moist and warm temperature, and uniform, with no change for the cooler. This, of course, is in direct opposition to the actual facts they have to meet in rooms which invariably grow colder at night. Another objection is that they grow so large and tall, and become so ungainly, that they are not fit for any length of time for any good position. They are too tall for hanging baskets, although would look very appropriate in the centre of a group of plants in a large flower stand. They are much more tender than the Achyranthes, will not bear the touch of frost, and a slight chill is death to them. Wherever they can have a warm position, with plenty of sunlight, (although not directly upon their leaves), and a moderately moist atmosphere, they will do well. The best varieties are :

Princess Royal, centre, reddish brown, light yellow margin.

Queen Victoria, rich bronzy crimson, bright yellow, edged with crimson veining.

Setting Sun, crimson centre, with bright yellow edge.

Albert Victor, centre purplish red, broad yellow margin.

Alternantheras.

These are dwarf plants with narrow lanceolate leaves, which make very effective edging; their leaves are variegated with crimson, pink, green, brown, orange and carmine, in some respects resembling our brilliant autumn leaves; are well suited for hanging baskets.

A. Latifolia, has broad leaves of olive, green, crimson and orange.

A. Amabilis, rich tints of orange, rose and green.

A. Amoena, is crimson, pink, brown and amber red.

Begonias,

Are purchased principally already started and potted, ready to be placed in the window for decoration. Keep the leaves away from the window pane, or they will turn black. The temperature of room should be 60° to 75° constantly, and warmth must be steady, not changing.

Begonia Rex, is the best variety yet grown in this country, and, as a showy plant, for picturesque ornament in the room or conservatory, it is unequalled. Leaves have an immense size, tinged with crimson, with here and there broad, silvery zones, and snowy spots, with emerald hues on the surface. It is perhaps the most popular plant now sold for house or parlor decoration.

PART III.

PARLOR DECORATIONS

Fig. 1.—Parlor Flower Stand for Tropical Plants.

CHAPTER XXVI.

The Decoration of Parlors and Living Rooms with Ornamental Plants and Flowers.

A subject like this is one of intense interest to the American flower loving public. Formerly little was done in the encouragement of it, because we all, like amateurs, and beginners, knew little of the best plants and methods, and waited to learn from those more experienced; but of late, amateurs, in their eager zeal for window and room decorations, have taken in hand their own impatient fancies, and led the way with experiments and trials of their own, while the florists everywhere look with admiration and respect upon the wide spreading taste for window and parlor gardening. The amateurs have outstripped the professionals in the rapidity of their progress, and the prettiest rooms to-day are embellished by the fingers of a fair plant lover, who a year before did not know one flower from another.

To speak with truth, nothing is prettier, more elegant, and in many respects easier, than the decoration of our parlors, reception rooms, halls, etc., with appropriate plants and flowers.

The very pictures, statues, vases, chandeliers, and other permanent ornaments, allow room for the exhibition of many kinds and varieties of beautiful plants.

In such rooms, however elegantly furnished, is the proper place for fine *Aquaria*, *Wardian Cases*, Flower Stands, Wire Arbors for climbing plants, flower baskets, or hanging baskets hung up between the curtains.

Flowers used for decoration will harmonize completely with any architecture or furniture of the parlor. Indeed, was there ever any flower out of place in a beautiful room?

A tasteful and carefully arranged composition of plants will captivate for a long time the love, attention and admiration of all classes of society.

Few American writers have devoted much attention to this subject, and we cannot now recall a single article in our horticultural literature which treats in detail of the use of plants for room decoration; but in English and Continental journals the topic is a common one, doubtless from the more extensive use of costly plants at parties, receptions, and large social gatherings. It is one of the higher branches of the florist's occupation, and really an art for the display of the most refined taste.

William Robinson, the author of "Parks, Promenades and Gardens of Paris," has perhaps described the Continental system of the plant decoration of apartments more completely than any other, and refers to it in these words:—

"The graceful custom of growing plants in living rooms is very much more prevalent on the Continent than with us. It is true that we often see a display of flowering plants in rooms, though we rarely rise to the use of subjects distinguished by beauty of form, or select those that are peculiarly adapted for indoors. But the day is approaching when the value of graceful plants as home ornaments will be very fully appreciated. Apart altogether from their effect as ornaments, what can more agreeably introduce us to the study of natural history? The influence of the graceful form of a young Palm in the hall, the fascinating verdure of Ferns, and fine leaved plants from many countries, in the drawing room, and flowers from the orchards of the uplands of Mexico, to the tiny bulbs of Europe, in your Lilliputian room-conservatory, is surely more eloquent in that direction than any book teaching. You cannot deny, as Kingsley says, that "your daughters find an enjoyment in it, and are more active, more cheerful, more self forgetful over it, than they would have been over novels and gossip, crochet and Berlin wool. At least you will confess that the abomination of "fancy work"— that standing cloak for dreamy idleness—has all but vanished from your drawing rooms since the "Lady Ferns" and Venus Hair Ferns appeared.'

Fig. 2.—Maranta fasciata.

Ferns, to be sure, have been a great help and a great attraction, but they are not altogether superior as to verdure and elegance; there are other plants much more readily grown in rooms.

"By a combination of all the plants suitable for this purpose, we may not only find very agreeable indoor imployment, but create the highest kind of ornament and interest in the house at all seasons.

"Merely displaying a few popular or showy subjects is not plant decoration in any high sense! Rooms are often over-crowded with artificial ornaments, many of them exact representations of natural objects; but in the case of plants we may, without inconvenience, enjoy and preserve the living objects themselves.

"Those we employ for this purpose, now are mostly of a fleeting character, and such as cannot be preserved in health for any length of time in living rooms. But if in addition to the best of these we select handsome leaved plants of a leathery texture, accustomed to withstand the fierce heats of hot countries, we shall find that the dry and dusty air of the living room is not at all injurious to them, and that it is quite easy to keep them in health for months, and even for years, in the same apartments.

"Many plants that in England are considered as Exotics, are sold in Paris in abundance for the decoration of apartments. The demand for use in private houses gives rise to a large and special branch of trade in many of the nurseries, and I know one Versailles cultivator who annually raises and sells 5,000 or 6,000 plants of the bright-leaved *Dracaena terminalis* alone, and by far the greater part for room decoration."

Although English plants are much better grown than the Parisian, yet those of the latter appear the best; the difference being caused by exceedingly tasteful and frequently peculiar arrangement, as well as by employing effective and graceful kinds What the Parisians do as regards arrangement may be best gleaned if we describe the decorations for one of the balls of the Hotel de Ville:

Fig. 3.—Gymnostachyum Verschaffeltii.

"Entering the Salle St. Jean, the eye was immediately attracted by a luxuriant mass of vegetation at one end, while on the right and immediately round a mirrored recess was a very tasteful and telling display, made as follows: In front of the large and high mirror stretched a bank of moss, common moss underneath, and the surface nicely formed of fresh green *Lycopodium denticula tum,* the whole being dotted over with the variously tinted Chinese Primulas,—a bank of these plants, in fact, high enough in its back parts to be reflected in the mirror, with the taller plants which surrounded it, gradually falling to the floor, and merging into the groups of larger plants on either side of the bank, the whole being enclosed by a low, gilt, wooden trellis work margin.

" The groups at each side contrasted most beautifully with this. Green predominated, but there was a sufficiency of flower, while beauty of form was fully developed. In the centre and back parts of these groups were tall specimens of the common sugar cane, (*Sacharinum officiranum,*) which held their long and boldly arching leaves well over the group. These were supported by Palms, which threw their graceful lines over the specimen Camellias, which were in their turn graced here and there by the presence of a *Dracæna* or dwarf Palm ; and so down to the front edge, where *Cinerarias,* forced bulbs, *Primulas* and Ferns, finished off the groups, all very closely placed, so that neither the lower part of the stems, nor a particle of any of the pots could be seen

" Any interstices that happened to remain between the bases of the plants were compactly filled with fresh green moss, which was also pressed against the little gilt trellis work, which enclosed the whole, so that from the uppermost point of the cane leaves to the floor, nothing was seen but fresh green foliage and graceful forms enshrouding the ordinary flowers of our greenhouses—that are infi-

Fig. 4.—Agave Americana.

nitely more attractive when thus set in the verdure of which nature is so profuse, and which is always so abundant where her charms of vegetation are at their highest.

" A scene such as this explains the prevalence of these graceful and noble-leaved plants in Paris gardens, and in Parisian flower shops and windows, for you may frequently see elegant little *Dracænas* ornamenting windows there, and as they

Fig. 5.—Dieffenbachia.

look as well at Christmas as at midsummer, I need hardly suggest how highly suited they are for purposes of this kind.

" The number of *Dracænas* cultivated in and around Paris is something enormous, and among the newer species of these—not alluding to the colored-leaved kinds—are some that combine grace with dignity as no other plants do combine them. They are useful for the centres of noble groups of plants in their larger forms, while the smaller species may be advantageously associated with the Maiden Hair Fern, and the *Cinerarias* of the conservatory bench.

"They are of the greatest utility in these decorations, and are largely used in all parts. So are most all kinds of fine-leaved plants, from *Phormium* to *Ficus*. Young Palms are also cultivated to an enormous extent about Paris; and so is every green and graceful-leaved plants, from the *Cycads* to the common trailing Ivy,—used to make living screens of.

"The wide staircase at the Hotel de Ville, ascending from the entrance hall, had also a charming array of plants so placed that the visitors seemed to pass through a sort of floral grove; fine-leaved plants arching over, but not rising very high, and having a profusion of flowering things among and beneath them.

Fig. 6.—Begonia.

"As the bank of *Primulas* and the groups of tall plants were placed opposite this staircase, and reflected in the great mirror behind, the effect when descending the staircase was fascinating indeed. A still finer effect was produced in a room near the great dancing saloon, and through which the guests passed to the magnificent ball room. Against each pillar in this saloon was placed a *palm* with high and arching leaves like those of the *Sieforthia elegans*, and others with larger leaves and pendulous leaflets. These meeting, or almost meeting across, produced a very graceful and imposing effect, while round them were arranged other plants, distinguished either by beauty of leaf or flower, and the groups at each pillar connected by single rows of dwarf plants, closely placed however, and well mossed in, as in the case of the more important groups.

"The very close placing of the plants is a peculiar part of the arrangement. You can not notice any dividing marks or gaps. Yet there is no awkward crowding.

"These arrangements were infinitely varied at the great balls, both public and private; rocks, water grottoes, and similar decorations, were occasionally introduced, both indoors and in the open air, and in the gardens behind private houses.

" The Tuilleries gardens at the time of the great fetes, were largely decorated in this way—each of the numerous lamp-posts having a bed of flowers around it, and the whole scene being turned into a kind of conservatory in a few days. The number of flowers required to do this was something enormous.

" The extent to which the floral embellishments of the Hotel de Ville were carried, may be judged from the great number of plants grown at Passy for that purpose,—the New Zealand Flax, which is so very useful for indoor or outdoor decoration, being grown to the extent of upwards of 10,000 plants and Palms, and all plants with fine leaves in great quantity.

"One plant, cultivated in great abundance a r o u n d Paris for winter blooming, is well worthy of increased attention, *Epiphyllum truncatum.*

" There are several varieties, and they certainly form most beautiful objects on dull December days.

" The variegated form of the common Roast-beef plant —*Iris foetidissima*—may be seen occasionally used with good effect. This is a true hardy native which will deserve culture. It forms a very pretty plant for room decoration, requires none but the most ordinary attention, and is easily obtained.

" The *Acanthuses*, too, and particularly *A. lusitanicus* used so effectively *out of doors*, are also grown abundantly in rooms, where they do very well. Everything

Fig. 7.—Yucca alœfolia.

proved to do well without the protection of a case is a gain to the very large class, who, from choice or necessity, like to grow plants in rooms."

A few years since a valuable communication on this subject of room decoration was given by a French gardener, Antonine Chantin, of Rue de Chatillon, Paris, to the Floral World of London. Mentioning the most popular plants used in the window embellishments of the French Capital, as their culture seems to be better understood in that city than any other, we take the liberty of quoting a few of his statements:

Palms.

" These play an important part in the embellishment of apartments in Paris.

Corypha Australis.   This plant, although but little known, is destined in a short time to occupy a foremost place in the decoration of apartments, where it makes itself conspicuous by its peculiar beauty, and the number of its leaves; it is, I believe, the most rustic in appearance of all the palms.

Cocos coronata and *flexuosa* are very elegant, and produce a charming effect.

Chamœrops humilis and *excelsa,* are two very fine hardy palms; *Latania borbonica* is certainly the most recherche plant of the family, and is valued as much for the beautiful green of its leaves as for its elegant appearance.

Fig. 8.—Alternanthera.

Phœnix dactylifera, leonensis and *reclinata* are also very much sought after and are highly esteemed.   *Areca alba, lutescens* and *rubra* are distinct and handsome."

Ferns.

Besides what we have said of Ferns in a previous chapter, there is need of little to repeat here.

Ferns cannot be dispensed with in elaborate decorations for the parlor or conservatory.   A single plant of the common Lady Fern, "*Athyrium Filix fœmina,*" is as useful in producing a graceful effect as anything we know.

Mr. Chantin in his remarks of Parisian decorations, says:

" The family of Ferns, although classed among plants with delicate tissues, and having a great dislike to dry, hot atmosphere, nevertheless furnish numerous examples which, with careful management, add very much to the beauty of apartments.   Thus, I have very frequently remarked, several species of *Adiantum,* which, wherever they can be preserved in good health, produces, without doubt, a most ravishing effect.

Pteris argyrea, P. cretica albo lineata, and *P. serrulata variegata* also produce a very fine effect, with their prettily marked foliage.

Alsophila australis, and *Balantium antarcticum* are also sometimes employed for decoration purposes in rooms of large dimensions, where their magnificent appearance never fails to produce a very imposing effect."

Select list of Ferns for Room or Table Decorations.

Adiantum cuneatum,
" formosum,
" hispidulum,
Asplenium flaccidum,
" marinum,
Blechnum brasiliense,
" corcovadense,
Athyrium Filix fœmina,
" F. f. Fieldii,
Scolopendrium vulgare crispense,
Lomaria gibba,

Lomaria ciliata,
Nephrolepis exaltata,
Pteris cretica albo lineata,
" serrulata,
Lastrea cristata,
" dilatata,
" Filix mas cristata,
Polystichum angulare,
" cristatum,
" proliferum.

Orchids.

" Until very recently I had believed that Orchids would never flourish if taken from the greenhouses, but a gardener of my acquaintance has introduced them while in bloom into a drawing-room with perfect success, the plants not having suffered in the least by the change of atmosphere."

The following *List of Orchids* is very suitable for rooms :

Barkeria Skinneri,
Aerides Warneri,
Brassavola Digbyana,
Calanthe vestita,
Chysis Limminghi,
Cypripedium barbatum,
" venustum,
" insignis,
Dendrobium nobile,
" pulchellum,
Epidendrum vitellinum,

Leptotes bicolor,
Lycaste Skinneri,
" aromatica,
Mormodes "
Oncidium ampliatum,
" flexuosum,
" divaricatum,
" cupreum,
Pleione maculata,
Sephronites cernua,
" violacea.

" All kinds of plants bearing flowers have paid their tribute to the ornamentation of rooms, from the humble mignionette, upon which the patient seamstress loves to turn her weary eyes, to the magnificent Orchid, that with its brilliant colors and fantastic forms fills with grace and beauty the apartments of the affluent."

Miscellaneous Plants.

" The following plants are very elegant in appearance, but require considerable care and attention, being somewhat difficult for ordinary window culture. They are more suitable for frames and cases, and are frequently cultivated in that manner :

Aralia, several species, especially Aralia Sieboldii.
Bambusa japonica variegata, and B. Fortunei variegata.
Bromeliaceæ, most varieties.
Carludovica, palmata and plicata.

Croton pictum, C. pictum variegatum, C. discolor.

Curculigo recurvata.

Ficus elasticus. This is a very elegant plant for a window ornament, but now a newer and much prettier variety, Ficus Chauvieri, is substituted for it generally."

Fig. 9.—Centaurea gymnocarpa.

Isolepis gracilis, a p r e t t y rush, is most elegant, requires plenty of water.

Musa. Several species are favorites, but principally M. discolor and M. rosea. *Musa ensete* is particularly suitable for window culture, but it is still so scarce and of such a price as seldom to be met with.

Pandanus amaryllifolius, and Philodendron pertusum, have been much sought after, and in most places thrive so well as to give general satisfaction.

Several varieties of Dasylirium and Beaucarnea are very suitable for rooms, and produce a very beautiful and graceful effect when grown in suspended vases or baskets.

Rhopala corcovadensis. This plant exhales a somewhat disagreeable odor, but is nevertheless much sought after on account of its very elegant and graceful appearance during the development of its young leaves."

In addition to Mr. Chantin's list, we give the following, which will live in a room throughout the year, provided the frost is kept out and the plants are kept free from dust. All are handsome :

"Lomatia elegantissima,　　　　Aralia leptophylla,
　　"　　ferruginea,　　　　　　"　　trifoliata,
　　"　　silaifolia,　　　　　　Rhopala Australis,
　　"　　Polyantha,　　　　　　Arundo donax variegata.
Nerium Splendens,

Pandanus graminifolius is peculiarly elegant, being well adapted for use in brackets.

Cannas, are all very proper subjects for the house. Take them up before frost, keep in a dry cellar through the winter, then bring to the light in the Spring, and they will start and grow well.

Mr. B. S. Williams, an eminent English florist, in some remarks upon the subject of ornamental plants, adds by way of caution, "a fact which should never be lost sight of, is this : That all plants with soft woolly leaves are ill-adapted for this purpose, but those with thick coriaceous leaves are always preferable—such as *Dracænas, Palms, Crotons, Anthurium, Aloes, Agaves* and *Ficuses*, amongst ornamental-leaved plants, and *Amaryllids, Begonias, Epiphyllums, Acacias, Azaleas, Coronillas, Cyclamens, Salvias,* and *Statices* among flowering plants.

"The ornamental-leaved kinds should be taken into an outer room occasionally, and have their leaves carefully sponged with warm water and soap, and stand until dry before removing them again into position. This operation removes all dust and dirt which may have accumulated, gives them a fresh and bright appearance, and is of vital importance to their well being."

He furnishes the following select list of plants eminently adapted for the decoration of apartments:

Ornamental-Leaved Plants.

Agave americana.
"   variegata.
Anthurium leuconeurum.
"   magnificum.
Aralia leptophylla.
"   Sieboldii.
"   reticulata.
Araucaria excelsa.
Aucuba japonica (vars).
Bambusa arundinacea.
Begonias (variegated).
Calamus asperrimus.
Caryota sobolifera.
Chamædorea Arenbergii.
"   desmoncioides.
"   Ernesti Augusti.
"   graminifolia.
"   Hartwegii.
"   Wendlandii.
Chamærops Fortunei.
"   humilis.
Cocos australis.
Coleus (many varieties).
Croton angustifolium.
"   variegatum.

Cyperus alternifolius variegatus.
Dracæna australis.
"   Cooperi.
"   ferrea.
"   gracilis.
"   indivisa lineata.
"   terminalis.
Ficus elastica.
"   religiosa.
Kentia sepida.
"   Bauerii.
Latania borbonica.
Lomatia silaifolia.
Morenia corallina.
Oreopanax dactylifolium.
Pandanus utilis.
Phœnix dactylifera.
Rhapis flabelliformis.
Sieforthea elegans.
Solanums (Weatherill's hybrids).
Yucca aloifolia variegata.
"   filamentosa variegata
"   quadricolor.
"   Stokesii.

Ornamental Flowering Plants.

Amaryllis (all varieties).
Acacia armata.
"   Drummondii.
"   grandis.
"   Riceana.
Azaleas (any varieties).
Begonia Digswellensis.
"   fuchsioides.
"   hybrida floribunda.
"   manicata.
"   odorata.
"   Weltoniensis.
Camellias (many varieties).
Callicarpa purpurea.
Chrysanthemums.
Coronilla glauca.
Cyclamen persicum (var.)
Daphne indica alba.
"   "   rubra.

Dielytra spectabilis.
Epiphyllum truncatum (varieties)
Eucharis amazonica.
Erica, many soft-wooded kinds.
Epacris (all varieties).
Erythrina Marie Belanger.
Genista Everestiana.
"   racemosa.
Gardenia radicans major.
Hebeclinium ianthimum.
Lachenalia (many vars.)
Leucopogon Richei.
Linum flavum.
"   trigynum.
Nerium Oleander.
Poinsettia pulcherrima.
Statice profusa.
Vallota purpurea.

CHOICE OF PLANTS AND THEIR ARRANGEMENTS.

Dracænas.

The most popular and suitable plants for gay decoration seem now to be the *Dracænas.*

After they have been once placed in the window box or jardinet, the attention they require is but ordinary, and they will live in the atmosphere of any moderately heated room the year round.

The variety most used is *D. terminalis*, very easily managed, and always ornamental ; the choice among florists often preponderates in favor of the *D. ferrea stricta*, which is still more beautifully variegated ; the *D. gilfilla*, with its stripes of white and green, still rare, is a great novelty. The colored leaved *D. Cooperi* and the green leaved *D. Australis, D. indivisa, D. Veitchii,* have all an elegant habit, and will do well in the temperature of any sitting room ranging from 60° to 75°.

Other varieties will do well, such as the *D. cannaefolia, congesta, rubra, stricta* and *umbraculifera,* but the most preferable of these would be the *rubra* and *stricta.*

Marantas.

Next in turn would be the *Marantas,* of which the best varieties would be *M. pulchella, Zebrina,* and also a dwarf variety of the latter.

The *zebrina* is much the most popular of all this class, and according to the experience of French gardeners, is the only one suitable for steady cultivation in apartments, as all the others succumb to the hot and dry atmosphere inseparably found in the living room. Another great difficulty in the use of the *Maranta* is the too great eagerness to display in the window ; the leaves being large, reach out and touch the window pane. When cooled with the touch they become at once of sickly look, turn yellow, and are greatly disfigured. They must be kept away from all cool winter air, and thrive best in a hot, moist location. Do not let the leaves rest or lie upon anything. The *Maranta Rosea Picta* is one of the most exquisite of this class, and to those who have conservatories, where it can temporarily be removed to and from the parlor, it will be well worth keeping.

The Poinsettia Pulcherima.

No plant of the present day has so striking a flower or is better capable for Parlor Ornament than this. It is not a plant for continuous room culture, but only for temporary purposes, being quite tender, needing a temperature of 75°, and even

Fig. 10.—Dracaena Terminalis.

at night not below 60°. For vases, for dinner tables, for floral decorations of some *Etagere*, or to be placed in front of a handsome looking glass, it will always be of more than ordinary merit.

The *Gymnostachyum Verschaffeltii*, is very suitable for vases, and in our illustration, Fig. 3, is used in a handsome silver stand and glass bowl as a decoration for the table.

Caladiums.

The variegated Caladiums are very desirable for decoration, for, besides their gracefulness, they will well endure the transition from the green house to a warm drawing room or boudoir, without any marked injury. The variegations of their foliage, spotted or shaded with tints of green, white, red and pink, are very unique and beautiful. The best sorts are as follows :

Argyrites, small foliage, prettily spotted and blotched with white.

Bicolor splendens, a strong grower, green ground with dark red centre.

Chantini, foliage red, centre spotted with white.

Wightii, foliage green, beautifully spotted with red and white.

Picturatum, long, narrow foliage, band of rosy red down the centre.

Verschaffeltii, green ground with crimson centre.

The best soil for the C a l a d i u m is fibrous loom, and plenty of leaf mould and silver sand.

Begonias.

In some respects the most gorgeous of all plants with variegated leaves. They should be mostly as single plants, *i. e.* only one plant in the centre of each box or basket. A large leaved Begonia in the window imparts an in-

Fig. 11.—Caladium.

describably rich appearance. The following are best varieties :

Begonia Rex, very showy, and a picturesque plant for exhibition purposes, leaves very broad, under side deep crimson, upper surface colored with various spots of silvery or snowy white.

Fuchsiodies, Saundersonii and parviflora are three very pretty varieties ; when in flower, the contrast of their scarlet rose and white flowers is very fine.

B. erecta multiflora, is mentioned by some florists, as especially desirable, for it combines the two qualities of flowers and foliage.

B. carnea pink ; *B. mamorata,* flesh color, may be added; the first are white, and produced abundantly, and the latter is a dark bronze of medium size, combined with an erect habit. If grown well it is very fine for the table.

Cultivation and Care of Palms for the House and Conservatory.

A few years ago the opinion was general, that palms were not only difficult in cultivation, but on account of their size, requiring a large space, only suitable for a big greenhouse and not at all for parlor decoration. Palms in the mind of people were imagined to be of immense size. For instance : the Indian Palmyra and Talipot palms, the slender high growing Cocos of the islands in the Indian Ocean and the Pacific Ocean, the graceful Sugar and Areca palms, or the Palma Real, in Cuba. So it happened that after some descriptions of our celebrated travelers, the cultivation of palms was nearly left untried. "Kings among the grasses," as Alex. von Humboldt relates in his "*Views about Nature*," how in South America the slender tops of several species reach above the highest trees of the forest. Admiration for glorious growth of the greater number of palms forbade the introduction into our small gardens and parlors, while the form of palms of pinnatisect fronds with fan or umbrella-shaped fronds, like Corypha and Chamaerops, Trinax, Mauritia and Sabal species called to great interest and induced to a study

Fig. 12. Begonia, grown on bracket.

of the physiognomy of them. Consequently numerous kinds of species came into trade and were civilized in our greenhouses. If we take in consideration how very few kinds of palms (in Linnæus time) were known (about 40 species), and how the lively period of culture of palms begins about 25 years ago, and how during this time nearly 400 species were cultivated in European Gardens, we comprehend clearly that palms are not difficult to cultivate, many of them even fit for small arrangement. Induced by Alexander von Humboldt, it was tried first to study their finding places and distribution in the primitive forests, in the Littorals and on the plateaus of the Andes, and according to this their culture commenced. Plenty of seed of a great many species of palms was acquired, and as soon as young plants were raised they showed the interesting habit of the old big plants. Dwarf kinds of palms were discovered and it was soon understood how well they were suited for parlor decoration. These species of palms, which grow often on the elevated points of the mountains by a sinking temperature, were also recognized to be fit for cultivation in the open air during the summer season. China, Japan, Hindoostan, Australia, Mexico, South America, provided us with the best species.

Fig. 13. Palm for Table Decoration.

We presume that now, as palms have been proved to be the most useful and durable parlor plants, and as they can be purchased at a low price, they will soon be favorites of our parlors and small house gardens. To cultivate palms well it is necessary to plant them into flowerpots, which are one-third longer than the ordinary kind of pots, of about the same proportion as Hyacinth pots. Nearly all genuine palms root deeply in the bottom.

Fig. 14. Decoration of Dinner Table with Palms.

We mention: The growth of the Cocos in loose sand on the sea coast, and several species which grow in dense moist woods, in the richest humus, or others in deep alluvial bottoms, near great rivers. The care of roots, letting them freely go deeply into pots, will be recompensed by the better and quicker growth of the plants. The mould for palms is to be a rich and well drained one; a compost of one part of good old manure, and the other part of rich loam, which could be mixed with some sharp sand and peat. The pots need a good drainage, and palms planted in this manner can be plentifully watered during the summer months. He, who will put his palms, which served for decoration for a parlor in the winter season, into the open air during the summer months, in some shady sheltered places, will keep them for many years, strong and healthy.

Several species endure to be planted in gardens and to be treated like bedding plants. But in replanting them into pots in the autumn, it is absolutely necessary to take great care of the roots. No defect must be done to the end points and very carefully they have to be digged out. The leaves of the palms are to be kept clean, free from all dust and insects, and we recommend to wet them sometimes with a sponge. Should big pots be used for palms, small ferns and plants may be grown with them at the same time, as this will not the least disturb the growing of palms, but will produce a splendid group, palms and ferns together.

We give an instance: with a Latania borbonica (Livistonia), the Pteris serrulata, Adiantum Capillus, Veneris, cuneatum, tenerum, pubescens, formosum, Pteris hastata, Davallia, canariensis, piidata, and several kinds of Selaginella, Tradescantia, Isolepis and Ficus stipularis. Other plants, with palm-like habitus, which are nevertheless no true palms, may be treated and used exactly like real palms, as: Cycas revoluta, Lamia, Encephalartos, Pandanus, Charludovica palmata, Lamatophyllum, borbonicum and Strelitzia, etc. We give in the following list only such plants, which are well suited, as we know by long experience for window gardening, and besides, are not expensive to purchase.

Our American ladies will surely not neglect this species of palms, as they deserve to take the first place among plants, on account of their beauty and durability.

Several kinds of palms grow slowly and serve thus for many years as decorations in rooms before they grow too big.

List of Palms for a well-heated room or parlor.

1. Palms with primatisect fronds: Areca rubra, pumila, lutescens, aurea, *Baueri; Astrocaryum Ayri, Elais guine-ensis; Caryola urens, sobolifera; *Ceroxylon andicola; Chamædorea gracilis, graminifolia, desmoncoides, elegans; Ernesti Augusti, *lunata, *Schiedeana, pygmæa, *elatior, *Mexicana; Cocos plumosa, oleracea, Euterpe edulis; *Jubæa spectabilis, (Cocos chilensis); Oreodoxa regia, Sancona; Oenocarysus frigida; *Phœnix dactilifera, *reclinata, *silvestris, farinifera, *Sieforthia elegans.

2. Palms with fan-shaped, or umbrella-shaped fronds: *Chamærops humilis,

*excelsa, *Fortunei, stauracantha, *histrix ; *Corypha minor (Sabal,) *Palmetto (Sabal and Chamærops,) maritima, miraguama ; Trinax barbadensis, argentea, *Livistonia australis (Corypha), sinensis ; *(Latania borbonica), Rhapis flabelliformis.

3. Plants with a habit like palms, belonging to the Cyclantheæ, Pandaneæ and Cycadeæ ; Charludovica atrovirens, palmata ; Pandanus graminifolius, javanicus, fol. var., utilis, odoratissimus, amaryllidifolius, pumilus, *Cycas revoluta, Ceratozamia mexicana, (Zamia) ; Macrozamia spiralis (Zamia), Zamia muricata. Those species marked (*) can be kept in a moderate temperature.

Floral Decorations—Suggestions and Plans for Arrangement.

Graceful Grasses, Lilies, Gladiolus, and other flowers with long flower stalks, stand best in vases or high urns; but Magnolias, Passion Flowers, Water Lilies, Pæonies, &c., look well in flat basins.

Plants for large flower stands, windows, or the back ground of a room, must be carefully chosen. Every plant which extends its leaves equally all around the central stem, may be advantageously used, either singly or as the centre of flower stands—such as Palms, Dracænas, Yuccas, Aralias, &c., &c.

Plants for windows must have a showy form to look well, not only from outside, but also in the room. Place the biggest plant just in the centre of the window to interrupt the monotony of the whole line. Choose, amongst other plants for this purpose, the following : Ficus Elastica, Dracaenas, Ardisia Crenulata, with red or white berries, or an Epiphylum Truncatum grafted on stock of Pereskia. Besides the season allows a proper selection of plants for decoration. Decorate your windows in early spring time with the following plants as: Lilies of the Valley, Crocus, Hyacinths, Narcissus, Jonquilles, Scilla Siberica, early Tulips, some kinds of Iris, Primula chinensis, Primula veris, Cyclamen persicum, Neapolitan Violets, Hepatica, Triloba, Cinerarias ; Dielytra Spectabilis, Roses, Amaryllis Formosissima. Or later in the month of April and May try to procure the following choice flowering plants as : Deutzia gracilis, Calla (Richardia) aethiopica minor, Azaleas in full bloom, Citrus sinensis, Camellias, with their splendid foliage and rich blossoms, some Ericas, Daphne Cneorum, Blue Lobelias, Nirembergia filicaulis, double Petunias, etc. Ladies or lovers of plants cannot well suppose that there is any scarceness in plants at this time in the year, for you will find enough in the flower market to satisfy every desire. And how easy is the cultivation and the treatment of the beautiful children of the Flora ! Only a regular watering and the moisture of air by saucers placed under the pots ; full light and fresh air by repeated opening of the windows on clear, sunny spring days is all which is required for keeping them in good condition. Their rich colors, their sweet perfume and delicate or interesting shape of flower will recompense fully each little trouble, which will be bestowed on them. In summer, when the parlor needs only an occasional decoration, as by festivities, parties, and so on, choose for decoration fine Fuchsias in flower, Gardenias, Hybiscus rosa sinensis fl. pl., double and single flowering Petunias, Heliotropes, different kinds of Coleus and Iresine Lindeni, or some small kinds of Ferns; or for a larger decoration only plants with large lucent leaves, as: Ficus elastica, Palms, Musa, Strelitzia, Aralias, Yuceas, Pandanus, Marantas, Cyperus alternifolius, and some larger kinds of Ferns.

Autumn offers a good variety of flowers and plants, which do not require much care. The longing for flowers awakens, when the rough winds of autumn tells us that winter is coming, and that the eye will in vain look out for joyful colors and shining leaves; when nature is dead, then comes the desire to have some laughing children of the Flora round our warm hearth, that we may enjoy their sweet odor and their graceful shape. It is a fact that a great many plants are cultivated by florists for decoration in the winter season. He who has a greenhouse of his own may have the pleasure to cultivate for himself: Hyacinth, Tulips, Crocus, Narcissus and other bulbous plants, which can be planted in fancy flower pots or Hyacinth glasses.

Fig. 15. Parlor Fountain and Flower Stand.

There is some poetical charm, having early in February or March, those messengers of spring at your home. We mention some other forced plants of incomparable beauty. For instance: Scilla sibirica, Hepatica triloba and H. angulosa, Russian and Neapolitan Violets, Cyclamen persicum, Hosteya japonica, Primula chinensis, Primula acaulis flore pleno, Delphinium formosum, Omphalodes verna, Phlox verna, Adonis vernalis, Irissusiana and persica, Fritillaria meleagris, Anemone nemorosa fl. pl., Pulmonaria virginicia, Sanguinaria canadensis and forced Rosa Thea, and Rosa bengalensis. For autumn decoration choose from the great number of blooming plants; the latest in the season and well suited for these decorations, by their compact low growth, is the Daisey-like or Pompone Chrysanthemums. Later in the winter season, when flowers become rare, you can have plants with large and beautiful foliage, whose form and lively green is very agreeable to the eye. Are you an admirer of Cactus? You find in November a certain species of Cactus flowering; the Epiphyllum truncatum. It is a matter of importance to arrange plants that every shape and part may be seen; to make the composition light and graceful by putting ferns and grass-like plants between others with large leaves, for instance: Ficus elastica, F. Cooperi, F. australis, Abutilon Thomsonii, A r a l i a Sieboldii, A. leptophylla, A. papyrifera, Camellias and Azaleas with Cyperus alternifolius, Panicum plicatum, Phorimum tenax, Polypodium aureum, Dicksonia umb r o s i a, Nephrolepis exaltata, Ophiopogon saburan, japonicum and spicatum, Isolepis pygmæa, Pteris arguta, hastata a n d serrulata, f o r o n e large group. Put following plants in the window: Ardisia crenulata, with red berries in the centre and for each side; Citrus sinensis, with small gold yellow oranges, Daphne odorata, Olea fragrans, Nardosmia fragrans (Tussilago,)

Fig. 16. Ornamental Flower Stand.

Convallaria majalis, Gardenia citriodora, blue Cinneraria, Rosa Lawrenceana, Bouwardia jasminiflora and splendida, Selaginella umbrosia, Eranthemum tuberculatum, Sanchezia nobilis, Eucharis amazonica, Vallota purpurea, Spreckelia lutea, Ornithogalum aureum and Adiantum Capillus, Veneris.

It will be nice to group in a flower stand some smaller plants round a big one. Take for instance for the centre: Curculigo recurvata, Dracæna congesta, Dr. ferrea, Dr. terminalis, Dr. australis, D. brasiliensis, Dr. rubra, Latania borbonica, Cryptomeria japonica, Araucaria imbricata, Yucca flaccida, Aralia papyrifera, longifolia; or a little orange tree, round which are grouped by size: Ferns with long fronds, as Blechnum australe, spicatum and B. frasineum, Pteris arguta, Pteris longifolium, Aspidium violascens, A. molle, Asplenium decursive, pinnatum, Cyrtomium falcatum, Osmunda cinnamomea and regalis, Struthiopteris germanica; and for the outline of this group, small plants of Camelia Azalia, Gardenia radicans, Myrtus, Aucuba, Magnolia fusca, Eugenia australis, Plectogyne variegata, Rhucus aculeatus, R. racemosus, Chenopodium lanatum, Alyssum maritimum, fol. var., and Carex japonica, fol. var.

Now to decorate a small parlor, which is daily used and has a higher temperature, take: Several Dracænas, small Palms, Pandanus utilis, Philodendrum pertusum, Alocasia macrorrhiza, fol.var., A. Jenningii, A. metallica, A. arborea, Croton pictum, and C. variegatum, and different species of Maranta, Amaryllis Tessani, A. solandræflora, A. vittata and A. regina, Vallota purpurea, Pitcairnea punicea, Aechmæa fulgens, Tillandsia farinosa, pyramidalis and amœna.

A composition of plants with thick and fleshy leaves and branches is attractive

Fig. 17.   Flower Box and tree trellis.

and interesting. For instance, for the centre of the group: Echeveria grandiflora, metallica, or E. sanguinea, or Sempervivum arboreum, fol. var., grafted Epiphyllum, or Opuntia brasiliensis, surrounded by Mammillaria, Echinocactus, Echeveria, secunda glauca, Aloe retusa, Sempervivum californicum, Aloe margaritifera, Sedum Sieboldii, fol. var.

It is some years since very successful and lasting efforts have been made to cultivate air plants (Orchids) in the room, (they have lately become cheaper.)

Nothing indeed can be more charming as flower stands in rustic style, covered with these interesting plants, mixed with Ferns, Selaginella, New Orleans moss, Tillandsia useoides, Nidularia, Aechmæa and Pitcairna. Of Orchids, are recommended the following: Cattleya, Lælia, Lycaste, Maxillaria, Oncidion, Odontoglossum, Schomburghia, Acropera, Acineta, Epidendron, Gongora, Lygopetalum and Brassia species.

For wardian cases the smallest species of Orchids and especially various kinds of Anectochylus, with their silver and golden veins in the leaves are very desirable; also the very interesting Dionaea muscipula which is one of our native orchids as well as Goodyera pubiscens; place them together with several kinds of ferns. A glass case filled with these plants is an elegant ornament for the parlor. Other Orchids only cultivated in pots will do well for window decoration. Take for this purpose: Bletia hyacinthina, Limodorum, Tankervillae, (Phajus grandifolius), Cymbidium oloefolium and C. ensifolium, Calanthe vestita and veratrifolia, and various species of Cypripedium. It shows of a refined

Fig. 18. Flower Box with arbor and climbing vines.

taste to decorate with air plants, ferns and fine climbing plants as: Cissus discolor, Ectrites Melalenca, Miconia speciosa, Pothos argyraea, Echites argyraea violacea, Passiflora trifasciata, kermesina, and P. princeps, Dioscorea discolor, Manettia bicolor, Thunbergia chrysops, Th. grandiflora and Th. laurifolia. Avoid plants with soft and downy leaves and employ more Ferns, Grasses or even Caladias, and plants with smooth leaves as they are more lasting for this purpose than the so-called Bedding plants which are more suitable for out of door cultivation.

For amples and hanging lamps, we recommend a plant of great value; it is Cordeline vicipara, now called Cloro phyton Sternbergianum; known a long time in Gardens. It produces on long hanging stalks a great many young plants with air roots; is therefore useful by this habit for Orchid stands and baskets. In larger parlors which are only moderately heated, plants from greenhouses and conservatories can be selected for a required decoration. The best selection

Fig. 19.   Flower Stand for Parlor Window.

would be: Azaleas, Camellias, Citrus sinensis and grafted Citrus **aurantium**, Daphne laureola, odorata, Cneorum; Olea fragrans; Eugenia australis; Crypto meria japonica, Cephalotasus Fortunei, Rhododendrums, Kalmia, Ilex aquefolium fol. var., Aucuba japonica and its varieties, Viburnum Tinis with fine white flowers in winter, Laurus nobilis, regalis and L. Camphora, Tristania laurina,

Eucalyptus globulus, Melianthus major, Melia Azedarach, Sida japonica, Cestrum aurantiacum, Melaleuca alba, decussata, ovalifolia and hypericifolia; and Eryobotria japonica. He who is fond of more tropical plants should use in such moderate temperature: Aralia Sieboldii, leptophylla, quinquefolia; Solanum Warsce-

Fig. 20. Decorative Flower Stand for Parlor, Window, or in front of Looking Glass.

witzii, robustum; Caladium violacum, cupreum (porphyroneurum), **Caladium** javanicum; Heclichium Gardnerianium, Bambusa Metake, Chamaerops Fortunei; Phormium tenax, Dianella coerulea, Ruellia varians, Solandra grandiflora,

Brugmansia arborea fl. pl., Sabal minor (Corypha), Chamaerops Palmetto (corypha) of Ferns especially: Balantium antarcticum, Blechnum australe; Cyrtomium falcatum, Cyathea australis and Cyathea medullaris. All these plants are very durable and easy in cultivation for a low temperature and do not require much light. They keep during the winter the full foliage and many of them will bloom at this season. Plants, like Acacia lophanta, drop the leaves often in winter and require much light and a careful treatment. It is, as we have said, most important to put saucers under the pots; it prevents the draining

Fig. 21. Aquarium, with arbor.

water from flowing over. The complaints of ladies that plants spoil the furniture will, if this caution is employed, be left away.

The following illustrations will explain the method how to treat, arrange and plant the different objects suitable for putting plants for decoration: This can be a guide for graceful arrangements to every one who has a passion for these sweet beings, leaving enough room to develop a refined good taste, and gaining with it the admiration of all. In some respects plants are like animals, looking out for their own particular society. You are not to mix Dracænas with Pelargoniums, or Ferns with high Calceolarias, Ageratum, Petunias, Matricarias, etc.; these combinations would be against the habit of such plants. But you may combine well Ferns and Grasses with plants, having beautiful lucent leaves like Caladias, Lilias, etc.; every Fern possesses the quality for softening the greatest contrast. Of plants with variegated and silver leaves, choose

Fig. 22. Combined Wardian Case and Flower Stand.

only such, which go well with other plants, and arrange like this: Centaurea gymnocarpa, candidissima and C. plumosa, Cinneraria maritima and Artemissia argentea, as a single plant; or in the centre of a group, surrounded by low plants, in rich flowering state, as: Rosa Lawrenceana, Lobelia ramosa and erinoides, Iberis sempervivens, Dianthus chinensis and imperialis flore pleno,

18

Cuphea, platycentra, Anemone coronaria, Sanoitalia procumbens fl. pl. Primula cortusoides, Gazania splendens, Geum coccineum, Ajuga reptans fol. var., Arabis albida fol. var., Cyclamen persicum and Coum, Saxifraga sarmentosa, Cerastium tomentosum, Myosotis azorica, Ornithogalum aureum, Erinus alpinus Calandrina umbellata, Viola cornuta, lutea and Viola odorata the Czar, Campanula pulla (pussilla), C. soldanellifolia, Vidallii, Garganica, cochlearifolia and Soldanella alpina. Collect of all these plants as the season allows.

Fig. 23. Flower Basket with Gold-fish basin.

Fig. 20 is a low flower stand, best placed in front of a high looking glass, or in summer in front of a fireplace. Such flower stand requires mostly plants with ornamental and variegated foliage, to be seen from above. For instance, all the varieties of Begonia Rex, hydrocotyledes, m a n i c a t a, Warcsewitzii, D r e g e i, smaragdina, stigmosa, Pearcei and riciniifolia; different Caladias, Sanchezia nobilis, Maranta zebina, pardina, vittata, regalis, and Lindeni, surrounded by Torrenia asiatica, Hoya carnosa, Tradescantia discolor, Gymnostachys Pearci, Peperomia argyræa, P i l e a m u s c o s a and various kinds of Gesneria and Gloxinia.

Fig. 21, an Aquarium covered by a little arbor, to be used for window d e c o r a t i o n or flower tables. Plants, as the cut shows us, are: Cyperus alternifolius, Calla athiopica minor, Iris fœtidissima, Acones graminifolius and Isolepis parlatoris. For climbing plants, which will well cover the arbor, take: Pilogyne suavis, Tropæolum tri-colorum or Smilax microphylla (Medeola asparagoides.)

Fig. 22 represents a Glass rotunda or Bell Glass, surrounded by different dwarf plants exposed to dry air, as: Lychnis Haageana, Spigelia marilandica, Mimulus quinquevulneris Convolvulus mauritanicus and Calcæolaria rugosa floribunda. The inside plants are like those which are proposed for Wardian cases, requiring the same treatment. Such well filled and well arranged Bell glasses are beautiful ornaments for the table at festivities.

Fig. 23. The flower basket, with goldfish basin, is very cheerful to look at when standing in a bay window or on a table. It is charming to see the lively and graceful little animals swimming about between the carefully arranged plants. Plant in this basket the neat: Rosa bengalensis, Agrippina, Crocus, Snowdrops, Lily of the Valley, Lephyranthus candidus; Verbena var., kinds: Nesembryanthemum cordifolium, Carex japonicus, fol. var., Sweet Alyssum and blue Lobelias.

Fig. 1 is a low flower stand for Tropical plants, covered with a falling veil to protect plants against the dust. Place it in front of a large looking glass, which will heighten the effect. Only large Tropical plants can be used here for decoration. Such are: Dracænas, Bambusa, Hedichium, Alpinia nutans, Curculigo recurvata, Pothos, macrophylla, Anthurium, Philodendron pertusum and Palms as: Chamaedorea lunata, elatior, gracilis;—Cycas revoluta, Rhapis flabelliformis, and large ferns as: Blechnun australe and brasiliense, Pteris, argyroneura and tricolor, Pteris arguta and hastata, Polypodium aureum, Nephrolepis exaltata, Cyathea medullaris and australis; Pteris cretica alba and Cyrtymium falcatum.

Fig. 24. This flower stand consists of wire or fine willow work prettily adorned at the bottom with Berlin-wool, or bead work done up by the fingers of a lady. It serves especially for keeping cut flowers which have to be put, to give them more durability, in wet sand. Toy or Passion flowers climb round at the sides, and Pelargonium pedatum, Fragaria indica, Saxifraga, Vinca major fol. var. Sweet Alyssum mixed with Lobelias decorate the upper part of the stand.

Fig. 25 is one of the handsomest parlor decorations; a sofa shaded by big plants with imposing foliage as on Fig 7.

Place for the warm season plants like this: Melianthus major, Canna, various kinds, Uhdea pinnatifida, Solanum robustum, laciniatum, Warcsewitzi; Amaranthus bicolor coccineus; Iresine and Alternanthera, Coleus, Fuchsia, Hybiscus, Plumbago, Gardenia florida, and Fortunei; Abutilon Thomsonii and mesopotamicum, fol. var., Chrysanthemum Sensation, Osmunda cinnamomea, Struthiopleris germanica, Adiantum pedatum, Onoclea sensibilis, Heliotrope, Jasminum gracile, Rosa Bourbon, Souvenir de Malmaison, Rosa Thea, Souvenir d'un. ami, Hydrangea hortensis, Lilium lancifolium and auratum.

Fig. 26 is much like Cut 9; but of greater importance is here the choice of single plants, as the whole arrangement shows small flower stands, tastefully grouped round the arbor. Fill the stands in the back ground with the following plants: Dracæna terminalis and D. ferrea, D. brasiliensis, rubra, congesta, australis, indivisa, Veitchii; also Ficus elastica, australis and Cooperi. For

Fig. 24. Parlor Flower Stand.

climbing plants decorating the arbor are well fit : Hedera algeriensis and Roegneriana, Cissus antarcticus, Rhuscus androgyus, Pilogyne suavis, Rubus mollucanus, Adlumia cirrhosa, Clematis azurea grandiflora, lanuginosa, and Fortunei.

Fig. 25. Parlor Sofa, surrounded with ornamental plants.

Fig. 27. The Flower fountain is, when small. determined for ornamental table decoration. In larger style it may be well suited for hall decoration or ornaments for a tent out of doors. The light and graceful wire-work can be covered with : Maurandia, Rhodochyton volubile, Eccremorcarpus punicus, Lophospermum, Tropaeolum tricolor

Fig. 26. Sofa with Ivied Arbor, and background of Dracænas.

or **T. pentaphyllum**, Thunbergia, Solanum jasminoides, Bignonia jasminoides, Medeola asparagiodes and Cardiospermum Flalicacaba. For the large shape take also:

various kind of Passiflora, Seneciomikanoides, Ipomoea, and fine ornamental gourds. The lower basin in the centre contains decorative plants with large leaves as: Begonia, **Maranta**, Caladia, Pothos, Sanchezia nobilis, Tradescantia discolor and **Warcsewitzii** :

Fig. 27. Floral decoration in the form of a fountain,

the basin above has only light delicate plants as: Ferns, Selaginella, various kinds, Isolepis gracilis, Torrenia, asiatica, Eranthemum Cooperi, Hybiscus Cooperi, Fittonia argentea, Alternanthera, Bambusa japonica, fol. var., and Cerastium tomentosum.

The decorative bird cage, on page 4, frontispiece to chapter 1, in a small shape, looks well on a table or in front of a looking glass; if bigger, it may be placed in the centre of a room. Here is a good opportunity for showing a fine cultivated taste in the arrangement of all kinds of plants. Below, in the stand at the bottom, you will perceive drawf plants of the following species: Stachys lanata, Coleus Beauty of Villamore, Nemophila insignis, Verbena tencrioides and Sanvitalia procumbens mixed with Sweet Alyssum and Lobelia; or, in a different style: Sempervivums Sedums, Mesembryanthemums, Cactus, Echeveria, Crassula, Aloe mixed with Phlox setacea and Cerastium tomentosum. Then higher

up on the stand you have in flat vases: Sedum Fabaria, Plumbago Sarpentæ, Epiphyllum truncatum, Daphne Cneorum. The four vases contain: Agave anuricana fol. var.: Corypha australis, Latania borbonica, Cycas revoluta, or Bromelia sativa fol. var.; Nidularia fulgens, Asplenium, Nidus avis, Echeveria metallica, Alocasia metallica, Statice Halfordii, or St. macrophylla. Yucca flaccida will produce the best effect in the vase on the top of the cage. Some small climbing plants decorate well the four corners of the cage. The lively songsters inside, thus surrounded by beautiful flowers, seem to forget that they are prisoners, and warble their lovely songs with perfect freedom and joy.

The plants recommended in this article are, throughout, handsome and convenient. They are to be had in any good nursery which makes a specialty of cultivating plants for decoration. Some florists take the delivering of plants by contract, renewing them from time

Fig. 28. Portable self-operating parlor fountain,

to time. We give you also a good hint how to clean plants. Take off the dust first with a small velvet scrap, then wet the leaves either with a sponge or syringe. Plants, of a lasting habit, as: Palms, some kinds of Orchids, Yuccas, Dracænas, Ficus elastica, will keep well some years by attendance and regular nursing, repaying the small trouble by their growth and fresh color.

Home Ornaments.

This department would not be complete without a word for the little ones of the house, some hint to them of what they can do to bring forth some glowing spot or sprig of living greenery. So we tell them how to make some pretty little contrivances in grasses, &c.

Plants with light, graceful foliage are every year becoming more popular; and to complete a picture of the highest order one requires a great variety of colors, and graceful pencilings; so in window gardening the culture of the grasses adds greatly to the whole effect. Their feathery plumes may not possess brilliancy of coloring, but their silvery and emerald tints are an offset to their more gorgeous companions.

Far prettier than many a pretentious and costly ornament is a simple bowl of grasses planted in pine cones, set in sand, in moss, or common soil.

If grown in cones—procure them from the woods, and sprinkle in as much soil as their scales will retain; then scatter the grass seeds over it, and sprinkle with water; place the cones in sand or moss—and be sure that they do not become dry—but water them sparingly at first, once a day, and set in a mode-rately warm place. Soon the seeds will sprout, and the tiny spears protrude in every direction.

Grass will sprout and grow in pine cones without any soil, but it serves to prevent the cone from closing too tightly when sprinkled, and also makes a more vigorous growth. The cones can be suspended in a window, either singly or in groups of three fastened together with thread wire; or a rustic basket or stand can be procured, and filled with cones with different kinds of grass, growing in each cone. There are three thousand different species of grasses in the world, and their study is a pleasing pursuit.

Fig. 29.   A Saucer Garden.

A very charming effect can be produced by placing a wet sponge in a glass bowl, and sprinkling over it canary seed, grasses and flax seeds; soon it will be covered with a thick growth of fresh bright green; it must be judiciously watered; if kept too dry it will wither away; if too wet it may damp off. Mustard seed may also be used, and its tiny yellow blossoms, will be to many, a novelty as well as a delight.

Children and invalids can derive much pleasure from raising a grass garden; it is better to select the dwarf varieties, as the taller kinds require more nourishment.

A Tumbler Garden may be constructed as follows: Fill a common tumbler of goblet with water, cut out a round of cotton batting, or of soft thick flannel of just the size to cover the surface, and lay it gently upon the water, upon this scatter the seed and grass, or flax or mustard, or all mixed, and gently set the tumbler away in a dark place. In a few days the seed will start; soon the roots

Fig. 30.   Grass growing in Pine Cones.

will begin to penetrate the cotton or flannel, slowly sending down their delicate white fibres to the bottom of the vessel, while the top will be covered with a little thicket of green; after the second day the vessel must be kept in a warm tight place, and two or three times a week carefully replenished with water by means of a teaspoon, or syringe inserted beneath the edge of the flannel.

A great advantage of such a miniature garden as this is that the roots may be plainly seen growing through the grass. Water cress has been grown this way, and a little story is related of a little girl who kept her invalid mother supplied all winter long with water cresses grown in this way upon wet flannel.

Peas.—Common garden peas will make a lovely vine, although sweet peas are much prettier, but either can be grown in water; fill a common tumbler with water; tie over it a bit of coarse lace, such as milliners use, and cover it with peas, pressing it down into the water. Keep in a dark place for two or three days, then give light and warmth. In a few days the roots will be plainly seen piercing through the lace, and the vines can twine around the casements, or a bit of a hoop skirt spring can be fastened about the tumbler, with springs attached to it in form of a globe, and the vines twined about them.

Fig. 31. Bracket for flowers under gas jets.

Keep the tumbler full of water, and add bits of charcoal to keep it fresh; every week turn in two or three drops of aqua ammonia, less if the tumbler is very small, but the deeper it is the better for your vines.

A *Saucer Garden* can be made with fresh moss, well wetted; in the centre place a pine cone filled with earth and common grass or canary bird seeds, and in a few days the tiny grass spears will appear, and soon you will have a verdurous cone of great beauty. Keep it secure from the frost, and give water enough, and you will have a lovely ornament.

The devices for growing grasses can be extended *ad libitum*, and none are so poor that they cannot secure a tumbler or a saucer garden, which will prove a delight and a joy to all beholders, while its care will be of the slightest.

If an acorn be suspended by a bit of thread tied around it within half an inch of the surface of water

Fig. 32. Chandelier Decorations.

contained in a small vase or tumbler, and allowed to remain undisturbed for one or two weeks in a warm place, it will burst its shell and throw a root into the water and shoot upwards, its straight and tapering stem covered with glossy green leaves. A young oak tree growing in this way is an elegant object. The water should be kept clean with bits of charcoal, and if the leaves turn yellow add a little ammonia to it. Chestnut trees can be grown in this way, but their leaves are not as beautiful and delicate as those of the oak.

Baskets of Green Cress, or Pepper Grass.

The common garden cress grows very rapidly, and can be used in various ways

Fig. 33. Flora Vase.

in making grassy ornaments for parlor or table decoration. A common basket of oziers can be transformed into a lovely greenery by planting it thus : Select a pretty shape of either ozier or wire, and line the basket with folds of cotton batting sewed on both outside and inside, covering the handle with the same, or thick white flannel can be substituted for the cotton wool and strips of it rolled around the handle.

Procure four or five ounces of cress seeds and steep them in warmish water for four or five hours , set into the basket a china saucer, (or the saucer of a flower pot will answer,) fill it with water, and when the soaked seed has become a little sticky spread them all over the flannel, to which they will adhere. Leave no spot uncovered, for it must be thickly strewn with plants. Set the basket in a warm, dark place for two or three days—longer if the leaves do not commence to sprout—then bring it out to air and light, and soon it will become a mass of feathery green foliage. You must sprinkle it every day with warmish water, holding it over a wash bowl ; and the water must always fill the saucer

A small fern can be grown in the saucer, or a Primula, or a cluster of Crocuses.

Another pretty device is that of the *Turnip basket,* which is made by simply taking a large Turnip, scraping out the inside so as to leave a thick wall of an inch all around, then plant in it some climbing or drooping vine, say a Morning Glory. Suspend the turnip with cords, and in a little time the vines will grow upward over the cords, while the turnip will sprout below and send forth leaves gracefully turning and curving upward.

The Sweet Potato would hardly be recognized by many who know it only to eat it, if they could see how pretty a parlor ornament it might be easily made.

Fig. 34 is a good illustration of one in a vase placed upon a bracket fastened to the side of a room.

Take a large sized Sweet Potato and drop it to the bottom of a vase or the bowl of a hanging basket. Cover the Potato with water nearly to its top, leaving perhaps a half inch uncovered, and always keeping it about at this point. It will soon put forth roots, and the top will shoot out a vine which will grow after a while with great rapidity. A sunny position suits it best,—and the tendrils will soon clasp the arms of the basket, or droop in long curls over the edge of the vase. Many visitors who have seen such a vine in the window of their friend, have inquired with admiration its name, thinking it must be some foreign plant. Had it possessed only some curious botanical or fanciful name, its praises would never cease being repeated, but the visitors are a little chagrined to find that their enthusiasm has been vented upon nothing but a *Sweet Potato Vine.*

Arrangement and Choice of Flowers for Wreaths, Bouquets and Vases.

Fig. 34. Sweet Potato Vine in vase.

The art of arranging flowers gracefully and well, is not so easily taught as their culture, for it requires an artistic eye to group them tastefully, yet fortunately they are so intrinsically beautiful that they can hardly be spoiled, though the best effect is not always attained.

The Germans, French, and even the Russian women are said to surpass the English and Americans in their various methods of weaving flowers into house decorations, and they seem born with a love of plants and flowers.

In our country flowers are chiefly regarded as accessories, while in France and Germany there is no family fete without its graceful door wreaths, its garlanded picture frames, and its coronals of flowers ; and not a toilette without its appropriate flower *parure*

In arranging flowers it is well to bear in mind the laws of worsted work, and when we desire to adorn our rooms with flowers we should consider the "grounding" to be prepared for them, as if it were a cushion.

White is often the chief ground work of a wreath, bouquet, or vase, yet it greatly impoverishes the other colors, and renders a brilliant assortment of flowers trivial, if little dabs of white are scattered all over them—yet if used as an outer edging it will heighten their colors, and in a bouquet, vase, or wreath of delicate, pale shades, it tends to make their colors more distinct.

Fig. 35. Vase of Cut Flowers.

Passion flowers are peculiarly lovely when arranged with pale pink roses, etc., but if w h i t e flowers are mingled with them, the effect is not pleasing.

Rose color and pale blue are exquisite when mingled ; white lilac or mauve with primrose ; dark blue and brilliant scarlet ; cerise or cherry and white ; dark purple and primrose, blue, white and rose color.

The shade of green should, as a general rule, harmonize with the natural foliage of the flowers ; if this is disregarded it will tend to overpower instead of increasing the brightness of the flowers. Very dark green looks well with only large, pure-tinted heavy flowers, like Roses, Camellias, Dahlies, etc., although it will look well with white flowers of finer structure, if their texture is thick and waxen and especially with wild flowers of the spring. Thin, yellowish green foliage would ruin the Camellia, which needs the intense dark color of its own leaves to show forth its statuesque beauty and elegance.

Indeed, the use of thin, quickly fading green sprays will injure all floral arrangements ; and young leaves of all kinds droop soon ; while older, thicker foliage will last a long time. The leaves of the scarlet geranium preserve many flowers by their velvety texture, which retains so much moisture, while their flowers will last well if a drop of gum arabic is dropped into each flower; and there are few that are more effective either in dress or table decoration.

Heath retains its beauty for a long time, as do nearly all flowers which possess a hard woody stem; while Fuchsias, Heliotropes, etc., with soft, succulent stems either drop their flowers, or turn black so quickly that their beauty is soon destroyed.

Carnations and Pinks are beautiful for floral decorations, and they keep their freshness for a long time. Verbenas and Chrysanthemums are also very desira-

ble. Hyacinths will make exquisite vases, wreaths, etc., and double and single Tulips are ornamental in decorating mantel pieces and tables.

Anemones are unequaled for a dinner table, as the full blaze of light exhibits their striking colors to great advantage, and the gorgeous scarlet, pink, pale blue and blue shading into white are perfect, but they require a soft mossy foliage of Lycopodiums or Ferns.

Azaleas are charming for every kind of adornment. There are no flowers more perfect for ornamenting the hair and dress, but they fade quickly unless damp blot-

Fig. 36. Basket of Cut Flowers.

ing paper or cotton or wool is rolled around their stems.

Dentzia gracilis is very beautiful for any decoration; and it is in much request so that the florists force large quantities of it every winter. Roses of every shade are always admirable; too many of them were never seen.

Stephanotis floribunda is ever welcome; its snowy, waxen, fragrant flowers being adapted to every floral ornament, and the same remark applies to the sweet Cape Jessamines, the Myrtle and the Orange blossom.

Bouvardias, Tuberoses, Mignonette, and all the sweet blossoms, are also to be desired for arranging in the various devices at present employed in decorating apartments, etc., for festive occasions.

Mounting and weaving flowers is a mechanical operation that is often useful.

The Parisian *fleuristes* can take a flower with less than half an inch of footstalk and make it very effective. The smallest piece of well soaked cotton wool is pressed around the stem, and a small piece of wire is wound about it to keep the wool close, and it is twisted closely together for a stem ; a fresh green leaf can

be rolled over the wool to prevent its being observed. Every one knows how often a lovely flower will snap from the stem and be seemingly useless, but with a bit of fine wire pierced through the calyx a stem is provided which will answer all the purpose ; then cotton wool thoroughly wetted can be wound tightly over it. White Camellias are ruined if the slightest moisture touches the petals, and the best way to mount the flower is to moisten a piece of white cotton wool about the size of half a dollar, then lay it on a piece the size of the flower itself, which should then be lifted up ; two ends of a loop of wire having

Fig. 37.   Bouquet.

been passed through the centre of the wool before laying it under the flower, lift up the loop of wire, and slip it between the leaflets or points of the thickest calyx and the flower, drawing it gently around it ; then reverse the flower, and pass the wire through the wool twisting it around a cluster of leaves of the Camellia, and concealing the wool with them. With pink flowers use pink wool, Melted isinglass is often used to make the flower adhere closely to the wool ; this helps to keep the flower from falling, and also moistens it. Isinglass is better in preparing flowers than gum or mucilage of any kind, because it is not so sticky, and is of a pure white tint. A crown or wreath of Camellias can be prepared in this manner, that will last for four or five days in great perfection ; even if the flowers drop their petals the wool retains enough of them to keep up the appearance of flowers.

Fig. 38.   A Cornucopia of Flowers.

To mount Geraniums, Azaleas, etc., the stems should be cut off within an inch of the cluster or single flower, and a drop of isinglass be given inside of the petals, hen the wetted wool and the wire should be arranged as described for Camellias.

Water Lilies can be treated in this way and they can be kept several days. In making wreaths, a delicate eye for combining color and light for arranging flowers are required, or clumsy garlands will be the result.

It is a mistake to suppose that a great variety of flowers is required; simple, small wreaths of Ivy leaves and Myrtle blossoms, or drooping racemes of Deutzia; of Geranium leaves mingled with white rose buds, and its own brilliant blossoms; of Pansies, and some thick textured leaves; of Azaleas and Primroses; or of any combination of two or three flowers are much more lovely for the decoration of the hair, dress and table.

The wreath can be tied with green zephyr wool upon a bit of thread wire, mingling the green leaves in a graceful form.

For the head or for a picture frame, the wreath is made more easily by commencing at each end, and arranging the flowers and leaves toward the centre—beginning with a few drooping branches, and filling the centre with a high coronal of knots of flowers.

In making up bouquets, frames of very fine green wire are much used, so that a single stem stripped of all its leaves, passes through each hole, and all of them are bound together underneath the frame.

The holes are arranged in circles, and the effect of the grouping is very good and lasting, but as soon as the flowers shrivel, or the petals fall it is no longer ornamental; but for decorating a dinner table, or carrying in the hand, it is a most desirable frame, as it is exceedingly light to hold, and takes very few flowers to produce a fine appearance.

The frame should be slightly conical, and a large flower is best adapted for the centre piece, and a fringe of some delicate fern, leaves or flower, should droop over the edges.

Fig. 39.   Wreath of Flowers.

The frames can be made at home with a little ingenuity; silver wire is the best, but copper can be used. The piece of wire for the outside circle of a large bouquet, should be cut half a yard in length, and the succeeding lengths should be three inches shorter, each one diminishing regularly until the last circle will be the size of a ten cent piece. Each of these wires, making six in all, should be neatly fastened together; and three wires must then be attached to the centre, one at equal distances, and passing in and out of each circle must be firmly hooked into the outer circle and arranged in a conical shape. Thread wire can now be twisted or netted in and out of the circles as close as the maker chooses. From the centre circle, three more wires can now be fastened and bent down straight to form a handle.

Fine wire can be used to form frames for covering vases, dishes, etc., and they can be made in the same manner. If very small flowers are to be used in forming the bouquet, place coarse netting lace, such as is used in millinery all over the frame, and it can be also employed in making the whole frame, using only one circle of rattan at the outer edge; but it will not last for only one occasion. Bouquets made on these frames affect a great saving of flowers. With but a small handful a large sized bouquet can be arranged. Various are the devices which can be appropriated in making up such bouquets. The centre can be of one flower, and a wreath of Rosebuds or Hyacinths or Blue Violets, or Pansies arranged all around it with a graceful ground work of green leaves.

Fig. 40. Parlor Stand for Cut Flowers.

In fastening on the handle, it is well to recall the shape of a parasol, and arrange the wires so that they will have a similar effect. In making such a frame for an oval dish no handle is required, and the dish can be filled with wet sand to keep the flowers fresh. If water is used in vases a few large pieces of charcoal are very needful to prevent it from being offensive.

It is a subject of dispute in arranging vases whether one should commence in the centre or at the outside, but in dishes of all kinds it is certainly the best plan to commence at the outer edge with a bordering of leaves; but for bouquets it is better to begin at the centre. Drooping flowers are always graceful, and are decidedly the best for bordering or edging both vases and bouquets.

Many a vase and bouquet of flowers are ruined by mingling too great a variety of colors and flowers. One sees that there are a great number of very pretty flowers, yet the effect is not exactly the thing, for they are decidedly crowded, and do not mix well together.

Two or three purple flowers in a vase of scarlet and white will ruin the whole. One must consult the colors of the flowers that are to be grouped together, rather than the great assortment of rich and rare blossoms.

Variegated foliage is exceedingly pretty for bordering bouquets, baskets and flat dishes. Begonia leaves and those of *Cissus discolor*, are much in request for this purpose.

A bouquet with a rich rose-colored flower as its central piece, and the next row of blue and white Hyacinths or violets tied to wires or broom corn splinters, and the outside mixed with rose color, blue and white, with a pretty, misty bordering of Gypsophila, or Clive, falling over deep crimson leaves, will be a most effective design. A pure white Camellia for the centre, with a wreath of white Heath mingled with Blue Violets, or Forget-me-nots, is very lovely.

The central flower white, and the outer wreath of scarlet Geraniums, is also pretty.

Carnations and Lilies of the Valley will mingle finely.

Among garden flowers how infinite the choice, ribbon grass, pear blossoms, tea violets, lily of the valley, with its leaves, white lilacs; dielytra, roses, in their season ; the fragrant lilies of July, and the bright geranium or verbenas. Saucers of pansies, edged with musk, are lovely ; so are balsams, with plenty of their own leaves.

A pretty design may be made as follows : Fill a glass dish with curled parsley leaves, put a white jonquil in the centre, from which let five sprays of the lily of the valley radiate ; or a star may be made of daisies and myrtle, or of blue and white larkspur.

A very novel bouquet may be made by taking an unripe melon, cut off one end, stand it up on the cut part, then surround with the stiff leaves of the Pæonia, and stick the melon full of dahlias and asters.

In one of our illustrations (43) may

Fig. 41. Ornamental Stand for vase of flowers.

be seen a beautiful design arranged with ferns. A few long fronds are arranged to fall over the vessel at the bottom, and a few sprigs of flowers are introduced to fill up the vase ; around the small staff which rises upwards, twines the Lypodium scandens, and from the top, which is in the shape of a cup, droops more plants, same description as at the base.

Bridal bouquets must be chiefly composed of the purest white flowers, with a

Fig. 42.　Basket of Cut Flowers.

little mingling of yellow, blue and blush white tints, but the snow white must predominate to produce the richest effect.

Green is essential in all bouquets, and the foliage of the respective flowers is always best fitted to show off their peculiar charms, yet a feathery and plumy green adds grace to all arrangement of flowers.

Nothing can produce a more lovely appearance than a vase of Lilies of the Valley, mingled with the emerald green folds of their own foliage.

Camellias, Azaleas, Orange flowers, white Jessamine, Myrtle, white Heath, and white Violets, mingle together in odorous beauty to adorn a bridal scene.

Rose-buds should not be forgotten, also the lovely waxen-petalled Stephanotis, and half-blown Gardenias.

As a general rule, all flowers of thin texture and pale delicate colors, fade so quickly that they are not suitable for decorative purposes.

They look exceedingly pretty while growing, but they will not improve any floral arrangement. Nemophila, Convolvulus, etc., etc., are lovely in their living beauty, but gathered they add nothing to the beauty of others; while Carnations, Geraniums, Rose, Asters, etc., etc., are always most brilliant and lasting. Fern leaves are also beautiful in vases, and so effective that but few flowers are required to make a brilliant display.

Fig. 43.   Table Decoration with Stand of Ferns.

Branches of Ivy are lovely and mingle well with scarlet and white Geraniums. When many vases are desired to be arranged, it is well to fill each vase with shades of one color, scarlet, crimson, pink, white, blue, purple, etc.

Hanging Baskets of cut flowers, much used for decorative purposes, and the style of flowers should correspond with that of the basket. In little lattice work baskets, the graceful fronds of Ferns, light wreaths of Ivy-drooping Fuchsias and sprays of Begonia, with Lobelias and Rose-buds, Cyclamens and Snowdrops woven in, present a most attractive appearance. The flowers are often arranged in tiny bottles, which keep them fresh a great while if a little salt and saltpetre are added to the water. These baskets are often suspended by wires, and long ivy wreaths can be twined about them.

Other baskets are arranged with a cross-bar of green, dividing them into four quarters, with a double row of white edging the green. Scarlet Geraniums and Blue Hyacinths fill up the interstices, but usually if one color is kept as a ground work, and another as a filling, the better will be the effect. Baskets can be arranged with branches of Ivy growing in bottles of water, mingled with

pressed fern and autumn leaves that have all the effect of growing plants, and can be suspended in a cool bay window where plants would never grow. The Ivy can be trained to creep up the cords and the ferns arranged in clusters by themselves. Pressed mosses can fill up all crevices, and the water with charcoal to keep it fresh, will not require any change, but only to be filled up once in three weeks. There will be no danger of its dripping upon the carpet, nor being chilled unless the temperature falls below freezing.

Long pieces of Ivy can be purchased at the florists, and they will soon strike root and grow finely.

In arranging vases that will stand far from close inspection, very large, bright flowers are the most desirable. Dahlias for the centre piece, surrounded with full blown roses, Chrysanthemums, etc.; little

Fig. 44. Stand of Ornamental Grasses.

delicate flowers are thrown away in such decorations.

For wreathing picture frames and looking glasses, nothing is more beautiful than evergreen, box, or myrtle boughs, thickly intermixed with Holly, Snowberries or Bitter-sweet, and the whole crowned by a bouquet of feathery Ferns with evergreens and berries.

For large green wreaths tied on the springs of hoop skirts firmly fastened together, the low growing evergreens of the pine woods are decidedly the best, and branches of spreading boughs of fir or hemlock can surmount each crown.

The gray woolly wreaths of the Clematis, when it has gone to seed, mingle well with the bright berries and the dark hued evergreens. There is no decoration which equals that of flowers on festive occasions, and those of our readers who live in the country can always avail themselves of the berries and evergreens of the forests and fields.

The mountain Ash berries are also extremely effective in trimming vases and rooms.

To Revive Faded Flowers.

Hot water will frequently restore flowers to freshness, even when every petal is drooping. Place the stems into a cup of boiling hot water, leave them in it until each petal has become smoothed out, then cut off the coddled ends and put into milk warm water.

Colored flowers revive sooner than those that are of snowy whiteness, as the latter turn yellow. A cool room is best adapted to keeping flowers fresh; they will wilt quickly in badly ventilated rooms, especially if filled with tobacco smoke. Take away each flower as it fades, else it will decay the others.

It is far better to gather your flowers for yourself and friends, than to let them fade upon the plants.

Cut Flowers, how to keep them

When gathering flowers, use a pair of sharp shears; a knife is better, especially for woody plants — roses, camellias, spireas, deutzias, fuchsias, and the like.

If you wish to sever a spray of blossoms or leaves, hold the stem to

Fig. 45.   Cross for Table Decoration.

be removed in the left hand, and at the back of the stem set the knife (held in the right hand) and cut in a slanting direction downward. If the spray springs from the head of the stalk, cut it as close as possible to the shoot next below it; it it be a side branch, cut it cleanly to the main stalk. Then there will be no outflow of the sap, no rough and withering sticks protruding their unsightly presence above sickly foliage and meagre blossoms; but, on the contrary, a symmetrical growth of verdure and florescence. Use the same method in removing a solitary flower or bud.

One great drawback to our enjoyment of cut flowers is the quickness with which they decay.

The moisture furnished cut flowers should be *rain water*, always of a moderate temperature, about blood warmth. The water should not be changed, but every morning its evaporation supplied with more of the same temperature; to which, after a few days, a little *aqua ammonia*—five drops to half a pint of water—may be added. It is well to place at the bottom of the dish or vase a layer of broken charcoal, about half an inch in depth—pieces about the size of small beans. In placing the flowers, let them have as much room as they need to show themselves naturally. At the expiration of a week, the stems should be examined, all decayed matter rubbed from them with a piece of flannel; and the tip of each end cleanly cut; and if any leaves or blossoms begin to look withered, those also should be cut away.

Fig. 46. Flower Stand for the Table.

Flowers decay much sooner when tied in bunches or bouquets than when arranged loosely. Too little air and too much water are the bane of most species. There ought to be a free current of the former around each spray or separate large flower, while the latter should not come above the calyx of any bloom; better be an inch or more below it. With most hardy plants, even if very long stemmed, two inches immersion will give water enough if they have plenty of air.

Branchlets of flowering shrubs and stalks of the lily tribe can be advantageously arranged in water held in deep vases in the manner just mentioned; but for a collection of the various orders, we prefer a perforated cover, (have used even the flat steamer of a dinner-boiler, but wish the "workers in clay" would provide for the necks of vases and flower-dishes plates similar to those prepared for drainers to soap dishes.) This rests upon the top of the vessel, and through its holes the stems can be passed to the water beneath without fear of too deep immersion, as

Fig. 47. Flower Stand for a Hall.

either by its leaves, or bud-stems, or stalks of surrounding greenery, each flower is lightly supported above the cover, which is hidden by the foliage hanging gracefully around. When water is to be supplied, the cover is raised without disturbing the stems.

For short stemmed flowers, a mixture of damp sand and powdered charcoal in equal proportions, answers very well; but care must be taken that the dish does not get too dry ; so also do baskets of creeping moss, in which they may be placed with fine effect; still the moss gets dry so soon that the flowers fare better if a saucer is hidden below, partly filled with water, which they can reach with the tips of their stems.

Fig. 48. Dish of Flowers and Ferns for the Table.

The prettiest and best arrangement for keeping cut flowers in beauty is a dish of velvet moss saturated with rain water.   When this moss is brought from the woods, if a few fronds of fern, especially those of the delicate Maiden Hair, are

Fig. 49. Ornamental Silver and Gold Stand for Fruit or Flowers.

taken with it, and suffered to form a part of the foliage of the group, you will find them a charming addition. Place the flower stems sparsely among the moss, and here and there a branchlet of green or a leaf. Just inside the edge of the dish pour a very little water twice a week ; and when any of the collection show signs of decay, remove them, and fill their places with fresh specimens; thus the dish may be kept filled with bloom and beauty for months.

Small bouquets for the hand soon fade if no effort is made to give them moisture; but a wrapping of a bit of wet cotton batting or a few wet threads of candle wicking, fastened lightly about the ends of the stems, will suffice to keep them in good condition several hours in a close, hot atmosphere. Those who do not like the formality of a bouquet holder, which this plan necessitates, can take a small vial—such as are used to hold medicine of homœopathists—partly fill it with water, and place the flower stems therein; and then cover the vial by tying a ribbon around it, just as they would the bare stems of a nosegay. Flowers used in decorating the hair and the dress can be kept bright and fresh in the same way.

If flowers are to be transported any distance after they are cut, they should be placed carefully in a tight box or case. If the box is not perfectly air tight, furnish it with a layer of damp moss or cotton batting.

When going for wild flowers, carry a tightly closing tin box, in which is a piece of wet, coarse sponge, and a basket. The smaller flowers are to be shut in the box. The sponge is laid in the bottom of the basket, and the stems of the larger flowers inserted in its pores. By so doing, even the most delicate can be brought home without withering.

Handsome wall decorations may be made by cutting long branches of ivy, clematis, woodbine, honeysuckle, or climbing roses, inserting a few inches of their stem in a bottle of rain water, and hanging the bottle behind a picture or a mirror, over and about which the flowers will bloom and the foliage flourish for many weeks, to the admiration of all beholders.

Fig. 50. Decorative Bird Cage for the house.

The beauty of so many flowers—hot house flowers especially—is tarnished by sprinkling. When they are drooping, it is best to try first a change to a cooler or a more airy department, and a double portion of ammonia added to their water; this frequently revives them very quickly.

CONCLUSION.

And now, regretfully taking leave of the interested readers who have followed us to the end, we cannot close without some slight but hearty expression of the genuine love and pure ennobling influence which comes from constant associations with flowers. Though Window Gardening has its difficulties, still its pleasures are as yet but partially told, and its capabilities only half revealed. How dreary our homes would be without some sweet presence of floral blossoms? Where they are, they seem to give a *"benediction of peace,"* for they beguile many a weary hour, and soothe many a feverish or anxious life. Would that all might be led ere long to study the beauties and acknowledge the sweet influence of the flowers, *"Nature's Jewels,"* whose life seems to be examples of humility, purity, and patience.

Ruskin says : "Flowers seem intended for the solace of ordinary humanity. Children love them ; quiet, tender, contented, ordinary people love them as they grow ; luxurious and disorderly people rejoice in them gathered. They are the cottagers' treasure, and in the crowded town, mark, as with a little broken fragment of rainbow, the windows of the worker, in whose hearts rests the *" covenant of peace."* To the child and the girl, to the peasant and manufacturing operative, to the grisette and the nun, the lover and the monk, they are precious always—

> "Bright gems of Earth in which, perchance we see
> What Eden was — what Paradise may be." '

ACKNOWLEDGMENTS.

The Editor would acknowledge with pleasure proper credit to the following Books or Journals which have been consulted for necessary information :

The Floral World	London, England.
The Gardeners' Magazine	" "
The Parks, Gardens and Promenades of Paris	By William Robinson.
Frauengarten, Illustriste Gartenbuch	By H. Jager, Leipsig.
Rustic Adornments for Homes of Taste	By Shirley Hibberd.
Flowers for the Parlor and Garden	Edward S. Rand, jr.
Practical Floriculture	Henderson.
Window Gardening, English Pamphlet	Robert T. Fish.
Indoor Plants	Miss E. A. Maling.
Hearth and Home, and American Agriculturist.	
The Horticulturist. N. E. Farmer.	
The Fern Garden	Shirley Hibberd.